BIBLICAL STRUCTURALISM

Method and Subjectivity
in the
Study of Ancient Texts

by Robert M. Polzin

FORTRESS PRESS
Philadelphia, Pennsylvania

SCHOLARS PRESS
Missoula, Montana

In memory of my mother,
Rose Ciolino Polzin

SEMEIA SUPPLEMENTS
Edited by William A. Beardslee

THE SWORD OF HIS MOUTH: FORCEFUL AND IMAGINATIVE
LANGUAGE IN SYNOPTIC SAYINGS
by Robert C. Tannehill

JESUS AS PRECURSOR
by Robert W. Funk

STUDIES IN THE STRUCTURE OF HEBREW NARRATIVE
by Robert C. Culley

STRUCTURAL ANALYSIS OF NARRATIVE
by Jean Calloud, translated by Daniel Patte

BIBLICAL STRUCTURALISM: METHOD AND SUBJECTIVITY
IN THE STUDY OF ANCIENT TEXTS
by Robert M. Polzin

TABLE OF CONTENTS

Preface

The plan of this book is simple. In part one I *describe* structural analysis; in part two I attempt to *do* structural analysis; and in part three I try to *describe how* examples of structural analysis might be found in the unlikeliest of sources: pre-structuralist biblical criticism. It is important, here at the beginning, to say something about the interrelationships of these three parts.

In part one I describe structural analysis in a special way: structurally. Thus the reader might look at chapter one as a kind of structural analysis of structural analysis. In structuralism it is believed to be a failing to speak too much to the point, as those readers who have tried to read structuralist writings have no doubt long since discovered. To achieve my purpose, therefore, I tried to say nothing essential (in the sense of *intrinsic*) about structuralism but rather to give the reader its contextual meaning. So the description of structuralism in part one is really a two-fold illustration: what I write there is determinately *about* structural analysis, and hopefully what I write there indeterminately *is* structural analysis. The intent is that the reader will attend to both facets of chapter one in his musings about structuralism.

In part two I attempt to do a structural job not on structuralism but on a biblical text, the Book of Job. Since structuralism is in my opinion a movement of mind, a vision, an imaginative approach to the study of anything, part one was necessarily abstract, vague, and up in the air. Part two is meant to be as specific as the Book of Job and as concrete as Job sitting on his dunghill scratching his sores. The reader should be warned here about another crucial relationship between parts one and two. It has been perceptively seen by some who have had an opportunity to read this manuscript before publication that part two makes few references back to part one and does not seem to continue what was begun there. Part two, it has been pointed out, seems almost to have been written to stand alone. (Actually, part two on Job was written first and parts one and three were written with it in full view.) This facet of the book deserves a response here.

One reason why there are in part two so few references back to part one is that I did not want to do an interpretation of my interpretation of the Book of Job. To adapt what Robert Scholes writes about artists (1974: 9-10), interpretations of their own work by critics are rarely attempted and seldom valuable. Moreover, as I will state in the introduction to part two, of all the aspects of structuralism discussed in part one the only one that I have any doubts about is the "deep subjectivity" of part two. And for me to argue that deep subjectivity *is* there would simply impose for a second time my own subjectivity upon the first instance of its presence. There is every reason to believe that the second attempt would not involve any deeper subjectivity than the first. That is one reason why part two largely stands by itself insofar as explicit references back to part one are concerned.

But I do insist that the connections *are* there. Part one is meant to be the context for part two in a very special way and I do not want to destroy this contextual connection by inserting parts of part one in part two. The connection between parts one and two must remain to a large extent indeterminate. Because I *cannot* relate the subjectivity embodied in part two to that subjectivity described in part one. And because, even if I could so relate them, I believe I would thereby destroy or at least seriously weaken the structural link between the two sections. Susan Wittig (1975b: 22) uses the insight of Wolfgang Iser about "indeterminate texts" to express the rationale I am invoking here:

> In these texts, he (Iser) suggests, it is not the creator's intention to frustrate or confuse us "so much as to make us aware of the nature of our own capability for providing links; in such cases, the text refers back directly to our own preconceptions—which are revealed by the act of interpretation that is a basic element of the reading process." (Iser 1974: 280)

So the indeterminate connection between the first two parts is as deliberate as the determinate connection between part one and part three. Part three is intimately connected with part one because *the way* in which Wellhausen's, von Rad's and Noth's studies are analyzed is to see whether their interpretations are like the description of structural analysis in part one. Whereas part two is related to part one primarily by the *doing* of a structural analysis (I attempted to *do* a structural analysis of structural analysis in part one and I attempted to *do* a structural analysis of the Book of Job in part two), part three is related to part one primarily by the *describing* of structural analysis (I attempted to *describe* structural analysis in part one and I attempted to *describe* how three classics were structural in part three).

What all this means from a structural point of view is that all three parts of this book *illustrate* what structural analysis is. Part one is intended to illustrate structuralism determinately by describing structuralism and only indeterminately by being one. Part two is intended to illustrate structuralism determinately by *being* a structural analysis and only indeterminately by describing one. And part three, like part one, is intended to illustrate structuralism determinately by describing and only indeterminately by being a structural analysis. The function of each part of this book is heuristic: the *descriptions* that are parts one and three and the *doing* that is part two are all transformations of this same function.

As for my intended audience I write for all those interested in the question of whether or not structuralism has anything to offer biblical studies. More specifically I address myself to those who are curious about the usefulness of this strange new academic creature in helping one to derive meaning from the Hebrew Bible. Any attempt to introduce biblical scholars to structuralism must delineate very carefully the strengths and especially the weaknesses of this new approach. Since *all* hermeneutical enterprises fall under the same semantic problems that face structural analysis, an adequate introduction to this topic must relate the strengths *and* weaknesses of structuralism to those aspects of approaches such as source criticism, form criticism and tradition history. Since we are all in the same semantic boat, my contention will be that most of the weaknesses that can be justifiably levelled against structuralism as a viable approach to the interpretation of biblical texts will also apply to established criticism as a matter of course.

It should be noted that an abridged form of chapter two appeared in *Interpretation* April 1974, pp. 182-200, and that another version of chapter seven appeared in *The Bulletin of the American Schools of Oriental Research,* February 1976, pp. 113-120. Both articles are gratefully used with permission. The biblical quotations on pages 107 and 108 are from the Anchor Bible translation by Marvin Pope. All other biblical quotations are from the Revised Standard Version and are used with permission.

Finally, thanks are due the editor of this series, William A. Beardslee, and his consultants for a number of suggestions that helped me in revising my manuscript for publication. And I am grateful for the constant love and support of my wife throughout the long genesis of this book.

Robert M. Polzin
Ottawa, February 1977

Part I

A Description of Structural Analysis

Chapter I

What is Structuralism?

This book is about structural analysis as a hermeneutic enterprise and maintains that structuralism as such is neither a science nor a distinctive methodology. At most it is a movement of mind (Scholes 1974: 1-7), a vision, an approach about which one may offer some descriptive statements. Three self-conscious aspects of structuralism seem to separate it from other hermeneutical approaches. First, structuralism is peculiarly self-conscious about the *object* it analyzes. It sees the text in a distinctive way: as a system of transformations that is self-regulating or closed. Second, structuralism is self-conscious about the nature of the *model* it constructs: a structural interpretation is a hypothetical-deductive interpretation. (In this respect a structural model is no different from any hermeneutical interpretation: in the sense in which I will be discussing the deductive / inductive dichotomy, there is no such thing as a truly inductive hermeneutics). Third, structuralism is peculiarly self-conscious about the *subject* who is doing the analyzing: it emphasizes self-reflection or (to adopt Roger Poole's expression) "deep subjectivity" (1972). To the extent that approaches emphasize these objective, deductive, and subjective elements in the self-conscious way in which I shall describe them, they can be considered examples of structuralism. This identification is often

1

difficult and sometimes impossible, but an attempt to describe what structural analysis involves seems at present a worthwhile enterprise.

First, what is distinctive about the way structuralism views its object, *the text*? It sees the text as a "structure" and Piaget's description of structure is useful here to start off (1970). Wholeness is the first defining mark of a structure. By this term Piaget emphasizes the operative distinction between structures and aggregates. Both a structure and an aggregate have elements of which they are comprised. But a structure is viewed as a *system,* that is, its elements are related in a law-like way which one postulates is discoverable, whereas the elements of an aggregate are not so related. The difference is between a heap of stones and a house of bricks. A heap of stones is only a collection of elements (or at least is considered as such for the moment); a house of bricks, however, involves an intelligible interplay of elements making up the whole. Now the soul of a structure consists in this, that it is neither the whole nor its elements that count but rather the relationships between and among its elements. Structuralism, then, deals with the law-like relationships that can be discovered between elements of a whole. If I claim to have discovered such relationships, I view my object of study as a whole; otherwise it remains for me an aggregate. In structuralism, therefore, everything is relative. But this is not to say that everything is arbitrary, because this would bring us back to a heap of stones. The term "law-like" is meant to distinguish relationships perceived between the stones in a heap from those perceived between the bricks of a house, when both objects are viewed from the same vantage point, for example, from that of functional intelligibility. A whole or system, like a house, has certain laws of composition that a heap of stones lacks. Now these laws of composition are referred to in structuralism by the term "transformations." What this term implies is that if the elements of a whole are related in an intelligible way, they are related in some kind of stable way. A structuralist expresses this stability of "law" or "rule" in much the same way as one says, "As a rule, a house has a roof." There are two kinds of stability that obtain between the elements of a structure or whole: the first involves those laws or rules whereby the whole was structured in the first place, and the second kind involves those laws or rules whereby the elements can interact with one another in certain ways. Thus there are rules according to which a house is built: one does not build a house on a foundation of sand. This is a structuring rule. On the other hand there are law-like relationships that obtain between elements of a whole once that whole is already structured. For example, because of the peculiar stability of that particular structure we call a house, it is possible to transform a living-room into a study, or a kitchen into a bath; but it is not possible to transform a basement into an attic (unless one turns a house upside down and installs a furnace on the former attic's ceiling!). What is to be emphasized here is that the rules by which a whole is structured and the rules by which it constantly structures itself are both implied in the concept of transformation.

This then is the second aspect of structure to be emphasized: it is a system of *transformations*. The key idea here is that the laws of composition of a whole determine its laws of transformation: it is because a kitchen *was built as a kitchen* that it can be turned into a bath so easily; moreover it is because an attic *is* at the top of a house that it cannot be transformed into a basement. Therefore when a structuralist talks about transformations, the first false impression to avoid is the idea that he is speaking necessarily about a temporal process. This is not always so. The kinds of transformations he deals with are of two types: either temporal or a-temporal. Transformation may or may not involve temporality. When I say, "four walls plus a floor plus a ceiling 'make' a room," I may be speaking of the initial temporal process of putting them together. On the other hand, I may be speaking of a kind of transformational situation whereby four walls, a floor and a ceiling "make up" a room in a non-temporal way. The term 'transformation' includes both possibilities and is meant, moreover, to emphasize that this is what makes a structure a structure: not the whole alone, nor the elements alone, but the laws of composition by which the elements "make up" the whole, both temporally and a-temporally.

The third aspect of structures is what Piaget calls their property of self-regulation. This means first of all that whatever transformations a particular structure allows, it only comprises those transformations that keep it the structure it already is. In other words, a structure is a "closed system" in such a way that the only kinds of transformations that belong to it, the only transformations that it can call its own, are those which do not transform it into another structure. In a particular house I can change a kitchen into a bath, I can even add a bedroom, without making that house something else. But if I knock out all the inner walls and ceilings, enlarge the front entrance and "house" a plane inside, I now have a hangar. Such a transformation does not "belong to" the internal structure of a house as the prior example did. A structure maintains itself by and is enclosed within the transformations that comprise it: this is what is meant by the self-regulating nature of a structure. Such a property of structure does not preclude in any way the fact that some structures can be related to others either as co-, sub-, or superstructures. In these cases the transformational laws of each structure are conceived of not as destroyed but integrated and the result is not a *loss* of transformational rules but the assumption of them into a larger network of rules. Thus an estate may include a separate building that houses the servants. Such a building is structured by all the transformational rules by which it is a house but these are subsumed and integrated into the transformational laws by which the estate, as the superstructure of which the house is a part, is regulated.

This idea of the essential closure of a structure is one of the more important facets of structuralism, an insight which will explain, time and time again, why a structuralist often will appear so bold as to analyze parts of an object of study without appearing aware of what his critics are so quick to point out: one's object cannot be *really* understood unless it is related to something "larger" of which it is a part, or "more fundamental" upon which it is based.

What is behind such criticisms is a view of knowledge which if carried to its logical conclusions would make impossible the development of any knowledge at all. The brashness of a structuralist who hopes to arrive at intelligibility of a whole which may itself be a part of a larger whole rests upon this essential postulate of his approach: whatever may be the larger relationships of a whole with larger wholes, if it can be considered in any real sense a structure itself, it will reveal certain stable laws that cannot be lost but only integrated with the rules of its superstructure. I can discover intelligible things about the servants' house even before I consider or even discover the fact that it is part of an estate.

These three characteristics, then, lie at the heart of structuralism: structuralism studies wholes, studies them as systems of transformations, and studies them as self-regulating or closed.

Let me apply these remarks to the general object of interest of biblical scholars, written products of language. The insights of structuralism would seem well-suited to the study of language in all its facets. Language is of its nature intelligible. If, as we have seen, a structure is such because of the intelligible relationships that exist among and between its elements, language would seem to be a prime suppository of structures. And so it is. The search for intelligibility is not only pursued *through* language, it is pursued *in* language. What is more obvious than that a language product is a whole, not an aggregate, of sounds or written units; that these units are related to one another in a meaningful way? Who can deny that a grammar is a prime example of a kind of structure or system underlying a particular language? To run through a particular declension or conjugation is to rattle off a series of stable transformations of a language. Again, it is obvious to every language-user that language is self-regulating. Indeed, the common experience that youngsters just learning a language can both recognize and produce "acceptable" utterances not part of their previous experience is the starting-point, not conclusion, of Chomsky's approach to language study. All of this is so obvious as to be devoid of insight. If this is all structuralism is saying, it says nothing new. Its insights are platitudes. However, we have only to probe beneath the surface of language as a system to see that one's view is beclouded by profound obstacles and shifting shadows. An example borrowed from A. G. Oettinger (1968) will illustrate one aspect of the complexities involved. Syntactic analysis by computer of the sentence, "Time flies like an arrow," yields three different syntactic structures which can be represented by conventional sentence-structure diagrams as follows:

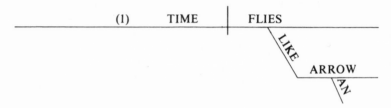

This structure would make our sentence similar to a sentence such as "A plane flies like a bird." This first structure has "time" as the subject of the verb "flies," with "like an arrow" a prepositional phrase modifying the verb.

In this second structure, "time" combines attributively to form a possible substantive "time-flies" as in the expression, "time-bomb;" "like" is interpreted as a verb. This structure would be similar to that of a sentence which reads, "Time-bombs utilize a clock." It might make sense if one were to picture insects called "time-flies" who happen to enjoy eating arrows for their meals much as termites are thought to enjoy wood.

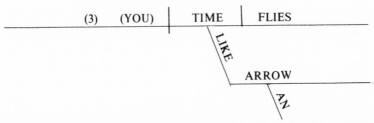

Here "time" acts as an imperative verb with "flies" the object. This structure might make sense by imagining an order to someone to take out his stop-watch and to time flies with great dispatch, or "like an arrow."

It is usually accepted that structural analysis has been able to make great strides in linguistics in the areas of phonology and grammar (taken to include both syntax and morphology). Problems involving semantics, which deals with the *content* of language, its meaning, have so far not lent themselves to such useful structural analysis. As Oettinger writes, "No computer techniques now known can deal effectively with semantic problems of this kind, but research in the field is continuing" (1968: 369). In other words, once you program a computer to recognize the syntactic structure as "legitimate" in English, you must deal with the *semantic* problem of which syntactic structure fits the semantic structure of this particular sentence. It does no good to program out the second and third structures from your theory of syntax because then the computer would not recognize as legitimate (syntactically *and* semantically) certain sentences such as "Time-bombs use clocks" or the order, "Time runners like a referee!" As Oettinger points out, "Semantics, the all too nebulous notion of what a sentence :neans, must be invoked to choose among the three structures syntax accepts for "Time flies like an arrow" (1968: 367). Not only computers but also their creators are unable to deal with this problem.

Here precisely is the point. Any approach, structural or not, that attempts to deal with the *meaning* of language products runs into the same *semantic* problem: we have not yet developed analytic tools precise enough and sufficiently formalized to help us discover, describe and relate the various semantic or meaning-related structures that lie beneath the particular language products we hope to analyze. When we deal with the *interpretation* of language products larger than the sentence we have been discussing, how can we hope to deal with such complexity, given the pitfalls inherent in the syntactic and semantic analysis of even the simplest sentences? Our attitude should be one of sufficient diffidence to avoid the *hubris* that often has characterized biblical criticism of recent times. One of the more valuable aspects of the structuralist approach can be its explicit self-understanding of the limits and vagaries of the hermeneutical quest. As I hope to show in detail later on, structuralism offers one a systematic understanding of why exegetes have not in fact accomplished many of the interpretative feats they mistakenly believe they have accomplished. On the one hand structuralism is ideally suited to the study of language products because here more than anywhere else one finds an intelligibility and a wholeness that is particularly suited to the human mind, the ground from which language springs. On the other hand, it is also in the study of language that structuralism finds one of its most difficult tasks. It is the paradoxical strength of structuralism that it recognizes not only its challenges but also its limitations.

A similar position is necessary when we talk about structural transformations. It cannot be denied that language presents us with innumerable examples of the law-like relationships that obtain between its elements, relationships we call transformations of a structure. But here, again, the problem faces us squarely. To say that we are not able to choose which *semantic* structure exists in the particular sentence, "Time flies like an arrow," is to admit that we do not know which set of transformational rules is at work at the meaning level of this sentence. And this means that we cannot be sure we have accurately described, let alone discovered, the "correct" structural interpretation of many a simple sentence. How much more difficult it is when we consider language products of greater length and complexity. If 'transformational grammar' is a commonplace approach within modern linguistics, transformational semantics is as yet only an ideal. We do not possess a "science of discourse" or, as Barthes calls it, a science of "translinguistics" (1970b). We have no "scientific" discipline centering around the structural analysis of language or language products on the level of meaning.

If, as we have seen, transformations are to be viewed not only as temporal but also as a-temporal, then no systematic understanding of a biblical text is adequate that fails to exploit the synchronic relationships waiting to be discovered within it. It is unfortunate that modern biblical criticism has concentrated on genetic and diachronic structures to such a degree that it often has ignored or largely misunderstood the numerous synchronic relationships which we call a-temporal transformations of a text. It is as if one believed the only (or most basic) way to understand a house is to understand how it got built. Unfortunately this is often the most difficult task at hand with the Bible because of lack of data, whereas an emphasis on how its parts correlate and co-exist is not beyond the resources at hand. To want to know how a house is made is certainly a necessary task for anyone who really wants to know about houses. However, one must also study a house by an examination of what makes this house what it is. Biblical criticism traditionally has confined itself to a search for internal signs of construction within the biblical house and has failed thereby to exploit many of the relationships that exist between the house's parts, as they now exist.

Thirdly, if self-regulation defines the third property of a structure, what does this involve in the structural analysis of language products? It is obvious that all language products, however large or small, are made up of self-contained units that normally satisfy this characteristic of structure. This means that language products are composed of combinations of structures co-ordinated as co-, sub-, or superstructures. In other words, parts of a larger structure are usually substructures in themselves: poems are composed of stanzas and each stanza encloses its own intelligibility apart from (but not unrelated to) the intelligibility of the whole poem. The third act of a play has *some* stable "meanings" apart from or in addition to its major structural relationship to the rest of the play. It is this self-regulating view of their object of study that by and large allows structuralists to appear arbitrary when they perform the first step of a structural analysis, segmentation of the text. Thus one structuralist will begin with superstructures and work his way down to the minutest structures. Another will start with substructures and work his way up. One will begin his analysis at the beginning of a product, another in the middle, another near the end. This "arbitrariness" can be present at all "discovery stages" of analysis, and is based upon a non-arbitrary stance: if indeed one's object of study (language products) contains various structures of whatever level, the path to their discovery is not predetermined in the sense of a hierarchical or mechanical route which must be followed.

Now that we have discussed what the general characteristics of structure are, we can describe certain major classes of structures that one may encounter in the interpretation of texts. Structures may be found on the plane of expression or on the plane of content. Secondly the kind of structures analyzed can be either diachronic or synchronic. And finally we can isolate and describe either syntagmatic or paradigmatic structures in a text. Let us look for a moment at each of these three dichotomies.

The study of language involves the plane of expression / plane of content dichotomy. The terminology employed here belongs primarily to the school of L. Hjelmslev (1953). Since language is composed of signs and since signs are composed of two elements, the 'signifier' and the 'signified' (following Saussure), that plane of language dealing with its signifier aspects is called the plane of expression and that dealing with its signified aspects is called the plane of content. Now because only the plane of expression deals, by definition, with the formal aspects of language (form as opposed to meaning) it is on it alone, according to many scholars, that structural linguistics operates. Inductivists such as Z. Harris and L. Bloomfield are of this opinion. These scholars maintain that since the plane of content deals with the non-formal aspects of language, its discipline, semantics, cannot be part of the science of linguistics. On the other hand, the followers of Saussure and especially Hjelmslev hold that semantics in principle if not in fact can be a part of structural linguistics.

Hjelmslev and his followers add a further distinction to these two planes which allows them to view semantics at least as a possible science. They recognize two levels or strata on each plane: that of substance and that of form. One sees immediately that "form," "formal" is used in a different sense from that used earlier. There, "form" was opposed to "meaning"; here "form" is opposed to "substance" in language products. Thus, say these scholars, it is the formal (vs. substantial) aspects of language which comprise the elements of a language system rather than formal (vs. meaningful) aspects of language. What this distinction means in practice is that each plane (expression and content) has two levels (formal vs. substantial) and it is only the formal level on each plane which comprises the structural relationships necessary to express "scientific" statements about language. Here are examples illustrating these distinctions: 1) an example of *substance of expression* would be the graphic or auditory aspects of a language product: the word 'paper-clips' is here written not spoken; 2) an example of the *form of expression* is the system of phonemes discovered and described in a given language; 3) an example of *substance of content* is the color continuum—whether this continuum is conceived of as mental or physical is a moot point; and 4) an example of the *form of content* would be the way a particular language carves up that continuum into a set of interrelated meaning units, each of which stakes out its own territory along the continuum. Thus in English, as John Lyons notes (1971: 56), that part of the color continuum signified by "blue" is signified in Russian by two separate words: *goluboj,* "light blue," and *sinij,* "dark blue," each of which represents in Russian separate colors, not different shades of one color.

In the light of these distinctions, it is possible to understand one reason why certain explanations of structural analysis bring in a misleading distinction between so-called "objective" and "subjective" methods of structural analysis. See, for example, a reference to this distinction in Addison Wright (1968: 318-319).

Based either upon an idea that interpretation is inductive in nature or upon the idea that a "scientific" analysis of language is only possible on the plane of expression, or often upon both misconceptions, this point of view holds that all textual analyses concentrating on meaning, ideas, or themes are subjective, vague and heaven-bound. How could it be otherwise, we are told, when one is working on that nebulous uncharted and shifting plane of content? On the other hand, they continue, an analysis concentrating on the plane of expression *can* deal "objectively" with a text. For what is more concrete and tangible, for example, than inclusions, anaphora, refrains, chiasms, etc., all those structural components of a text's plane of expression? We are here in a situation analogous to the hierarchy of levels honored by the inductivist who "hugs the phonetic ground" (Hockett's phrase, quoted by Bach) as he constructs his phonemic analysis. Then he hugs the phonemic ground as he constructs his syntactic and morphological analyses. Finally, he hugs the morphemic ground, tied down snugly by syntactic ropes lest he float up into the subjective heavens of semantics where such vague and fluid creatures as semes and mythemes abound. In short, content-plane analysis is thought to be subjective because one believes the expression-plane to be the only domain of formal language study. (This is often equivalent to believing that the inductive method—*the* scientific method—has no business on the content-plane of language).

My understanding of the interrelationships between the plane of expression and the plane of content in all language phenomena leads me to accept the following positions: 1) structural analysis is possible on the plane of content as well as the plane of expression; 2) in principle, analysis on the plane of expression is not more secure nor less subjective than analysis on the plane of content; 3) there is therefore *no* hierarchical order of analysis of a given text, i.e., first on the expression plane, then on the content plane; 4) nevertheless, the analyses articulated on each plane must be compared and interrelated as a means of complementing and adjusting discovered patterns one with the other. If indeed signs operate on both planes simultaneously, the structures of both planes must somehow interact. An analysis on only one plane is as incomplete as expression without content or content without expression. I can be more specific about these four convictions, using two studies of the Books of Chronicles. Polzin (1976) contains a grammatical analysis of Chronicles and, as such, concentrates on the plane of expression. On the other hand, Wellhausen's *Prolegomena* contains, in chapter six, an analysis of the books of Chronicles that concentrates on the plane of content. Grammar concerns itself with the form, not the meaning of language whereas content analysis of language focuses on its meaning not its form. The differences between these two analyses of Chronicles depend primarily upon the plane of language studied in each case. For example, when my study discusses the synoptic and non-synoptic segments of Chronicles insofar as they show contrasting patterns in the use of '*et,* infinitives, forms of pronominal suffixes, etc., I am concentrating on the systematic form of expression used in these segments, that is, on my construction of the *signifier* of the language of Chronicles. On the other hand, when Wellhausen writes about "the complete difference of general conception and the multitude of discrepancies in details" between Chronicles and Sam / Kings, he is concentrating on the systematic form of content used in these corpora, that is, on his construction of their *signified* aspects.

Secondly, I believe that in principle neither type of analysis is more nor less secure than the other. It may appear at first glance that the object of analysis in grammar is more concrete than the object of analysis in content, but this impression rests upon a mistaken understanding of the objects structured by the analysis, as Bach points out (1965: 121). Phonological or morphological analysis does *not* deal with the structuring of actual utterances in a corpus, nor are the forms it isolates "actually occurring forms of the language." Phonemes and morphemes are just as much abstractions and hypothetical constructs as sememes or mythemes. It cannot be denied that linguistic abstractions in phonology and grammar have in fact produced results much more generally accepted and satisfying than those in semantics have. But this is not the same thing as stating that the situation is *necessary* by the very nature of the objects studied. The only difference here is that the signifier is the mediator of the signified and not vice-versa. On this point see Roland Barthes (1970a: 47). However this is not the same thing as saying that it is 'signifiers as system' that leads to an understanding of the signified as system.

A third conviction follows from the second: there is no *a priori* hierarchical order of analysis of a given text. A content-analysis need not be preceded by an expression-analysis nor vice-versa. We know in fact that both planes enter into each analysis in contrasting ways. For example, in linguistics the very isolation of phonemes depends upon at least an intuitive grasp of changes in meaning brought about by the commutation of one sound with another. Likewise in grammatical analysis: the emphasis may be on construction of a structure of grammatical expression, but such a structure is constructed by an intuitive interpretation of differences in meaning or content brought about in the commutation of grammatical forms. In the same way, content analysis cannot be totally independent of judgments depending upon some type of subsidiary grasp of the expression plane of a text. This is even more so the case when we leave the confines of linguistics and enter the world of literature as it is analyzed in our two examples from Chronicles. The very identity of literature depends upon an individuality and an anatomy largely concentrated on the plane of expression. Herein lies a special challenge to the biblical scholar and one of his most difficult problems. The challenge is needlessly magnified by an imagined order of investigation.

Thus my last conviction concerning the two planes of language: the sign system we call language, the language products we call literature, exist on the two planes of expression and content, upon each of which language simultaneously operates and interacts. This means that content-analysis of a text must somehow complement its expression-analysis. In the case of our two examples from Chronicles, we have a fortunate corroboration of the individual results of each analysis. The hypothesis that the Chronicler's grammar is later than Sam / Kings' grammar (Polzin: 1976) is corroborated by Wellhausen's hypothesis that the total impression of the Chronicler's message places it later than the message found in Sam/Kings, when accounts about the same persons and events are analyzed. Had these two analyses resulted in conflicting or confusing hypotheses, the very idea of the interconnection of expression and content-structure would demand a confrontation between the two analyses, an adjustment of one or the other or of both. To use another example, a *preliminary* analysis of the non-massoretic psalms of llQPs*a*, (the Psalmsscroll from Qumrân), shows a grammatical structure that is predominantly classical in nature, so that one would at first place their composition before the Late Biblical Hebrew (LBH) stage of the language. On the other hand, key ideas contained in them, that is, an examination of their content, make us very suspicious of this preliminary impression. And indeed, a closer examination of the plane of expression shows that our content plane suspicions are justified. See on this point the present writer's study (1967). Again, the book of Esther on the basis of grammar alone does not appear to be as late as other LBH compositions. Its content, however, helps us to correct this misconception and to recognize many of its expressions as archaistic rather than archaic. To give a final example, two books appeared in 1878, each arguing the opposite conclusion about the dating of the Priestly Source. Ryssel maintained on the basis of an examination of the expression plane of the Priestly source that it was the earliest of the Pentateuchal sources, whereas Julius Wellhausen, as we shall see, maintained P was the latest of the sources on the basis of an analysis of the content-plane of P. Neither could be held wrong simply because he confined his analysis to only one of the planes of language. However once the two conflicting *results* became known, the conflict had to be faced squarely. Was the expression archaic and the content only apparently late, or was the expression archaistic and the content actually late? Or perhaps Ryssel was simply wrong and P's expression was neither archaic nor archaistic but rather late. With our advance in knowledge since then, we can now be fairly sure that Wellhausen's late dating of P is correct. Had Wellhausen's content-analysis not been so admirably fashioned, perhaps the incorrect early dating of P would have continued to hold sway longer than it actually did. Wellhausen was right in this specific case not because he was less subjective than Ryssel (on many points he was more so), but because he constructed a better hypothesis based on premises, some of which, at least, have borne the test of time. As he himself writes, "But history as is well known has always to be constructed. . . The question is whether one constructs well or ill" (1965: 367).

All this underlines the view we shall shortly discuss: that all brands of hermeneutical interpretations are *hypothetical constructs* whether they be on the expression plane or the content plane. Semantics may not yet be an accepted member of the linguistic family; however, it is no longer under a cloud, as it was for a number of years following Bloomfield's book, *Language*. As Stephen Ullman remarks, "Now the pendulum has swung in the opposite extreme and semantics has become one of the growing points of linguistic study" (1973: 86).

synchronic vs diachronic

We now come to that distinction which perhaps has most relevance to the present situation in biblical studies: Structural analysis can emphasize either synchonic or diachronic structures of a text. Briefly, diachronic structures involve the text along and across its various temporal phases of development. A diachronic description represents its object according to the various changes or transformations it undergoes in time. Such a description of a man's weight would include the information that he came into the world weighing five pounds, weighed 180 pounds at age forty and now weighs 195 pounds in his sixtieth year. It is a genetic description. On the other hand, synchronic analysis studies an object at any one phase or moment in its development, if indeed it does develop. A synchronic description might tell us that a given individual is five feet tall, weighs 150 pounds, has brown hair and eyes, and walks with a limp. Or such a man might be described as he appeared fifteen years ago. Each description taken separately is synchronic, non-genetic. Were I to compare and relate this man's appearance fifteen years ago with his appearance now, I would then be offering a diachronic description. Another example might be the question, "How is this building constructed?," an ambiguous question which can be answered both synchronically and diachronically. A synchronic answer would be: "it has a cement foundation with a wooden superstructure, dry wall and brick-facing." A diachronic answer would be: "first the cement foundation was poured. Then they erected the wooden superstructure and finally they covered the inner walls with dry wall and the exterior surfaces with brick." Structure as process and structure as product are not to be confused. Each aspect corresponds to either temporal or a-temporal transformational laws as we have described them at the beginning of this chapter.

At least two factors have contributed to the general view that structural analysis is centrally concerned with synchrony. First of all the *magna carta* of modern structural linguistics composed by Ferdinand de Saussure emphasized, perhaps too strongly, the primacy of synchronic analysis over diachronic analysis. Since then it has become increasingly obvious that if the emphasis was needed, the distinction itself is not as clear-cut as Saussure supposed. This last point has been underlined, for example, by Roman Jakobson (1971a: 720-721). The value of Saussure's insight lay nevertheless in his emphasis on synchronic aspects of language hitherto neglected by the predominantly diachronic investigations that characterized his discipline and its history. Since his time, however, the importance of describing the synchronic structural relationships obtaining in any language has been adequately recognized, together with a new insight: synchrony can also be dynamic. Piaget's emphasis on structures as self-regulating points in the same direction.

A second factor which has contributed to the emphasis on synchronism in structuralism has been the essentially synchronic approach of perhaps the best-known and least understood structuralist, Claude Lévi-Strauss. Having been largely responsible for making structuralism something more than a scholarly pursuit by exciting the interest of the world at large, Lévi-Strauss has become synonymous with structuralism. Thus the new movement is understood often only in reference to the synchronic-agenetic approach that characterizes Levi-Straussian structuralism.

In reality, structural analysis can concentrate either on synchronic or diachronic structures, depending on the type of relationships it wishes to isolate, describe, and explain.

In principle, neither approach contradicts the other any more than a synchronic description of a painting denies the diachronic process whereby the painter produced it. Indeed, the value of many of Jackson Pollock's "paintings" is perhaps a function of the unorthodox process whereby he produced them. One can describe the relationship of these two types of structural analysis as complementary approaches to the analysis of any object that has a history of development. The hundreds of years during which the Hebrew Bible was shaped until it reached the substantial form we have today make it an apt object of diachronic as well as synchronic analysis. The Bible's diachronic dimensions are not in any way to be denied. However, its synchronic dimensions unfortunately have not been sufficiently exploited because of the almost exclusive emphasis on diachrony that characterizes most of modern biblical scholarship.

One final distinction concerning contrasting types of structural analysis. Structuralism may emphasize syntagmatic relationships in a text or it may concentrate on paradigmatic relationships in a text. One may consult Lyons for a clear explanation of this dichotomy (1971: 70-81 and 1973: 12-13). When applied to the study of various types of literature, e.g., narratives, certain theoretical considerations separate analysts. Thus for example Propp, Todorov and Dundes hold that temporal succession, or the order of functions as they appear in a narrative is necessary to the syntax of a narrative's structure whereas other scholars such as Lévi-Strauss apparently think otherwise. In effect this difference of opinion produces analysts who emphasize paradigmatic relations in a text whereas others emphasize the importance of syntagmatic analyses.

Second, the *models* that embody a structural analysis are self-consciously hypothetical-deductive in nature. In this respect structuralism emphasizes an aspect of analysis that it believes belongs to all hermeneutic approaches. The inductive/deductive dichotomy, as it relates to a philosophy of science, involves terminological distinctions well stated by Karl Popper (1968: especially 30). In the area of linguistics, the non-inductive nature of language study is argued for by Emmon Bach (1965) and given due emphasis by Piaget (1970). I want to apply these insights specifically to semantic questions since this is such a crucial area for anyone interested in hermeneutical approaches to biblical studies. I intend to describe what an inductivist view toward study of biblical texts would entail and why this approach does not exist. Then I will try to articulate the hypothetical, deductive thrust of hermeneutics as I understand it. Before I begin, it is important to emphasize that I am *not* using the dichotomy, inductive/deductive, to distinguish those analysts who bring a model to the text to aid analysis (the "deductive" approach of e.g. A. J. Greimas) from those analysts who prefer to discover a pattern within a text (the "inductive" approach of e.g. Todorov: 1969). It is clear that both types of analysts do indeed exist and largely do what they say they are doing. The distinction I am now going to discuss states that a truly inductive hermeneutics does not exist.

What would be the view of an inductivist who is asked to articulate a methodology or approach aimed at the formal analysis of a specific language corpus such as a biblical text? In other words, can one fashion an inductive methodology that is equipped "scientifically" to arrive at one or another of the meanings of a biblical text? The answer and attitude of a biblical scholar who is convinced of the possibility of the inductive approach to the philosophy of science can be described as follows. First, he is convinced that there must be a definite mechanical procedure (containing unambiguous rules of operation) whereby the various units of the language corpus, the "text," can be initially *identified.* It is by means of this rigorous formal first step that one is able to segment a text into discrete units whose relations will form the structural description one is aiming at. Now since this first step must be done in as rigorously formal a fashion as possible, it is immediately obvious to an inductivist that a semantic analysis of a language corpus (often called discourse analysis) fails to take even this first step, since in actual practice its division of the text into segments is partly intuitive rather than strictly formal. "Meaning" belongs to that aspect of language which is of its nature and by definition the opposite of "form" or "formal" in linguistic science. If the first requirement of language analysis is that it must be "formal" both in its object and its procedures, then it must be concluded that no semantic analysis can be "scientific" in the sense of being rigorously formal. Language is composed of two basic components, "form" and "meaning." The scientific enterprise can only concern itself with the formal aspects of language. Therefore, there can be no science of semantics or of discourse analysis and any attempt at an analysis of a text according to its various meanings is at once arbitrary, fluid, subjective, non-formal, and unscientific. It is important to point out that the inductivist *in principle* denies the application of the term, science, to semantics or semantically based disciplines, whereas there are many scholars who only assert that *de facto* we have articulated no analysis of language that can be even remotely called scientific on the plane of meaning. This means that, for an inductivist, every analysis of the *content* of biblical texts or any systematic treatment of meaning-relationships is doomed to arbitrary subjectivity from the outset. For there is no conceivable formal method whereby one initially can segment a language-corpus into meaning-units able then to be analyzed as having structural relationships with any other meaning unit of the text. In other words, there is no conceivable mechanical procedure whereby I can divide up, for example, the book of Job into meaning-units whose semantic relationships can be analyzed in a systematic way.

However, to help complete this description of an inductivist confronting hermeneutical questions, let us assume that our inductivist considers possible this initial step of a rigorously formal segmentation. What then? As Bach points out in his description of this kind of language-analyst (1965: 119-121) there is a strict hierarchy of levels of analysis which must be recognized before analysis can be correctly accomplished. Were one to allow even the *possibility* of a "scientific" analysis on the plane of content, this analysis would have to be based upon prior analyses on the pre-linguistic, phonemic, morphemic and syntactic levels of language. There is a definite *order* of analysis that must be followed if rigor is to be preserved. And just as this order must be followed at the pre-semantic stages of analysis, so would it be necessary to follow some kind of order of analysis on the semantic level, were one to admit (as inductivists do not) the possibility of rigor in semantic analyses. We see clearly now why a structuralist's apparent arbitrariness in the first segmental step of structural analysis can be scandalous to many commentators. A good deal (but not all) of the embarrassment can be explained by an inductivist paradigm of language analysis. Any attempt at an analysis of the thematic content of the Book of Job would have to be preceded, according to inductivism, by extensive systematic pre-semantic analyses upon which content-analysis rests as on a foundation.

Let me go a step further. If for the sake of argument these first two steps were possible of achievement (which inductivists deny), what then? The inductivist would come now to the heart of his analysis. He aims at *describing* whatever patterns he is able to discover existing somehow in all the inductive evidence he has been able to gather and analyze. He sees this analysis as a set of cautious generalizations, limited only to the inductive evidence he has assembled. As Leonard Bloomfield has written, "The only useful generalizations about language are inductive generalizations" (1933: 115). What this understanding of language-analysis means for the exegete is this: one may not develop any theories or hypotheses about the structure of any text that are not *verifiable* by inductive observation. As Bach points out, this approach to language study "amounts to a denial of the possibility of a science of linguistics" (1965: 116). This is so because the actual hypotheses which scholars produce cannot be verified in this inductive way. Moreover, in the area of biblical exegesis, the inductive approach relegates all exegesis that is not based on phonemic and grammatical investigations to the arena of arbitrary, subjective, non-scientific analysis of language. I will return to this point in a moment when I describe the creative, deductive nature of biblical structuralism. What I want to emphasize at this point is that, for an inductivist, analysis must be rigidly formal not only in its initial phases of *identifying* units of a language corpus but also in its essential phase of *describing* the patterns encompassing these units' relationships. Moreover, no rigorous or unambiguous analysis is possible on the semantic level of language. The inductivist view of hermeneutics describes a creature that, it thus appears, does not exist. Why is this so? We can retrace our steps over the various phases of inductive analysis and relate them to the key idea of structure. We shall see at each step that there is no point of contact between the inductivist viewpoint and what is involved in the discovery and description of a text's meaning.

First of all it must be pointed out, as Nattiez has emphasized (1973: 231-234), that when one speaks about structure in language the initial isolation and discovery of language units, phonemic as well as morphemic, is always arbitrary and to a very great extent intuitive. It may be true that the particular domain of semantics (the plane of content) adds certain dimensions of "arbitrariness" and intuition that are not present on the level of phonology and grammar. However it is that "arbitrary" nature common to *all* language domains about which I am here primarily concerned. If the first step on the road toward discovering the semantic structure of a text is the proper segmentation of the text into the various meaning units comprising that structure, there simply is no formal scientific procedure whereby such segmentation must be accomplished. As Bach points out (1965: 121), phonemes are "completely hypothetical constructs." So also are the basic

content-units of a text (variously called sememes, mythemes, etc.).
The inductivist view that one can articulate scientific procedures
of discovery has been laid to rest, in my view, by the well-known
work of certain philosophers of science such as Karl Popper and
Michael Polanyi. Popper is very definite about the procedures of
discovering an hypothesis:

> If we distinguish, with Reichenbach, between a 'procedure of
> finding' and a 'procedure of justifying' a hypothesis, then we
> have to say that the former—the procedure of finding a
> hypothesis—cannot be rationally constructed. (1968: 315)

We also read:

> The initial stage, the act of conceiving or inventing a theory,
> seems to me neither to call for logical analysis nor to be
> susceptible of it. (1968: 31)

Now this view of Popper's holds not only for our first step
(discovery of units) but also for the essential discovery of
relationships between units (description of structure): there is no
rational reconstructible procedure whereby accurate
segmentation or accurate structuration can be discovered. This is
not to say that the discovery of patterns or structures does not
demand method or that the process need not be methodical; it
means fundamentally that a major element in such a process is
creative and intuitive in nature, that is, what an inductivist
pejoratively would call subjective and arbitrary.

Michael Polanyi is no less specific on this point. The position
that one cannot hope to base one's hypothesis upon an inductive
marshalling of evidence, inductively arrived at, flows from the
nature of discovery itself. There is an essential irreversibility and
inarticulateness inherent in all discovery:

The irreversible character of discovery suggests that no
solution of a problem can be accredited as a discovery if it is a
procedure following definite rules. For such a procedure would
be reversible in the sense that it could be traced back stepwise to
its beginning and repeated at will any number of times, like any
arithmetical computation. Accordingly, any strictly formalized
procedure would also be excluded as a means of achieving
discovery. (1962: 123)

Polanyi, like Popper, emphasizes the creative element so
necessary in the construction of an hypothesis:

. . . So we see once more that discovery is creative, in the
sense that it is not to be achieved by the diligent performance of
any previously known and specifiable procedure. This
strengthens our conception of originality. The application of
existing rules can produce valuable surveys, but does not
advance the principles of science. We have to cross the logical
gap between a problem and its solution by relying on the
unspecifiable impulse of our heuristic passion . . . . (1962:
143)

It is because of the very nature of human discovery as creative and
unspecifiable that even the so-called scientific branches of
linguistics, phonology and grammar, are rooted in their first steps
in "subjective," "arbitrary" or conventionally bound processes. As
Bach points out, "The hypotheses and constructs of phonology
are neither more nor less secure than those of syntax" (1965: 121).
And neither of these are more nor less secure than those of
semantics.

Because this first step involves the discovery of semantic parts
or structures underlying the biblical text, such a process of
segmentation can be, indeed must be, as arbitrary and
unspecifiable as the creative discovery of any pattern whatsoever.
One is at this point "searching for" a structure, attempting to
discern a pattern, and the discovery might be here no more than a

hope, a passionate concern. Feel for the text, experience, background, knowledge, scholarly hunch and intuition, orderly examination of the material, all play their part even at this beginning phase of segmentation. Mechanical rules of procedure, however, in the strict inductivist meaning of this phrase, do not play an absolutely necessary role in the discovery of those parts of a whole whose interrelationships make up a structure.

Secondly, any language analyst who is an inductivist supposes a hierarchy of domains or levels of analysis. In this view one analyzes more fundamental levels before going on to other levels. Thus an exegete must base his semantically related analysis of a text upon a thorough-going and systematic grammatical analysis, which in turn should be based upon a phonemic analysis of the text in question. Here again the inductivist trap does not succeed in understanding the nature of structure. This hierarchical view mistakenly assumes that in language analysis, some structures (e.g. phonological) are closer to reality, more objective, more physical than other structures (e.g. syntactic or semantic). For now, it will be sufficient to point out that the very nature of a structure as *closed* implies that, whatever its relations to a co-, sub-, or superstructure, it can be studied in and for itself. On this point see Piaget (1970: 13-16). This view effectively rules out the *a priori* necessity of studying a number of interrelated structures in any established order.

Thirdly, an essential step of structural analysis aims at *describing* whatever structure or structures have been discovered. For an inductivist, this description is *based upon* all the inductive evidence he has gathered and analyzed. He has studied the units his prior segmentation had helped him to discover and he has articulated a cautious generalization that is only as valid as the evidence he has marshalled. Here, even more clearly than in the first step, he has ignored what Polanyi calls the "logical gap" that separates a problem from its eventual solution. In the case of exegesis the inductivist ignores the "logical gap" existing between the text in its concrete form and the structure (on any level) discovered within and behind that text. "To discover" a structure is, as Piaget emphasizes, "to construct" a structure.

The essential incompatibility between the inductivist and the hermeneutical enterprise may be summarized as follows. The inductivist believes that rigid formality and rules of procedure are necessary before one can *identify* units of a structure and especially before one can *describe* the structure composed of such units. A more realistic approach, on the other hand, recognizes that "structure" as an abstract, hypothetical, construct is incapable of inductive discovery. Popper writes "For a theory of induction is superfluous. It has no function in a logic of science" (1968: 315).

If structural analysis is not inductive, how may we then describe it? We may attempt to do so by calling it a hypothetical deductive approach, as long as it is understood that this is not thereby a claim that structuralism is in fact scientific or that it is necessarily built upon the scientific paradigm.

Perhaps the two examples I discussed earlier can help to describe what I mean by the deductivist nature of structural hermeneutics. Both examples concern the Books of Chronicles, first on the level of grammar, then on the level of semantics.

My first example illustrates the various steps that comprise a specific analysis, grammatical in nature, of the books of Chronicles. The classic work is that of A. Kropat (1909) and one may consult most recently the present writer's study (1976). The first step in analysis consists in the preliminary segmentation of the books of Chronicles into two major segments. The first segment comprises all those passages which duplicate similar passages in Samuel/Kings and is called the synoptic section of Chronicles, and the second major segment comprises those passages of Chronicles not so duplicated and therefore is called the non-synoptic section of Chronicles or simply the Chronicler's language. Now it is important to realize that this first example of segmentation does not rest upon any formal mechanical procedure inherent in the nature of grammatical analysis but rather on an accident of history, namely, that a body of traditions was preserved in two separate historical "books" of the Hebrew

Bible, Samuel / Kings on the one hand and Chronicles on the other. Another way of describing the nature of the initial segmentation is to say that the criteria of segmentation are not systematically linguistic in nature, that it is not the formal grammatical features of each segment which allow us at this point to segment Chronicles into synoptic and non-synoptic sections. This initial segmentation is, from a linguistic point of view, *arbitrary,* however useful it is for the analysis itself. At this point a set of "axioms" are employed which comprise the point of departure of the analysis. For example, central axioms will be that the Chronicler's language represents the grammatical situation of biblical Hebrew prose (= BH) in the 5th-4th centuries B.C. whereas the language of the synoptic passages represents an earlier stage of BH grammar. These statements are called axioms because they are essentially undemonstrable from a linguistic point of view. Also, even were these statements or "axioms" elsewhere the consequences of other deductive argumentations, they nevertheless still would be only hypotheses based on other "axioms."

We now come to the essential step in the grammatical analysis: the procedure whereby each major segment is analyzed with a view to discovering those features of its grammatical structure related in any way to the grammatical features of the other segment's structure. In other words, one *describes* the grammatical structure of the synoptic segment *in relation to* the grammatical structure of the non-synoptic segment. Here specific linguistic criteria are used which enable the analyst to describe and distinguish the grammatical nature of both major segments. A systematic inspection of each segment is here necessary. But it is important to note that this procedure is not an inductive *proof* for the resulting grammatical description. It is only the specific explanation or full articulation of the grammatical structure one claims to have "discovered" in the segments analyzed. Just as later when no amount of inductive investigation can really *verify* or *validate* the hypothesis at which we arrive, similarly here in the discovery procedures leading toward the hypothesis, no amount of inductive investigation *establishes* the structure as discovered. It is this false idea of a necessary phase of even a scientific investigation that M. Polanyi condemns when he writes about " . . . the hollowness of the assertion that science is simply based upon experiments which anyone can repeat at will." In reality, Polanyi continues, " . . . any critical verification of a scientific statement requires the same powers for recognizing rationality in nature as does the process of scientific discovery even though it exercises these at a lower level" (1962: 13). This power for recognizing rationality in nature is what Polanyi calls "personal knowledge" and it is diametrically opposed to the inductivist view that minute investigation is the sufficient cause of scientific discovery. I would maintain that inductive investigation is often a *necessary* step, but never the sufficient step, toward discovery since there is always a "logical gap" between the examination of a problem and its solution. It is the *sufficient* role of inductive investigation, not its usefulness nor normal necessity, which I oppose when describing discovery procedures.

Thus, a minute investigation of each segment helps to reveal a grammatical pattern that distinguishes the synoptic from the non-synoptic segments. In contrast to the synoptic passages, the Chronicler's language shows a radically reduced use of *'et* with pronominal suffix. Moreover, it reveals an increased of *'et* before nouns in the nominative case (so-called *'et* emphatic). In contrast to the synoptic passages, collectives are construed as plurals almost without exception. The Chronicler often uses plural forms of words and phrases which are singular in the synoptic passages. For example, see ᶜārê (ham) mᵉṣûrôt of 2Chr 11.10.23, etc., as opposed to ᶜārê māṣôr of 2Chr 8.5, etc. Again, the Chronicler has a reduced usage of the infinitive absolute and contrasting features concerning the infinitive construct. The Chronicler also shows a merging of the third feminine plural suffix with the third masculine plural suffix, which is not apparent in the synoptic passages. There is a contrast also in the order of cardinal numerals in appositional relationship with their substantives: the Chronicler prefers to place the substantive before the numeral whereas the opposite order is the general practice in the synoptic passages. Other contrasts involving weights and measures could also be mentioned here. For a full presentation and evaluation of the material see R. Polzin (1976). In short, one discovers a series of features that distinguishes and contrasts the grammatical structures of each major segment.

The stage is now set for the *deductive* phase of the analysis. Since the analyst's axioms involve the diachronic assumption that synoptic passages represent an *earlier* grammatical stage of BH than the non-synoptic passages, it follows as a major consequence that the grammatical structure of the synoptic passages, as *discovered* and *described,* represents BH at a stage prior to that stage of BH discovered and described in the non-synoptic passages. It is important to point out that this consequence has the character of an hypothesis since it ultimately rests upon indemonstrable axioms. *

This example of a grammatical analysis of Chronicles illustrates the hypothetical-deductive associations of structural analysis. In its operative procedures structuralism is hypothetical because the analysis proceeds from starting points which can be described as something like indemonstrable axioms to consequences that may be described as *something like* hypotheses. Similarly, structuralism can be described as deductive since the process going from axioms to hypothesis is *something like* an act of deduction. The "logical gap" or creative nature of structuralism rests not only on all the myriad, often non-specifiable, factors that lead the analyst to accept a set of axioms as an essential part of his analysis, but especially on the often non-specifiable and mysterious process whereby he discovers the structures he sets in relation to his "axioms" to produce certain "hypotheses."

A second example illustrating the hypothetical deductive associations of structural analysis is drawn from Julius Wellhausen's analysis of Chronicles in his classic work on the History of Israel (1965 [1878] : 171-227). In a following chapter I shall delineate his methodology in greater detail. Here I want to discuss only in a limited way the deductive associations of his

* Yes. Reasons other than different temporal stages in Hebrew might account for the different grammatical features (i.e. regional-dialectical differences, different authors, etc.).

methodology. Wellhausen, as a proponent of *tendenz-criticism*, worked predominantly on the semantic level, and it is for this reason that I have chosen him for my second example. He wrote his book in order to establish that the Priestly source was the latest of the Pentateuchal sources. Briefly, he sought to establish that the semantic structure of P could be seen to be representative of a later stage in the history of Israel's religion than the semantic structure of the other sources. He assumed that the sharp tools of higher criticism had accurately segmented the Pentateuchal (read for him Hexateuchal) traditions into three major sources: JE, D, and P. He also assumed that JE was earlier than D. He saw his task as showing that P is not earlier than JE and D but later than they are. His method of argumentation was to explain how the semantic structure of P, that is, the interrelationships of meaning units comprising the main message of P, everywhere *assumes* the existence of the semantic structure of D, whereas the main message of JE is everywhere *ignorant* of D. He believed that an examination of the various legal and narrative portions of each source bears out his conclusions.

Part One of the *Prolegomena* treats the legal sources of the Hebrew Bible, and Part Two concerns its narrative traditions. The first chapter of Part Two treats Chronicles, and Wellhausen explains why he begins this part of his work with an examination of Chronicles. Changes in prevailing ideas necessarily reveal themselves in the shape of the traditions of each successive age. Some periods in Israel's history allow us to apprehend prevailing ideas with greater certainty than other periods. Thus, we are told, he begins the inquiry where the matter is clearest—the books of Chronicles. Wellhausen intends to show that the varying ways in which Sam / Kings and Chronicles respectively represent *the same facts and events* are explained by the mere difference of date of their compositions. We see immediately that his main concern is an analysis of the meaning or inner significance of each corpus. He thus provides us with an investigation on the plane of content, rather than on the plane of expression which was the domain of my first example. Wellhausen indicates his main concern when he writes, " . . . here the difficulty . . . is not to collect the details of evidence, but so to shape the superabundant material as to convey a right total impression" (1965: 172). This is clearly an emphasis on pattern or structure rather than on individual details of content.

The first step in any hermeneutics is the process of segmentation and Wellhausen indicates that a preliminary stage of this first step has already been accomplished by historical forces:

> . . . we are here in a favorable position of starting with the objects of comparison distinctly defined, instead of having as usual to begin by a critical separation of sources of various age combined in one document. (1965: 171)

If my first grammatical example utilized a segmentation of Chronicles into synoptic and non-synoptic *passages*, this semantic example moves up to the plane of *content* and compares meaning units from Sam / Kings with meaning units from Chronicles. Wellhausen further segments synoptic content into three sub-segments: varying treatments of David, of Solomon, and of the succeeding kings of Israel. He closes the chapter with a treatment of some non-synoptic segments of Chronicles, segments he calls the "additions" of Chronicles: primarily 1Chr 1-9. Throughout his analysis of Chronicles vs. Sam / Kings, he concentrates on the *signified* not *signifier* aspect of language.

Before I describe the essential step of his analysis, that is, his discovery of the differing semantic structures of each major segment—what he calls "shaping the super-abundant material as to convey a right total impression"—it is necessary to mention certain "axioms" that form the starting point of his deduction-like argumentation. Just as my grammatical example began with the diachronic axiom that the synoptic passages of Chronicles represent an earlier stage of BH than the non-synoptic passages, so too Wellhausen has similar axioms concerning Sam / Kings and Chronicles respectively:

and, what is more, we can also date the rival histories with
tolerable certainty. The Books of Samuel and of Kings were
edited in the Babylonian exile; Chronicles on the other hand
was composed fully three hundred years later, after the
downfall of the Persian empire, out of the very midst of fully
developed Judaism. (1965: 171)

Another axiom used in this chapter is the basic content-structure
of the Priestly Code which Wellhausen has just fully described as
part of his argumentation in Part One. This point will be dealt
with in more detail later in this book, but for now one need only
emphasize that Wellhausen's description of the Priestly Code and
his hypothesis concerning its dating are used in this chapter on
Chronicles like axioms which fully account for the varying ways in
which the two histories represent the same facts and events.

Using such axioms as his starting point, Wellhausen will argue
in the following deductive manner: since Sam / Kings is early and
Chronicles late, and since Priestly content is found in Chronicles
but not in Sam / Kings, the differences between the two rival
histories is explained by positing the composition of P in the
interval between them. In other words, the content-structure of
Chronicles supposes the existence and influence of the Priestly
Code whereas the content-structure of Sam / Kings does not. The
book of Chronicles is a function of the Priestly Code; Sam / Kings
is not.

Note well that just as his diachronic axioms concerning the
relative dating of Sam / Kings and Chronicles are discoverable but
not demonstrable—that is, even those "axioms" that are
hypothetical conclusions of previous deductive arguments are
ultimately based upon other indemonstrable axioms—so also his
description of the structural pattern of each segment on the plane
of content is discoverable but not demonstrable in the strict sense
of the term. Wellhausen's detailed descriptions of the varying
semantic treatments of "the same facts and events" are not a *proof*
that such structures exist but are more precisely his full
articulation of the structure he has discovered, an articulation of
what he calls the right "total impression" (1965: 172, 182) or "the

complete difference of general conception" (1965: 222). There exists a logical gap between what he calls "the multitude of discrepancies in details" and the "complete difference of general conception." One does not go from the former to the latter by a process of inductive logic. Rather one deductively arrives at, as it were, an hypothesis that best explains not only the axiomatic structures one accepts to begin with but also the various patterns one discovers along the way. Some kind of methodical, inductive process may be preliminarily useful for the construction of the hypothesis. Such a process, however, is never its sufficient cause.

The third self-conscious aspect of structuralism involves the subject who does the analyzing; deep subjectivity (Poole 1972) might be an appropriate phrase here, and I would like to borrow it to describe this aspect of structuralism as applied to the hermeneutical problems of biblical studies. Somehow or other this aspect centers around the relationships existing between the reader (exegete, interpreter) and the text. If in the text part relates to part and if a text's structure is the complex of relationships between those parts, the structure of the process of interpretation is constituted by the relationships of the "givens" a reader brings to his reading and those of the text itself which is read. For an analysis to be structural there must be a self-conscious awareness (Polanyi's subsidiary awareness) of the law-like relationship between the analyst's model, the structure as constructed, and the personal structures (the structures structuring) within the analyst which enabled him to construct or "find" such a structure of the text in the first place. Structural analysis confronts both the object investigated and the operational laws of the subject who constructs the model. It seems to me that it is the conscious awareness of and relationship between the object constructed and subject constructing that constitutes the contextual understanding, i.e. the structural understanding, of structural analysis. It follows therefore that it makes no difference what the specific *content* is of the structure constructed or what the specific system is by which such a structure is constructed by the analyst. It is not the nature or essence or positive input of the model itself, nor the methodology by which the model was constructed, that makes an analysis "structural." Rather, structural understanding is the *conscious* or self-*conscious* articulation of any structure whatsoever within the context of or viewed simultaneously with the subject's system of organization, each phase of which, 'structure as structuring' (within the analyst) and 'structure as structured' (within the object) is the context of the other.

Structuralism in this view is neither a theory nor a methodology. Rather, an analysis is 'structural' to the extent that an analyst consciously constructs a model of which he has subsidiary awareness of its relationship to the very set of procedural tools he used to construct it in the first place. It might be helpful to describe a structural analysis as involving an implicit story about one's search for an object, the successful conclusion or climax of which story is not precisely the description of the object (a necessary but insufficient part of the story) but an awareness of the paths that led the investigator to find or construct his object. Without this "climax" the story is not structural since the object is not structurally understood. For it is only structurally understood when it is related in some way to the *context* in which it was constructed in the first place. Here it is form, not content, that specifies structure, both the structure of the object studied, and the structure of the "methodology" or approach by which it is studied.

A structural analysis is like a syntagm in language: its value, meaning, form is *relational* in the most fundamental sense. Not only must we know *what* is said, but *who* said it and *in what context* it was said. Viewed in this way, structural analysis is nothing else than the semiotics of knowledge. It is neither theory nor practice. It is rather the conjunction of theory and practice considered as *sign*.

To illustrate what I mean by the self reflexive or subjective aspect of structuralism, I can describe the hermeneutical process with the help of a semiotic system based on Saussure (1966) and Hjelmslev (1953).

Saussure explained a sign as constituted by the relationship of "signifier" (*signifiant*) and "signified" (*signifié*). Similarly every explanation of a text, insofar as it intends to articulate a text's significance, is a statement about a statement in the sense that it defines or analyzes the text as a *signifier* having a certain content or *signified* which it, the explanation, attempts to articulate. Every explanation of a text is the substitution of one "word" for another since it is the substitution of one statement for another. Every text is a sign whose *signified* aspects cannot be re-presented except by a sign other than the text itself. When I make any statement whatsoever about a text's meaning, I am saying something about it as a *sign* and I thereby relate it in some way to another *sign*, my own statement about it. This new relation which I thus set up is one in which the text itself is considered as relating to my statement about it as *signifier* to *signified*. But now there are two statements instead of one, two signs instead of one. Since I intend these two signs to be related to one another as *signifier* to *signified*, this implies that my statement about a statement in reality constitutes a third sign. This process of explaining one text by means of another text is equivalent to joining two signs together to form a new sign, a new object of study whose parts or constituent elements (*signifier* =original text and *signified* =statement about that text) cannot now be studied or analyzed except in relation to one another. My statement about a statement cannot be studied by itself but must be studied insofar as it is part of a sign, i.e. in relation to the statement it is supposed to "explain."

Now suppose one wants to analyze my statement about a text in order to judge its "validity" in relation to the text itself. This procedure would produce a *third* statement which attempts to assess the validity of my claim, namely, whether my statement is related to the original statement as *signified* is to *signifier*. Now this third statement can either reassert aspects of this relation or deny them. If it reasserts certain aspects of the second statement, one now has a third statement, which purports to be the significance of or a signified aspect of the second statement. In other words, this third statement sets up another sign composed of the text and my exegesis as *signifier* and a further statement as *signified*. If, on the other hand, this further statement denies aspects of the relation of signifier to signified which my statement set up, it in effect is denying the particular significance of my statement. It is saying that the original text does not have all or some of the significance I said it has.

The implication of all this is important in the understanding of structural analysis. *Every* statement about a statement involves the constituting of a sign in which something "significant" (the *signified*) is said about something else (the *signifier*). But even when one is supposed to be talking about "things" or "objects," e.g. "the man Abraham has been chosen by Yahweh," rather than statements, what one *says* are *words* so that every exegesis is a statement about a statement, every exegesis is a sign. To talk about things which are not language is still to *talk* so that even when I want to assess statements about things I can only do so by articulating statements about a statement. To assent to a statement about things is still to assent to the sign constituted by that statement. There is no way out of the semiological circle and it is precisely the self-reflexive power of structuralism that enables it to recognize and to emphasize this basic weakness.

I would describe a structural analysis as the intersection of at least three sign-systems. First of all, since every structural analysis is itself a language-product, it can be considered a sign-system comprising a *signifier*, its expression plane, and a *signified*, its content-plane. It is a sign like every other language product. Secondly, since I am here talking about a structural analysis of a biblical text, I view a structural analysis as a statement about another statement, a sign explaining, or relating to, another sign. From this perspective, since the analysis purports to *explain* or *give the significance* of a biblical text, the structural model is related to the text from which it was derived as *signified* to *signifier*. In other words, the object studied and the structure constructed *together* constitute a sign, a statement about a statement in which the former purports to articulate the content or, *significance* of the latter. Just as the biblical text is already a sign-system and the structural analysis as language is another sign-system the relation between these two sign-systems itself embodies a sign system. Thirdly, since the construction of a model involves not just an object to be structured but a structuring subject, namely an analyst, the model or structural analysis can be viewed as pointing toward, or indicative of, the system within the analyst by which it, the model, was constructed. In other words the structural analysis is the *signifier* of a particular content, namely the structures (within the analyst) viewed as the *signified* of the analysis. This combination of model as *signifier* and subject as *signified* constitutes the third-sign system that intersects a structural analysis. We can imagine the structural process as composed of these three elements:

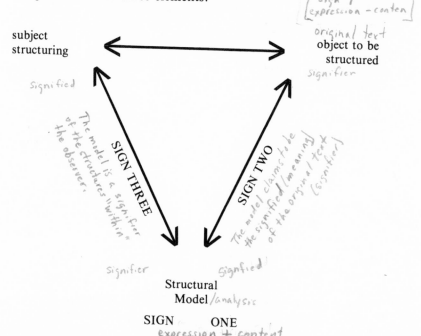

Structural
Model /analysis

SIGN   ONE
expression + content
(signifier)   (signified)

Structural analysis, viewed as the intersection of sign-systems can be described as

a) the *signified* aspect of the object structured, the latter seen as its *signifier* (SIGN 2)

b) the *signifier* aspect of the subject structuring, the latter seen as its *signified.* (SIGN 3)

c) itself a sign composed of signifier (expression) and signified (content) (SIGN l)

(Of course, since the object studied, the biblical text, is already a language product, it constitutes a *fourth* sign system; indeed, from a semiotic point of view, *every* object in the world can be viewed as part of a sign-system).

One can view these various interrelationships as follows:

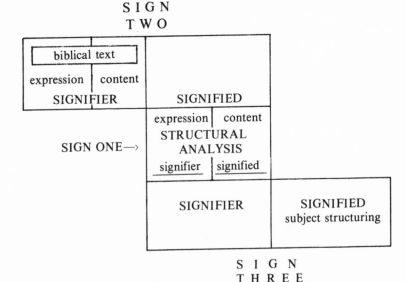

Structural analysis as sign can be viewed in its dual role as the *meaning* (=content) of an object but the *expression* of a subject. It is the crucial awareness and self-consciousness of the latter role of analysis that most often signals the study of an object as truly structural.

Susan Wittig (1975b) has provided us with a parallel account of what I call the subjective nature of structuralism. Her impressive paper is based in part on the American semioticians / and Semanticists Morris, Peirce, and Stephen Ullman, together with useful insights about the "phenomenology" of the reading act drawn from Wolfgang Iser (1974) and Roman Ingarden (1973). Wittig's analysis is intended to be a semiotic discussion of New Testament parables and moreover questions the usefulness of the sign-system of Saussure and Hjelmslev in this regard. Nevertheless, her paper accurately describes the self-conscious subjectivity that is in my opinion structuralism's most valuable contribution to the quest for an adequate hermeneutics. In the following citation with which Wittig concludes her study, what is said about "the parable" is equally valid when applied to "structural analysis." (It is to my mind more than accidental that American attempts to apply structuralism to New Testament studies have largely concentrated on the parables):

"The meaning of the parables—the meaning of any text . . . lies in the reader's own act of structuration, in his efforts to achieve significance, to understand both the parable and his own system of values and beliefs which is called to his attention by the parable. Indeed, if the parable has any single dependable meaning, it is that the human mind creates significance, and can understand itself completely only when it can comprehend itself in the act of making meaning" (1975: 28).

Now that I have completed my description of what I think are the key aspects of structuralism as a hermeneutical approach, I come to the only important part of this discussion: how my description should be understood. Since I believe that structuralism is a particularly valuable way of understanding things, my description of structuralism was an attempt to describe it *in a structural way*, and I believe that the reader will only understand what I am driving at if he succeeds in looking at my description of structural analysis structurally.

One sign that the reader may be on his way toward a structural understanding of my description of structural analysis would be his awareness of a certain degree of frustration that my description did not say anything *essential* about the intrinsic nature of the structuralist approach. I wrote about how a *text* is a system of structures and how an *interpreter* is a builder of structures and when I came to discuss what a structural *analysis* is, the most I could say about it was how it was like all other hermeneutical approaches. So far I have written nothing really concrete or distinctive about *how one can identify a structural analysis itself.*

The reader who is aware that I talked around and about structuralism without saying "what it is in itself" is on his way to understanding my description in the very same way as a structuralist understands something. If structuralism proclaims the importance of looking at things in a new way, this means that its own description of itself should be looked at in this new way. The description is a "something" like everything else. Therefore, to understand the structuralist message means something more than understanding what it says about itself or anything else. One must understand what it says *according to the very way structuralism claims a thing can be profitably understood: not in itself but in its relations with its context.* Thus to see my description of structuralism as frustratingly skirting the issue is to become aware that I attempted to describe structuralism by remaining faithful to its central vision: seeing and describing something relationally and contextually.

This is why I believe structuralism cannot be a distinctive discipline or methodology. To label it such is to believe it has a specifiable *content* that can be discovered and analyzed. But then structuralism's paradoxical message, that you really do not understand something in itself but only in its context, would be understood, by some kind of madness, in and for itself according to the very mode of understanding it is trying to counteract or at least complement. Such a misunderstanding would be as incomprehensible as promoting the abolition of the death penalty by making it a capital crime to oppose such abolition.

We can conclude this discussion of structuralism with some remarks on one of structuralism's obvious failings: structuralists are often obscure in their enthusiastic but stuttering attempts to explain what it is they think they are doing. That is to say, we structuralists often appear to be a confused and confusing group. Starting from the archetypal high priest of structuralism, Claude Lévi-Strauss, and extending all the way down to the enthusiastic writers working at the lower depths of the movement, clarity of exposition is not a common commodity. It is as though there were an assumption that the idea of "deep" in deep subjectivity necessarily implies "dark," "difficult to see," even "surrealistic." Structuralism does not necessarily involve the convoluted statements, bewildering neologisms, shifting terminology and mystical dimensions that characterize many structural analyses or accounts sympathetic to such approaches. This monograph, I realize, is open to this same criticism of obscurantism. Two recent articles are especially illustrative of the state of affairs to which I refer. Both of them are written by competent young scholars, contain valuable insights concerning structuralism, and have been helpful to me in structural matters. But this has been so in spite of, not because of, their clarity of expression and content.

A recent review article by William Doty (1973) illustrates that penchant for neologisms and awkward expressions which characterizes much structuralist writing. It is clear that many of the following citations derive from the scholars to which Doty refers rather than to his own style of presentation. We owe a great deal to scholars like Doty who take on such difficult but necessary tasks. Nevertheless, this article bristles with such expressions as "the textual pole of communication contact," "grammaticality," "a speaker may not miscontext *bits* of meaning." We learn about "text-contextual structure" and about "fundamental category-projection." There is reference to studies about "the special qualities of narrated time and narrated world." We read about the "primality of access through language" and about "a category-confusion error." The article discusses Güttgemanns' reference to "macrosyntactic matrix(es)," "paratagmatic" elements, "nar-remes" and "textemes." We learn from Güttgemanns that "The "genres" are therefore to be understood as generative phenomena of "text-competence consisting of selections and combinations of linguistic functions." The evangelists were responsible (according to form criticism) for an "arbitrary superimposition of perspectival frameworks."

More important than these examples from the plane of expression is the misleading assumption that all these new insights about which Doty is commenting serve as "improving upon form-critical procedures by incorporating disciplined linguistic analysis" (119). Doty adds, "I share a sense of the importance of non-religious literary criticism and linguistics, both as a means of disciplining what has come to be an extremely chaotic and methodologically unclarified field" (121). The truth is that linguistics is methodologically disciplined *as an accomplished fact* only in those areas of language study below the sentence, not beyond it. And even here semantics has been a problem for decades. To promote linguistic insights in order to improve biblical studies is a task I share with Doty. But to promote these insights precisely in order to bring discipline and a clear methodology into biblical studies is to invest them with powers, in my opinion, far beyond their present abilities. I cannot escape the perhaps unfair impression that the preponderance of neologisms and borrowed linguistic terminology in many structuralist works somehow is supposed to impress one with an image of methodological discipline, whereas in fact within linguistics itself there is at this level of language study a self conscious awareness of unattained goals and methodological groping. My conviction here is that a great deal of false advertising is provided by enthusiastic promoters of what in itself is a good thing: the opening-up of disciplines one to the other. One must face the fact, already sufficiently emphasized, that analysis is at present only a hope and a dream. And like many dreams it is confused and confusing.

A look at a second article illustrates such confusion. As with Doty's article, the review article by William Hendricks (1973) contains valuable insights into the structuralist movement but is at the same time confusing. Entitled 'Verbal Art and the Structuralist Synthesis," the article discusses two issues occasioned by the publication of *Structural Analysis of Oral Tradition* edited by Pierre Maranda and Elli Köngas Maranda. The first half of this article discusses amongst other things what Lévi-Strauss and A. J. Greimas each mean by the threefold structural scheme: ARMATURE (FRAMEWORK), CODE, and MESSAGE. Showing how these terms mean quite different things for each author and pointing out the difficulty of arriving at some assurance concerning what they *do* mean to each author, Hendricks goes on to show how Greimas' "discussion of the notion of code provides a needed clarification of Lévi-Strauss' ideas; also it makes an independent contribution of great value—a ground-breaking first step toward the integration of myth interpretation into semantic theory" (249). The trouble here is that whichever scheme is preferable, they both depart from the usual meanings of CODE/MESSAGE as developed by communication theory and applied to linguistics by scholars of such stature as R. Jakobson (1971a: 224). So that in the structural study of folklore, when one comes across the terms CODE, FRAMEWORK, or MESSAGE, does he understand these terms as understood by Lévi-Strauss, Greimas, Hendricks, Jakobson, or whomever? And how does he know he understands what, for example, Lévi-Strauss himself means by these terms? The problems of communication here are quite significant.

It is one thing to stutter; it is quite another to stutter without being aware of it or, if aware, unable to admit it. Present attitudes toward structuralism would be freed from many unnecessary complications were structuralists to admit that they have a tendency to stutter. As Jakobson has so clearly shown, even asphasiacs have much to teach us about the acquisition and use of language. Ultimately the less aware a structuralist is of his stuttering attempts, the less structural his analysis is. In spite of Barthes' inimitable brilliance, even he is not immune from justified criticisms about obscurantism. For example John Updike (1975: 194) concludes "He [Barthes] teaches us to see multiple layers of reader-writer interaction hovering above every page; above his own pages there is, faint but obscuring, a frosted layer of irony that blurs opus and commentary into a single plane."

Bibliographical Remarks— Part One

1. *"Structure" in Language*

Three linguistically oriented treatments can be mentioned here. Roman Jakobson (1971a: 711-722) surveys the territory in a simple yet profound way. Emile Benveniste (1971b) also clarifies for us what structure means in linguistics. Finally, "Structural Linguistics" is the subject of an article by André Martinet (1953). A more recent treatment is A. Martinet (1965). One can get a taste of what structure in language means from a more philosophic point of view in G. Granger (1965). Raymond Boudon, a sociologist, gives us two detailed examples of structure in language (1971: 64-78, 103-115). John Lyons has recently written on "Structuralism and Linguistics" (1973: 5-19). And Jean Piaget devotes a chapter of his monograph to structural linguistics (1970: 74-96).

2. *Structuralism and Deep Subjectivity*

In order to put this aspect of structuralism in perspective, a few remarks about an otherwise admirable introduction to the structuralist approach. Raymond Boudon (1971) presents us with a picture of the structuralist enterprise which strongly denies the present usefulness of structural analysis in the study of literature. There is a crucial distinction, he writes, between the structuralism of linguistics and anthropology and that of literary studies. Whereas the former can be scientific and valuable, the latter is at present non-scientific and useless. The one is truly structural, the other is only "magical" insofar as it succeeds in only chanting the name, "structuralism." Boudon's initial insight, that structuralism should be defined contextually rather than essentially, is a valuable one. But his application of this insight is misleading since he bases his *syntagmatic* description of structuralism upon a prior

44

paradigmatic understanding of certain aspects of *modern science.* Whether or not Lévi-Strauss is correct when he asserts that syntagmatic analysis is meaningless unless it rests upon the paradigmatic relationships that exist between various syntagms and their parts (1970: 307), it appears to me that Boudon's description of structuralism ultimately fails not because his syntagmatic description is based upon a paradigm but more precisely because it appears to be based upon an unfortunate paradigm. By basing his "structural analysis of structuralism" on a particular *scientific* paradigm, essentially that of K. Popper, he appears to me to fall into the essentialist trap of faulting literary structuralism because its last step is at present non-verifiable (or in Popper's terms, "non-falsifiable"). This means it lacks an essential characteristic that "scientific" structuralism possesses, namely "falsifiability." However, to analyze structural analysis structurally, and not "scientifically," is to see that the last step in "scientific" structuralism, falsifiability, and the last step in literary structuralism, intelligibility, are in fact structural variations within a common pattern which transcends the notion "scientifically falsifiable."

If the object of Boudon's analysis is structural analysis, he *must* describe it "contextually" not "inherently" as he himself recognizes. But since he assumes that "a structure is either a scientific hypothesis or it is nothing" (1971: 101), he fails to carry through his *contextual* analysis of structural analysis. He has in fact invested it with the paradigmatic nature of 'science.' However, if we were to view the transformation in science, hypothesis——>falsifiability, as a variant of the transformation in literary analysis, hypothesis——>intelligibility, we might recognize a crucial aspect of structuralism apparently denied by his description: the "logical gap," as Polanyi describes it, between the *testing* of a theory and the assertion that it is false. In other words, his agreement with Popper concerning the necessary falsifiability of all true scientific hypotheses forces Boudon to neglect the *creative* quality of this last step of scientific structuralism just as he fails to recognize any *'scientific* quality' in the last step of his "magical" literary structuralism. It is the crucial value of structuralism to recognize the truly arbitrary and subjective nature of *all* analytic and synthetic inquiry, be it scientific or not. The same creative impulses which are a necessary part of the discovery of a scientific hypothesis are present in attempts to validate or falsify it. This is a key insight of Polanyi's philosophy of science and marks a crucial advance over Popper's description, which, it appears to me, does not accurately describe the process of testing theories.

There are any number of bibliographic sources, some more obviously structuralist than others, which help to clarify this crucial attitude of structuralism which we are attempting to describe as "deep subjectivity." Whether they approach the problem by discussing science and literature as R. Barthes (1970c) does, or theory and practice as M. Horkheimer does (1972), or subject and object as P. Caws does (1970), or linguistic phenomena and extra-linguistic context as R. Lakoff does (1972), or subjectivity and objectivity as Roger Poole does (1972), the effect is the same: to blur the illusory clarity of the distinction between each element of the dichotomy.

R. Barthes (1970c) discusses the well-known criticism of the approach of literary structuralists which usually takes the form of asserting that literary structuralists at best produce verbal art which only masquerades as science. Besides Boudon's criticisms, mentioned above, we see the 'methodology' of Barthes criticized from a scientific viewpoint by J. C. Gardin (1967), Jean Molino (1969) and George Mounin (1970). But as Barthes points out, it would be a mistake for structuralism to model itself after the human sciences and thus to present itself as a science 'yet to be born.' For this aim would ultimately be self-defeating since structuralism would then still subscribe to the 'scientific' illusion that the language it produces is *expression* whereas only its *content* is "science." Structuralism will actually be selling out to science if it continues to recognize the distinction between language and metalanguage, the usual way some scholars resolve the dilemma of analyzing a vague and formless object (language) in a language-like way that is sufficiently scientific (metalanguage). Barthes recommends a blurring of this distinction so that language-centered structuralism and its object tend toward homogeneity. It seems to me that Barthes' criticisms about the scientific study of the meaning of language have a direct bearing on the role of 'scientific method' in biblical exegesis. Biblical exegesis cannot claim to be 'scientific' in the usual sense of the term.

Other critics of Barthes find his hermeneutics unsatisfactory for reasons other than those concerning his lack of "scientific method." For example, John Updike writes "Barthes compels our respect more by what he demands than by what he delivers; his criticism lacks only the quality of inspiring trust. It is never relaxed" (1975: 194).

Concerning descriptions of the subjective aspect of structuralism, Susan Wittig's paper (1975b) appears to me to be at present the clearest and most comprehensive explanation. For those who want to explore more deeply the phenomenology of the reading act, Wittig finds Roman Ingarden's *The Cognition of the Literary Work of Art* (1973) a valuable source.

My choice of the phrase, deep subjectivity, is not meant to assert the primacy of some sort of "subjectivity" over "objectivity" in structuralist thought. Rather I want to emphasize an aspect of structural analysis that has not been sufficiently emphasized: the *structural* role of the interpreter in producing an analysis. In this regard I am in general agreement with Richard E. Palmer (1975) when he describes the postmodern turn of hermeneutics as involving an aspect of "beyond subjectivity."

Finally on the question of obscurantism as an aspect of many structuralists' writing, there are some telling points made by Bernard Bergonzi in a perceptive review of a number of recent structuralist books (1975).

3. *Important Dichotomies Relevant to Structural Hermeneutics*

a) *Inductive/deductive.* The essentially noninductive nature of the study of language is brilliantly described by Emmon Bach (1965). As I have already noted, Bach argues for the hypothetical-deductive nature of linguistic studies. I see no reason to exclude his insights from similar importance in the study of literature or discourse. By far the clearest treatment of the hypothetical-deductive nature of structuralism as it applied to the social sciences is that of Raymond Boudon (1971). As mentioned above, Boudon's over-dependence on a paradigm drawn from the natural sciences leads him to brand most literary structuralists as purveyors of a "magical," not a "scientific" structuralism. His distinction is especially relevant when he discusses the question of how to "verify" a particular structural analysis of an object. A classic defence of the position that a theory of induction has no place in the logic of science is that of K. Popper (1968). As my chapter indicates, my stance has been to adapt Popper's insight to the domain of language and literature studies through the corrective use of M. Polanyi's philosophy of science (1962). This latter work clarifies the *creative* nature of even the verification process in science, a feature not sufficiently recognized by Popper or Boudon. Finally, C. Lévi-Strauss (1967: 54-65) also emphasizes the hypothetical deductive nature of the structuralist enterprise as opposed to inductively oriented approaches.

b) *Synchronic/Diachronic Hermeneutics.* Paul Ricouer in his dialogues with Lévi-Strauss, maintains that in the semitic and Judeo-Christian spheres diachrony should prevail over synchrony in one's methodological approach. See Ricouer (1969: 48ff). Nevertheless, as recently as November 1975 (at a AAR Seminar in Chicago) Ricouer admits that he has no answer on how to meaningfully relate diachronic or genetic biblical interpretations to synchronic ones. He also stated that he feared "historical obscurantism" more than he did structural analysis. Lévi-Strauss (1963) maintains that the only difference between his sphere of myths and the Judeo-Christian sphere from the point of view of the diachrony / synchrony dichotomy is one of *documentation*, or rather its paucity, for studying past societies. Jakobson (e.g. 1971a: 720-721) and Lévi-Strauss (1967: 87-89) both emphasize a weakening of this dichotomy by means of an appeal to the *dynamics* of linguistic synchrony.

c) *Plane of Expression / Plane of Content.* The key importance of this dichotomy for understanding structural hermeneutics is not always recognized. In my opinion, this dichotomy helps to put into perspective the work of rhetorical criticism as seen, for example, in James Muilenberg (1969) and Addison Wright (1968) both of whom concentrate on the plane of expression, as opposed to structuralists such as Polzin (1974) or Via (1971, 1973) who either concentrate on thematic structure or use formal literary considerations in an attempt to discover "deep structure" and to develop a systematics on the plane of content. As we have noted, this dichotomy is basic to the theory of language proposed by Hjelmslev (1953) and his followers (e.g. Jean-Pierre Paillet [1973]). Note however Wittig's caution on the use of Hjelmslev here (1975b).

d) *Paradigmatic / Syntagmatic.* Rooted in theoretical linguistics, this dichotomy is helpful in interrelating various examples of structural hermeneutics. Moreover in specific questions, such as occur in the study of narrative structures, structuralists differ in their opinions. For example, some analysts discover structural laws in the very *sequence* of narrative units whereas others do not. In other words, is a myth or a folk tale like a Latin sentence in which word order is often not crucial to its meaning or rather like an English sentence in which word order is crucial? On one hand Lévi-Strauss (1967: 202-228) will analyze the Oedipal myth and disregard sequence to discover *paradigmatic* structure. On the other hand, V. Propp (1968) holds that the corpus of Russian folktales he investigated shows the order or sequence of narrative units to be remarkably stable. Thus Propp discusses the *syntagmatic* structure of his narratives, as A. Dundes points out (See Propp [1968: XI-XVII]). The central importance of this problem is discussed by R. Barthes (1966: 12-14). Another important theoretical discussion of this problem can be found in Todorov (1971). Scholes (1974: 143-147) summarizes well the important points Todorov makes on the nature and function of structuralist *reading*, especially the significance of the ordering of elements in a literary text.

4. *The Structural Study of Literature*

a) *Structuralism and Literary Studies.* This topic is so vast that my choices here are even more eclectic than in the other sections. We can first mention some journals. *Poetics: International Review for the Theory of Literature* started publication in 1970 and defines its identity as "being interested exclusively in theoretical and methodological work" and explicitly includes Structuralism within this category. Another periodical, *Poétique: Revue de théorie et d'analyse littéraire* publishes from time to time structuralist authors; two of its editors are T. Todorov and G. Genette, two of the best-known promoters of the present structuralist movement. Volume 8 (1966) of *Communications* (Ecole Pratique des Hautes Etudes) is devoted to "L'analyse structurale du Récit," and contains an introductory article by Roland Barthes (1966) and other articles by A. J. Greimas, Claude Bremond, Umberto Eco, Jules Gritti, Violette Morin, Christian Metz, Tzvetan Todorov, and Gerard Genette. Volume 12 of *Langages* is devoted to "Linguistique et littérature." When one determines to launch out into a systematic study of discourse, he immediately confronts immense problems such as whether the aspect of "*énonciation*," as opposed to "*énoncé*," belongs to his object of study. Since this question is analogous to the role of "*Sitz im Leben*" in form-critical studies, one might profitably consult a recent issue of *Langages,* Volume 17 (1970), devoted entirely to the question of "*L'énonciation*" and containing articles by Benveniste, Ducrot, P. F. Strawson and Z. Vendler; see also the work of Claude Germain (1973) and a fine article by Robin Lakoff (1972), both about linguistic context.

A useful survey on the structural study of literature is Robert Scholes' *Structuralism in Literature* (1974). Besides containing a balanced annotated bibliography, Scholes' book aims at detailing how structuralism is both a movement of mind and a method. He is largely successful in conveying the vision, imagination and mind-set that is present day structuralism. Unfortunately he is not successful in showing how his survey of key structuralist work reveals a distinctively recognizable method. Scholes perceptively sees that one of the valuable movements of structuralism in recent years is *toward* a reading of individual literary works, after initial and necessary investigations which Scholes calls *micropoetics* and *macropoetics,* This emphasis on individuality and uniqueness of texts is precisely the main strength of Scholes' book: he succeeds in conveying the sense and importance of *individual* structuralists. At the same time, Scholes is unable to describe *how* these authors, so different from one another in their work, can meaningfully be termed proponents of a structural *method.* Jonathan Culler has written an important book about the literary uses of structuralism (1975) in which he apparently disagrees with Scholes on the need for "proliferating interpretations of individual texts." Culler had already published a helpful introduction to the linguistic dimensions of literary structuralism (1973) and his book, published two years later, is in my opinion the best treatment of structuralist poetics that I have so far read.

Gerard Genette and T. Todorov are two important literary structuralists. Consult Scholes' bibliography (1974) for references to their writings. Roland Barthes has articles on "Science Versus Literature" (1970c) and on historical discourse (1970d). A recent article by Joseph Blenkinsopp (1975) contains a Proppian analysis of the Gilgamesh Epic. George Steiner (1973) has a helpful and illuminating article on the relationship of linguistics and literature. Other examples of literary structuralism may be found in the introductions to Structuralism edited by Lane (1970) and Ehrmann (1970) and in the book by Oswald Ducrot *et al.* (1968).

Finally the vast literature on Semiotics must be mentioned as a source for literary structuralism.

An example of polemic against structuralism in literature is

George Watson's recent article (1975).

b) *Structural Study and/or Semiotics of the Bible: Theory.*
(Consult bibliographic remarks at end of part two, pp. 126-28 for
references to *attempts* at structural analysis of the Bible.)

The bulk of the material in this section is contained in five
sources: Leon-Dufour ed. (1970), Bovon (1971a), *Langages* 22
(June 1971), *Interpretation* (April 1974) and *Semeia 4* (edited by
John Dominic Crossan). Additional articles may be found in
Linguistica Biblica.

The April issue (1974) of *Interpretation* is devoted to structural
analysis of the Bible and contains theoretical articles by Robert
Spivey (1974), Richard Jacobson (1974), and Robert Culley
(1974). The May 1973 issue of *Esprit* contains three articles on
method in biblical exegesis, one by Paul Beauchamp (1973), one
by Luce Giard (1973), and the third by Louis Marin (1973). They
all confront the structuralist approach from various points of view
and the latter two articles are especially good. The June 1971 issue
of *Langages* 22 contains three theoretical articles concerning
"Semiotique narrative: récits bibliques": C. Chabrol (1971)
introduces the issue with a study of the problems surrounding
narrative semiotics of biblical texts; R. P. E. Haulotte (1971)
discusses structuralism as a method of biblical exegesis; and L.
Marin (1971) offers a fine concluding article. The issue includes a
select bibliography. Theoretical considerations concerning
structuralism, exegesis and hermeneutics are interwoven with
examples of structural analysis of specific biblical texts in *Exégèse
et herméneutique,* R. Barthes et al., (Leon-Dufour 1971).
Contributors to this volume include R. Barthes (1971a), P.
Beauchamp (1971), Joseph Courtes (1971), Louis Marin (1971a),
Henri Bouillard (1971), Paul Ricouer (1971a, 1971b) and Edgar
Haulotte (1971). Alain Blancy (1973) has written an article on
structuralism and hermeneutics. Robert Culley (1972) offers some
valuable comments on E. R. Leach's attempts to apply structural
analysis to biblical material (the Old Testament). Paul
Beauchamp (1972) offers a brief introduction to structural
analysis as an exegetical approach. F. Bovon (1971b) briefly

introduces biblical structuralism à la Barthes and Lévi-Strauss. *Semeia 4* contains Paul Ricouer's most recent statement on biblical hermeneutics (1975). Consult also Ricouer (1974) and Ricouer (1975/6) for other studies relevant to biblical hermeneutics. In *Semeia 3* (1975) Hugh White provides an important comparative study of the biblical methodologies of Hermann Gunkel and Roland Barthes. Way back in 1966, Robert Funk wrote *Language, Hermeneutic, and the Word of God*, a book which Norman Perrin asserts (1975: 372): "represents a major development in New Testament hermeneutics." Norman Petersen (1974) has offered some important methodological remarks on genre in relation to a literary-structuralist analysis of parables by Dan O. Via Jr., whose most recent work (1975) contains an excellent introductory chapter on literary structuralism and its implications for the study of the Bible.

Part II

An Attempt at Structural Analysis: The Book of Job

Introduction. I have labelled this part an attempt at structural analysis because I am not at all sure that one will find herein one of the characteristics of structuralism about which I wrote in chapter one. It is a fairly easy matter to see the "movements" of chapter two, the "transformations" of chapter three, and the "indexes" of chapter four as synchronic *structures* of the Book of Job (Ch. one pp. 2-19). It is also clear to me that as far as the *deductive* nature of a structural analysis itself is concerned (pp. 19-33) these chapters involve models that are not built upon or derived from an inductive marshalling of evidence as discussed in chapter one. In any case, since my belief is that all hermeneutic conclusions are deductively arrived at, so I believe are the conclusions of these chapters *in principle.*

But when one attempts to evaluate the third aspect that I discussed in chapter one, the *subjective dimensions* of a structural analysis (pp. 33-39), how can I establish or even convincingly assert that my attempt is true to that movement of mind, that vision, that imagination I referred to as "deep subjectivity"? I would have to assess chapters two, three and four in terms of the deep subjectivity necessary for a structural analysis. But by what kind of analysis would I arrive at a conclusion in this regard? Would it be by a structural analysis? But then how would I assess whether this analysis (of my first analysis) actually contains the deep subjectivity necessary to validate *it* as truly structural? Perhaps a third analysis is necessary, putting my second analysis to the structural test. And so on, leading nowhere.

Accordingly I will leave the assessing of these three chapters to someone else. But whoever undertakes to analyze and interpret Part Two, or the whole work of which it is a part, will produce an analysis and render an assessment that *itself* will be structurally understood not when its object is understood (the present book) but precisely when its subject (the book-reviewer) is. Every statement about a statement is a *signified* in relation to its subject matter; but it is also a *signifier* in relation to its author or source.

In any case, whether this second part is an example of structural analysis or simply an exercise in hermeneutics is not within my power to say.

In order to put into perspective the scope of part two, let me call attention to the three elements which are at the heart of this structural analysis of the book of Job: the "framework," the "code," and the "message" of the book. Chapter two will only concentrate on the first of these three elements, the "framework" of the book of Job. Here we will address ourselves to the problem of dividing up the discourse into its largest analyzable unities. This is a process of segmenting the discourse, a syntagm, into its largest (rather than smallest) component parts, *respecting the order of those parts.* For example, the statement, "He drank some coffee yesterday," offers a variety of possibilities for segmentation. Do I consider it as composed of the following unities: he + drank + some + coffee + yesterday (word segmentation)? Or rather, would I divide it up as follows: he drank + some coffee + yesterday? In other words, how best may we prepare the discourse for discovery of some *system* underlying the syntagm?

Besides being a *syntagmatic* analysis, chapter two will confine itself to the plane of content and therefore is primarily a *thematic* analysis of the book of Job. As I shall make clear, it is also a *synchronic* analysis, largely in reaction to the unsatisfying diachronic interpretations of literary- and form-critical scholars.

Chapter three, on the "code" of the book of Job, will attempt to offer some remarks on the problem of "finding the invariants in variations," as R. Jakobson describes the central problem of linguistics in the last 100 years (1971a: 224). It therefore will build upon chapter two in the hopes of discovering aspects of a system underlying the framework. This is the *paradigmatic* stage of my structural analysis.

Chapter four, on the "message of the book of Job," will treat those aspects of the book (besides its components and its system) which must be known before its message(s) can be grasped. This last step will take into account Barthes' level of narration (1966) and the idea of *énonciation* as opposed to that of *énoncé*. Here too we will consider questions that concern the form-critical concept of "*Sitz im Leben.*"

We may characterize these three parts of an analysis as going from a level of internal variance in discourse: *framework of the message*; to that of internal invariance in discourse: *code of the message*; and finally to a level of external variance: *the giving of the message*. Put another way, we are in this part analyzing our discourse primarily in its internal relations of metonymy (chapter two), then analyzing it according to some of its internal relations of metaphor (chapter three), and finally discussing it in its external relations of metonymy, (chapter four).

One final point. I make no apologies for introducing here operative distinctions, models, or descriptions suggested in previous studies by Barthes, Lévi-Strauss, Jakobson, Todorov, etc. It would be a mistake to view any of these models as constituting my analysis as "structural." As I insist in chapter one, structuralism is not a distinct methodology or procedure of analysis. In the last analysis, what must be asked of the following three chapters is how self-conscious are they concerning the three aspects of structuralism discussed in chapter one?

Chapter II

The Framework of the Book of Job

Few books in the Old Testament have discrepancy and contradiction so central to their make-up as the book of Job. Many scholars have solved the problems these contradictions entail by employing a process of subtraction, that is by eliminating What-Does-Not-Fit. Otto Eissfeldt summarizes very well the results of this de-husking procedure (1965: 456-62). First of all one separates the outer folktale (1:1-2:10 and 42:7-17) from the inner speeches because they offer different solutions to Job's problem: in the folktale there is an outward restoration of his fortunes by God, in the speeches an inner conquest of his sufferings by Job. Then, a majority of scholars regard Elihu as a second-class citizen of the story, inserted at a later stage, since his appearance is not anticipated nor does it have any effect on what follows. His speeches interrupt what is clearly intended as a direct movement from the speeches of Job to the speeches of God. Moreover, Elihu's view that suffering is a source of blessing contradicts God's speeches which point out that no solution to the problem of suffering is possible. The precious chaff of the wisdom poem in chapter 28 is the next to go, since it does not fit into its present context as part of Job's speeches in chapters 27-31. If Job had indeed at this point proclaimed this hymn to divine wisdom, it no longer would have been necessary for God, in chapters 38-41, to direct Job to His wisdom which surpasses all human understanding. No small number of critics also reject the speeches of God and Job's replies (38-42:6) as insertions. Finally we must not forget to mention whatever in chapters 3-27:10 and 29-31 shows *Inconsistency*, such as weak and doleful statements from the rebellious mouth of Job.

I find these and similar attempts at analysis counter-
productive. Indeed, confrontation of inconsistencies appears to
be as much a feature of the book's structure as of its content.
Attempts to remove these inconsistencies can be characterized as
academic "failure of nerve" just as the platitudes of Job's friends
are a "failure of nerve" in the face of Job's problems. By removing
the book's inconsistencies, some scholars have succeeded in
removing its message. This chapter begins to describe how these
many inconsistencies are essential to its message.

The major contradictions in the story appear to be connected
with a major theme of the book: for any thinking person there is a
contradiction between what he has been taught to *believe* about
divine justice and what he experiences almost daily in his life.
God, who is all powerful and all just, rewards with good fortune
those who obey him and punishes with inexorable might those
who disobey him. The good prosper and the bad suffer. So we are
taught to believe. Within the Hebrew Bible this theme is not
simply representative, for example, of the Deuteronomic strain in
the text, although it finds a classic formulation in such sources. It
pervades the Tetrateuch, the Prophets, and the wisdom literature
of Israel. Personal experience, however, contradicts this article of
faith. The evil prosper, the good die young and often we
experience ourselves suffering unjustly without any hint of what
we are suffering *for*. Innocent suffering is a fact of common
experience. Now this theme of the contradiction between a man's
religious beliefs about the justice of (the) god(s) and his own
personal experience is not peculiar to Israel. It is well known
within the wisdom literature of the Ancient Near East of which
Job forms only one small example. However, the book of Job
presents the problem and works towards its solution with a genius
that is characteristic of that type of literature often called myth. A
central concern of the book can be expressed in terms of a
contradiction between what a member of society should believe
and what he actually experiences. The fleshing-out of this theme
in the story takes place in such an obviously inconsistent fashion
that one realizes—as it were intuitively—that this clash must be

essential to the story.

Consider the words and actions of Job himself. For eighteen chapters he audaciously denies or questions much that his faith had apparently led him to believe. Something is rotten in heaven because, he says, "I know I am innocent and yet I am suffering!" Within these eighteen chapters of Job's speeches can be found examples of some of the most anti-Yahwist sentiments of which we have any record in literature. 9:22 is especially strong:

> It is all one. Therefore I have said 'He destroys the wicked and the innocent. If a scourge kills immediately, he mocks the despair (*l^e massat?*) of the innocent. He has handed over the earth to the wicked. He covers the faces of its judges. If not, then who *is* He?

After eighteen chapters of audacity, defiance, and self-righteousness, there intervenes the vision of God from a whirlwind. In the blinking of an eye, Job recants and repents. He says in 42:5-6:

> I had heard of thee by the hearing of the ear, but now my eyes have seen thee; therefore I despise myself and repent in dust and ashes.

It is so instantaneous and violent an about-face, it is seen by many scholars to be almost unbelievable. What Job denies for eighteen chapters, after the theophanic speeches of 38-41 he affirms: although he still cannot *understand* it, God *must* reward the good and punish the evil. What he affirms for all these chapters, after the vision he now somehow denies: his own experience of innocence and God's injustice. It is no wonder that literary critics have attempted to remove the words of the repentant Job from the book. That the repentant Job of 42:1-6 is "obviously" not the same Job as in the rest of the book is so patent to some critics that it is with the greatest of ease that they remove these and similar verses from Job's mouth as the rather amateurish insertions of later authors unworthy of the genius of the book's main author. It is paradoxical, however, that they are unaware of a larger inconsistency: this "amateurish solution" to Job's problem has somehow struck the most responsive of chords within men's hearts down through the ages. The effect and its cause are mysteriously disproportionate. Either we are all amateurs at heart or the solution manages to be somehow profound in its simplicity.

A second major inconsistency centers around Job's friends. For ten chapters and with few exceptions they collectively affirm the Israelite doctrine of divine retribution: God rewards the good and punishes the evil. It is true that one can with some success delineate precise differences between the positions of each of the friends. However, it remains true that, concerning the binary opposition between traditional Israelite belief and personal experience, they in general take the former as fundamental and incontrovertible. Eliphaz states the position succinctly in 4:7-9:

> Think now, who that was innocent ever perished? Or where were the upright cut off? As I have seen, those who plow iniquity and sow trouble reap the same. By the breath of God they perish and by the blast of his anger they are consumed.

But after ten chapters of this, following the words of God in 42:7-9, they dutifully offer sacrifice to God "for not speaking of Him what is right." And the Lord accepts their recanting. The relationship of God's words to the friends' position is similar to that of the vision and Job's position: What they affirmed before the vision/word of God, after it they deny.

Finally we come to what is perhaps the most amazing inconsistency in the whole book: some of God's words seem to contradict his actions. He states to Eliphaz in 42:7 that Job was right and his friends were wrong:

> My wrath is kindled against you and against your two friends; for you have not spoken of me what is right, *as my servant Job has* (italics added).

Note that this statement appears to be inconsistent not only with

Yahweh's speeches in 38-41 but also with what follows verse 9 in the epilogue (where he proceeds to act in accordance with the principle of retribution: he rewards the good Job and forgives the repentant friends). One might of course assume here that in the original folk-tale Job's words were a confirmation of the principle of retribution, not a denial as they presently stand in the poetry. Such an attempt to remove the inconsistency rather than describe its function in the present story is wholly unsatisfactory. We must face squarely the relationship of God to Job and to his friends. Immediately after God *says* that Job was originally correct in questioning the universal validity of the principle of divine retribution, He proceeds to reward Job for his repentance. God apparently acts like the kind of person he praises Job for denying him to be. Concerning Job's friends, at the same time as He *says* they are wrong in their naive insistence that he always punishes the evil, He threatens to punish them for being evil, "for not speaking of Him what is right." He will avert disaster from them if they repent and admit that He does not always avert disaster from the repentant! Clearly what God *says* in the book of Job and how he *acts* within it provide us with its central paradox.

I have mentioned that the usual literary- and form-critical analyses of our text resolve its inconsistencies by removing one or the other of the clashing elements. Such attempts at analysis seem to me ultimately to destroy the message(s) of the book and moreover make impossible the first step toward understanding how, *in its present form*, it has affected men so profoundly down through the ages. ⟶

The present chapter aims at isolating and analyzing the largest primary unities contained in the text. These unities will derive from the kind of discourse which constitutes the object of our investigation. Even though a typology of discourse has not yet been fully or successfully constructed, we may in general acknowledge three main types of discourse: metonymy (e.g. story, narrative, novel, etc.), metaphor (e.g. lyric poetry) and enthymeme (e.g. philosophic treatises) (Barthes: 1966: 4n.1). In its present form, the book of Job tells a story. We intend to investigate our text, therefore, from the point of view of its being a sequence of sentences constituting a narrative.

The first task at hand is to isolate the largest unities which appear to be essential to the very framework of the story. Secondary developments of the narration will, for the time being, be disregarded. The level on which we are centering our remarks is the level of functions and not the level of actants / actions. The lowest level of a story is the functional level. Its basic unities are "cardinal functions," veritable hinges of a story in that they are nuclear actions or events without which the story would be essentially different. These functions are unities of *dynamic* content or the dynamic roles certain lexemes have in the discursive framework of the story. What is important to emphasize here is that, although everything in a story is in some sense "functional," the functions we want to isolate in our narrative are the *largest* functional units discursively set out in the story. This means, first of all, that they are not catalytic or filler functions, but at least cardinal functions, that is, the action to which they refer opens up, maintains, or closes a subsequent alternative in the course of the story. In short, it "inaugurates or concludes an uncertainty" (Barthes: 1966: 9). Moreover, in a story, a group of cardinal functions may be united into *sequences* or groups of functions united by a certain solidarity. For example, on a level more minute than that upon which we are concentrating, the "sequence" of getting a phone call involves certain functions: the phone rings, one answers it, speaks and finally hangs up (Barthes: 1966: 13). Every story can be described as a series of sequences (groups of cardinal functions or nuclei). Finally, sequences can be united into larger unities which we can designate provisionally, *movements* or *segments* of the story. Now it is the dynamic role each movement plays in the story which determines it (the movement's) *major* function in the syntagmatic development of the story. This main functional role of each movement we have designated the *main sequential* function of the movement. The nature of the main sequential function in the Book of Job is to set up or mediate some conflict or contradiction. Centering the movements around conflict or contradiction and its resolution recalls immediately structural analysis *à la* Lévi-Strauss. I may point out here that such a model is utilized not because I subscribe to the theory that this is the essential model for all myth or all narrative discourse but rather because, in my opinion, it "fits" when applied to the story contained in the book of Job.

These dynamic roles which we have called functions have specific lexemes (persons, places, things, actions) filling them in the story. To simplify our analysis of this functional level, we are arbitrarily limiting it on the personal level to those relationships that develop between the two most obviously essential characters of the story, God and Job. The other "actors" in the story, Satan, the comforters, Job's family, Elihu, will not be treated in this study on functions. This decision has the advantage, we hope, of making our first attempts at analysis less complicated and will allow us to focus more clearly on chief elements of the narrative. Completeness is being sacrificed for clarity. Moreover, in this study I will not consider the question of whether the very *order* or sequencing of major functional unities found in a narrative is necessary to their syntax. This is one of the central questions dividing analysts of narratives, be they "structuralist" or not. Thus, for example, Propp, Todorov, and Dundes hold that temporal succession is necessary to the syntax of narrative functions, whereas scholars such as Lévi-Strauss, the Marandas, etc., think otherwise. We intend in this section to respect the order of the sequence of events narrated in the story. "Before vs. After" will be seen as a necessary property of the framework as we describe it and of each of the movements that comprise that framework.

Before we continue it might be useful to visualize the functional components we have been discussing in this section. We give first a general model:

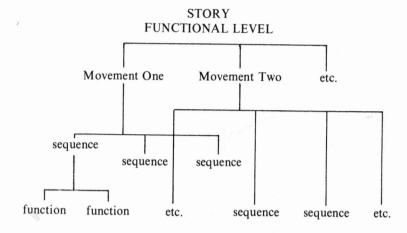

FIG. ONE

Notice the imbricated nature of such a model: one sequence may still be in progress when another is initiated. One can also point out that on the functional level, *narrative* functions are not to be systematically identified with *linguistic* unities. Functions can be represented by unities larger than sentences, (e.g. groups of sentences or even the entire discourse) or by unities smaller than sentences (e.g. the phrase, word, or even parts of words [Barthes: 1966: 8]). The aim of this study is to isolate the main movements or segments of the story.

Secondly we can give a specific model relating to the book of Job:

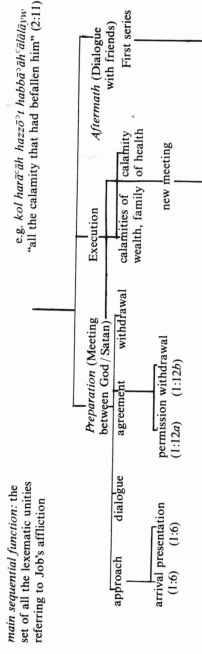

Fig. Two

One moves upward on the schema from the lowest elements (cardinal functions) to series of hierarchically related sequences (e.g. *Approach* and *Preparation*) to the main sequential function (the afflicting of Job by God) of the movement. This diagram is only an approximation for the purposes of illustrating our methodological remarks. It does not represent a detailed analysis of the 14 chapters contained within its parameters.

just relationship between God and Job

There seem to be four main segments or movements in our story: (1) God afflicts Job by removing his health, wealth and family (1-37); (2) God appears to Job out of the whirlwind (38-42:6); (3) God states that Job spoke correctly of him (42:7-9); (4) God acts in behalf of Job by restoring everything to him twofold (42:10-17).

FIRST MOVEMENT
Preparation. A contradiction is set up and expounded (Job 1-37): *God afflicts Job.*

This first movement centers around the afflictions imposed upon Job by God through Satan's agency. The two parts of the dramatic movement are a description of the state of affairs *before* these afflictions and secondly after these afflictions. In chapters one and two the sequences of this movement are combined by "alternation," that is, first Job loses his wealth and family and responds accordingly (1), then he loses his health and responds accordingly (2), then his friends come and a long dialogue ensues (3-37). Before his afflictions, Job is described as a good man and uniquely blessed by God. His afflictions then set the scene for a confrontation in the dialogue between elements in the sphere of religious belief, e.g. the traditional retribution scheme in Israel (God rewards the good and punishes the evil, e.g. 4:7-9) and certain facts and interpretations in the sphere of personal experience (Job sees himself as innocent yet suffering, e.g. 9:22-24). The afflicting of Job appears to be the main sequential function of this movement: a conflict is thereby set up between the sphere of belief and that of experience. Job's afflictions enable the dialogue of 3-37 to confront the apparent contradiction between what one *believes* as a member of a religious community and what one *experiences* as an individual. A detailed analysis of the individual speeches is not possible in a study of this length; however the general picture is quite clear: the friends, in the face of conflict brought on by the afflictions, side preponderantly with the sphere of belief instead of the sphere of personal experience;

Job in general assents to the impact of his own sufferings as opposed to the traditional belief-positions of his friends. If Zophar, for example, mouths the trite statements that the good are secure and the eyes of the wocked will fail (11), Job answers in 13:12, "Your maxims are proverbs of ashes, your defenses are defenses of clay."

It is important here to delineate what belongs to the *before* and to the *after* of the main sequential function, "God afflicts Job." Since, as we have explained, this function sets up a contradiction between the sphere of belief and that of experience, it is important to notice that the conversations between God and Satan in chapters one and two *already* set up this conflict before the actual sufferings are inflicted. Before the afflictions, God holds that Job is blessed because he is righteous (sphere of belief) while Satan suspects that Job is righteous because he is blessed (sphere of experience). In the same way, after the afflictions come upon Job, his friends hold that he is afflicted because he is bad (sphere of belief) while he holds he is righteous in spite of being afflicted (sphere of experience). The two conversations therefore (between God and Satan on one hand and Job and his friends on the other) belong to the *after* portion of this movement in that they function as the verbalization of the conflict which the very act of affliction embodies in the context of the story. Thus the *before* section of this movement comprises only chapter 1:1-5 where Job is described as being both righteous (v.1,5) and blessed (vv.2-4). The *after* section of this movement comprises the rest of the section. We may characterize this movement as one in which *at first* both the belief sphere and the experience sphere coincide, but then, because of the afflictions of Job, these spheres are brought in conflict.

FIRST MOVEMENT

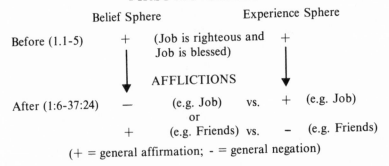

Belief Sphere   Experience Sphere

Before (1.1-5)   +   (Job is righteous and   +
                                 Job is blessed)

                                 AFFLICTIONS

After (1:6-37:24)   —   (e.g. Job)   vs.   +   (e.g. Job)
                                       or
                        +   (e.g. Friends) vs.   —   (e.g. Friends)

(+ = general affirmation; - = general negation)

SECOND MOVEMENT

The Theophany. First Contradiction is resolved but a new one set up. *God appears to Job out of the Whirlwind.* (38-42:6).

In describing the before / after sections of each movement, it should be made clear that the state of affairs representing the "after" of a previous movement becomes the "before" section of the next movement. The existing conflict exemplified by the opposing sides in the dialogues (between God and Satan and between Job and his friends) is thus the "before" section of the second movement. Narrowing our focus on the relationships between Job and God we have God answering Job "out of the whirlwind" in chapters 38-41. It is this theophanic series of speeches, whatever their semantic content, which brings about a change in Job's position as outlined in his speeches within 3-37. Whereas he was overwhelmed by the impact of his sufferings to such an extent that he had to deny elements of the sphere of belief, he is now overwhelmed by the theophany to such an extent that he can now generally assent to what he previously denied. This is clearly the basic import of his speech in 42:1-6 especially, "Therefore I have uttered what I did not understand, things too wonderful for me, which I did not know" (v. 3) and "I had heard of thee by the hearing of the ear, but now my eye sees thee; therefore I despise myself and repent in dust and ashes" (vv. 5-6). Because of the force and power of the theophany, Job throws his complete assent to the sphere of belief and, in so doing, repudiates his previous position (" . . . I have uttered what I did not understand"). This means that, in effect, the vision of God has effected a twofold change in him that can be visualized as follows:

SECOND MOVEMENT

Belief Sphere   Experience Sphere

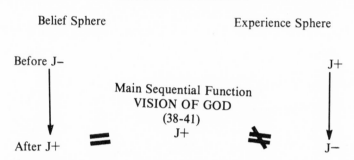

Before J—   J+

Main Sequential Function
VISION OF GOD
(38-41)
J+

After J+   J—

The functional nature of the vision of God is to enable Job to deny the validity of his own suffering experience in order that he might assent to those elements of the belief sphere he previously denied. The vision of God thus dissolves for Job the contradiction between these two spheres as expressed primarily in chapters 3-37. However, the theophany thereby sets up a new conflict in Job, viz. between itself as just affirmed by Job and his own personal experience as just denied by him. Whereas in this movement the vision functions as a mediator between apparently contradictory spheres, by so mediating, it becomes one of the opposing terms in a new contradiction. In other words, how can Job now reconcile the contradiction between the vision of God and his own afflicted experience? By assenting to the vision he has had to deny part of himself, the validity of his own previous experience. This conflict within Job is the subject of the third movement of the plot. Before we go on, however, let us emphasize our conviction that the second movement is the central movement of the whole book. The main conflict of our text is that described for us in such detail and verbal artistry in the speeches of 3-37, and its resolution the main

goal of the text. The third and fourth movements are almost a
"mopping-up" affair after the main battle has been won. They are
short and to the point, comprising the main task of 42:7-17.

THIRD MOVEMENT
The second conflict resolved but a new one set up: God
states that Job "spoke of (Him) what is right" (42:7-9).

The contradiction set up by the second movement is visualized
as follows:

Vision of God   Experience of Affliction

This contradiction must be somehow reconciled and it is the
function of God's statement in 42:7-9 to mediate this
contradiction. The vision of God was more overwhelming to Job
than his own terrible afflictions; he thus in some sense could
repudiate his former interpretation of them. The author of this
work is not content to allow this repudiation to stand and so God
himself speaks in defence of Job's former position. If one
maintains that God is here referring to Job's repentance speech in
42:1-6 then one is left with the problem of how God could then
characterize Job's friends' position as wrong. If Job was right and
his friends wrong, it appears that God is referring to the
statements of each found in the dialogues. In speaking to Eliphaz,
He says, "My wrath is kindled against you and against your two
friends: for you have not spoken of me what is right, as my servant
Job has (v.7) . . . for you have not spoken of me what is right as
my servant Job as (v.8)." The function therefore of this speech,
with regard to God and Job, is to mediate between the conflict set
up in the last movement between the vision of God and Job's
interpretation of his own experience. Job fulfilled God's role for
him in the speech of 42:7-9 (he is to pray for his friends, for he was
right and they were wrong): "the Lord accepted Job's prayer." Job
thus is enabled by this divine speech to assent once more to the

validity of his interpretations concerning himself and God uttered in 3-37 and we may express this stage as follows:

THIRD MOVEMENT

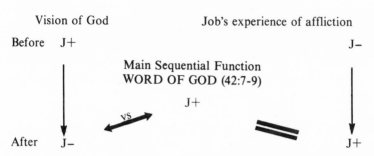

Vision of God   Job's experience of affliction

Before   J+   J−

Main Sequential Function
WORD OF GOD (42:7-9)

J+

vs

After   J−   J+

We see here, as in the previous movement, a double role of the main sequential function: as a mediating term it resolves one conflict but sets up another in the process. By assenting to the word of God in 42:7-9, which in effect sanctioned Job's previous speeches, Job is led to the implicit denial of the theophanic speeches of 38-41 which had in effect condemned his previous position. Put another way, there is an apparent contradiction between the content of God's speeches in 38-41 (God says, "I am powerful; Job you are wrong") and his speech in 42:7-9 (God says, "Job you were right!"). The fourth and last movement of the book will confront this contradiction.

THE FOURTH MOVEMENT

The last conflict resolved and equlibirium re-established. God restores everything to Job twofold (42:10-17).

The final verses in the book (42:10-17) recount how "the LORD restored the fortunes of Job, when he had prayed for his friends; and the LORD gave Job twice as much as he had before (v.10) . . . Job died an old man and full of days (v.17)." Clearly the action of God in restoring Job's fortunes twofold serves here as the main sequential function of this movement acting as a mediator between the conflict inherent in the word of God and the Vision of God. The main thrust of 38-41 is that since God is all powerful, Job is wrong in his attitude. The main thrust of 42:7-9 is that Job was right, which statement threatens to attack the main assertion of 38-41, namely that Job was wrong. By restoring Job's fortunes twofold, God's act both confirms his word of 42:7-9 and confirms *by deed* what he had only asserted *by word* in 38-41: his omnipotent power. In 42:7-9 God only *said* Job was right; in 38-41, God only *said* He was all powerful: in 42:10-17 God's action rewards Job for being correct and *proves* his own omnipotence over all the affairs of the world. Moreover the original equilibrium with which the book begins is re-established with no apparent contradictions left to confuse its message. Far from being a gratuitous "Hollywood ending," chapter 42's final verses dialectically resolve the subsidiary conflicts which the central event of the entire book, the theophany of God, had engendered. The fourth movement can be pictured as follows:

FOURTH MOVEMENT

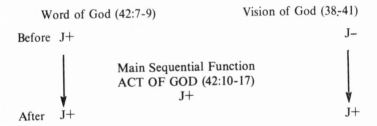

Word of God (42:7-9)   Vision of God (38-41)

Before J+   J−

Main Sequential Function
ACT OF GOD (42:10-17)
J+

After   J+   J+

The book of Job ends as it began, with no contradiction. Between the beginning and the end, the set of contradictions initiated from 1:6ff is resolved.

The framework of the book of Job, viewed as a dramatic narrative and centering on the sequential relationships between Job and God, appears to us to be a dialectical working out of a series of contradictions by means of four major sequential functions: (1) God afflicts Job; (2) God appears to Job; (3) God states that Job spoke correctly of Him; and (4) God restores all to Job twofold. The first and fourth functions either set up or resolve contradiction; the second and third movements both resolve and set up contradiction. The central movement is the second where the conflict (minutely detailed in 3-37) between the belief and experience spheres is resolved through the awesome theophany of 38-41. The last two movements in chapter 42:7-17 almost automatically settle the conflicts this vision sets in motion. We can recapitulate our narrative "reading" of the story with the following diagram:

4th Seq. Function	3rd Seq. Function	2nd Seq. Function	1st Seq. Function	Belief	Experience	Read: ↙
				+ Job is "right-eous"	+ Job is rich	Initial Situation of Story ch. 1:1-5
			Affliction: →	−	+	Movement One 1:6—37:24
		Vision: →	−	+		Movement Two 38:1—42:6
	Word →	−	+			Movement Three 42:7-9
Act: →	+ Job is "correct"	+ Job is twice rich				Movement Four 42:10-17

N.B. (1) In movements two and three, the function of the previous movement becomes the denied *term* of next movement.

(2) Each sphere and function is affirmed before story ends.

Note that the story ends up with precisely that information that is lacking in the first chapter. When God and Satan discuss Job, the crux of the problem and the element that allows the story to develop is precisely not knowing *for sure* whether Job was righteous because God has blessed him or whether he was blessed because he was righteous. We are only told that Job was *both* righteous and blessed in 1:1-5. 1:6ff then proceed to spell out the problem: what is the relationship between these two facts in Job's life? The journey the reader takes to solve this initial problem takes him along a path which *apparently* allows him to deny the equation "righteous, therefore blessed; blessed therefore righteous" by allowing him to assert "cursed yet righteous." However the vision of God and what follows, as it were, turns the reader upside down, as it did Job, and one ends up where he began: except that instead of a suspicion, we now have a certainty that Job was blessed because he was righteous. As happens so often in life one ends up where he began with no apparent progress achieved. But there is change: that of being wiser than he was when he began.

The framework of the story, then, is a work of genius. By means of its remarkable resources it takes the reader on a journey, the beginning of which may be described as equilibrium without insight and whose conclusion is appropriately equilibrium with insight. The genius of this journey is that insight is conferred not by the avoidance of contradiction and inconsistency but precisely by the courageous integration of contradiction and resolution. In other words the story is a paradigm. What is on the surface a diachronic linear treatment of a problem reveals itself as containing an underlying or latent synchronic structure. This paradigmatic pattern will be the subject of the next step in structural analysis: the "code" of the book of Job.

Before we go on to the next chapter, it might be interesting to discuss this discursive framework of the Job narrative in the light of Lévi-Strauss' formula on the structure of myth. He originally published his programmatic article "The Structural Study of Myth" in 1955. Toward the end of the article, he introduces a formula in the following way: "Although it is not possible at the present stage to come closer than an approximate formulation which will certainly need to be refined in the future, it seems that every myth considered as the aggregate of all its variants corresponds to a formula of the following type:

$$F_x(a) : F_y(b) \cong F_x(b) : F_{a-1}(y)" \ (1967:225).$$

His explanation of this formula is extremely laconic: "Herewith two terms, a and b, being given as well as two functions, x and y, of these terms, it is assumed that a relation of equivalence exists between two situations defined respectively by the inversion of *terms* and *relations*, under two conditions: (1) that one term be replaced by its opposite (in the above formula, a and $a-1$); (2) that an inversion be made between the *function value* and the *term value* of two elements (above, y and a)" (*ibid*).

Since 1955, although Lévi-Strauss has published four monumental volumes in Mythology, he has referred to this formula only once, asserting that it had not ceased to guide him since he formulated it. (See Maranda: 1971: 28.) We utilize his formula here not because we believe that every "myth" corresponds to it (so Lévi-Strauss), but solely because we find it remarkable that such a formula, conceived first of all in connection with the structure of North American myths, agrees very closely with the discursive framework of the book of Job. Some might point out that it is because the prologue and epilogue of the book were originally a folktale that this formula seems to find some relevance to our text. They would say that the *story* comes from the folktale whereas the *text* is primarily poetic speeches, so that the original structure of the tale remains in fragmented and incomplete form. It is this remnant, they would suggest, which the formula "picks up" in the reading of the discursive framework of the book. Since I am limiting my analysis to the book's synchronic relationships such an insight is for my purposes irrelevant. *Whatever* the origin and shape of the prose beginning and ending to our book, in its present form and structure (the only form we have any real assurance of) it participates in a set of relations both with parts of itself and with aspects of the poetic portions of chapters 3-42:6. Moreover the key mediating term of the formula in the second movement comes from the poetic section, the theophanic speeches of 38-41, and its final outcome is the Joban speech of 42:1-6. [Thus, whatever one wishes to say about the prehistory of this text, the prose and the poetry have been so skillfully woven together that any attempt to separate them rips apart the fabric of the narrative, destroys its unity and succeeds only in talking about hypothetical prior states of discourse.]

Interpretations of Lévi-Strauss' formula are not quite so numerous as his followers and opponents, yet for the sake of consistency we shall apply the formula as interpreted by Elli and Pierre Maranda (1971: 24-34) with one major caution: the Marandas' understanding of "function" is somewhat different from the description of narrative functions given by Barthes. I have described briefly Barthes' understanding of "functions" in narration earlier in this chapter and one should also note Barthes' shifting use of this term (see now Bovon: 1971b: 19). The Marandas understand terms to be sociohistorical symbols; thus they are lexematic in character. Functions for them are "the roles held by (these) symbols." Reference is made to the work of L. Tesnière and E. Richer and apparently the Marandas' precise idea of function is analogous to "grammatical role" in linguistics. One major difference, therefore, between Barthes and the Marandas is that Barthes explicitly warns against functions being systematically identified with linguistic unities (so that a function can be represented variously by groups of sentences, a sentence, a clause, a phrase, a word, or even a particle in a given story) whereas, if I understand them correctly, the Marandas conceive function to be on a higher level than Barthes. Perhaps it would be accurate to say that Barthes' "functions" are closer to the Marandas' "terms" and the Marandas' functions are closer to Barthes' narrative unities on the higher level of action/actants. Lévi Strauss' formula is not to be understood as a strict mathematical formulation but is intended only to be a convenient shorthand which appears to describe accurately and concisely the narrative structure under discussion. Its components are gross analytic units: (1) terms, i.e. lexemes such as $^{\circ}iyy\hat{o}b$ "Job," $^{\circ e}l\hat{o}^ah$ "God," $hezy\hat{o}n$ "vision," $r\bar{a}^c\bar{a}h$ "calamity," etc., thus any specific thing person, place, thing, action performing a dynamic role in the story; and (2) functions, i.e. unities of content or the dynamic roles certain lexemes or combinations of lexemes have in the discursive framework of the story.

The four movements of the story are (1) God afflicts Job; (2) God appears to Job who "repents"; (3) God states that Job spoke correctly of him; and (4) God restores all to Job twofold. Since there is no mediating term in the first movement (whose goal is essentially the setting up of the contradiction which opens the second movement) we can proceed to the second movement to apply Lévi-Strauss' formula.

The Second Movement: The Theophanic Speeches of 38-42:6

1. Formula: $f_x(a) : f_y(b) \cong f_x(b) : f_{a-1}(y)$
2. Terms and Functions:
   a = all the lexemes relating to Job's afflictions.
      A set of all these could be enumerated:
      a_1 $^{\circ}\bar{e}\check{s}\,^{\circ e}loh\hat{i}m$ "lightning" (1:16)
      a_2 $ka\acute{s}d\hat{i}m$ "Chaldeans" (1:17)
      a_3 $\check{s}^ek\hat{i}n\,r\bar{a}^c$ "a foul pox" (2:7)
      a_4 $hakk^e{}^{\circ}\bar{e}b$ "the anguish" (2:13)
      a_5 $h\bar{a}^{\circ e}loh\hat{i}m$ "God" (2:10)
   b = lexemes relating to the theophany of 38-41.
      A set of all these could be enumerated:
      b_1 $wayya^can\;YHWH\,^{\circ}et\,^{\circ}iyy\hat{o}b$ "God answered Job" (38:1)
      b_2 $wayyo^{\circ}mar$ "and he said" (38.1)
      b_3 any part of the divine speeches in 38-41 or all of them taken *in globo*, etc.
   y = affirmation of faith. This is one of the two functions of the mediating term of this movement (b) which

function becomes a term value according to Lévi-Strauss' formula.

f_x = negating function of a term. In this movement term a tends to negate elements in the sphere of belief, e.g. the traditional retribution formula of 'God rewards the good and punishes the evil' and term b, the mediating term, tends to negate elements of Job's experience. e.g. that God is punishing him unjustly.

f_y = affirmation function of a term. In this movement term b, the mediating term, affirms elements of the belief-sphere discussed in the book. e.g. God is all powerful and decides who is to be righteous or not and acts accordingly in justice.

f_{a-1} = spiritual gain function. Just as a is material affliction so its opposite, a-l, is spiritual gain, i.e. the spiritual gain of Job's affirmation of faith in 42:1-6.

3. Explanation of formula:

The negating function of Job's material loss (which negates elements in faith sphere) is related to the affirmation function of the theophany (which affirms elements of faith sphere)

JUST AS

the negating function of the theophany (which denies elements of Job's suffering experience) is related to the spiritual gain function of Job's affirmation of faith.

4. Commentary:

As Maranda explains, "the first two members of the formula refer to the setting up of the conflict, the third to the turning point in the plot, while the last member refers to the final situation" (1971: 27).

"To put it metaphorically, the inverse of, say, a loss which expressed the actual impact of a negative power is not only a loss nullified or recuperation, but a gain . . ." (*ibid.*). Thus Job's confession of faith and repentance (in 42:1-6) by means of and because of the mediating force of the theophany in 38-41 is a replacement of a material loss by a spiritual gain. The Marandas continue, "Another way of explicating our interpretation of Lévi-Strauss' formula is to point out that its first three members $f_x(a)$, $f_y(b)$ and $f_x(b)$ express a dynamic process whose final outcome, expressed by the last member, $f_{a-1}(y)$ is the result or a state, i.e., the end of the process of mediation." (*ibid.*). In other words, the spiritual gain function of Job's affirmation of faith is the end of the process of mediation of the theophany. One final quote: "In other words, if two opposite tendencies x and y in the opening of a folkloristic item actualize the deep opposition of two terms a and b so that a conflict, a 'problem' results, then the following operation (*) takes place:

$$[f_x(b)] * [f_x(a)] \longrightarrow f_{a-1}(y) \text{ " (1971: 28)}$$

In the book of Job, this means that in the second movement the negating function of the theophanic speeches (- experience) "operates on" the negating function of Job's material loss (- faith) so that he is enabled to affirm faith and repentance, which affirmation functions as spiritual gain for him.

Here is how I would apply the Marandas' remarks to the framework of the Book of Job, movements one and two:

A.   In the first movement a contradiction was set up:

$f_x(a)$ vs $f_y(b)$ Job's suffering experience functions as a denial of the faith-affirming function of the orthodox retribution theory.

B.   Then, with chapters 38-42:6, all the lexemes connected with God's theophany replace the lexemes that articulate the orthodox retribution theory in their faith-affirming function. That is, b in movement one was any lexeme representing the orthodox retribution theory, but b in movement two is now any lexeme representing or expressing the significance of God's theophany.

1.   In the second movement, the contradiction set up in the

previous movement now has the following form:

$f_x(a)$ vs $f_y(b)$ Job's suffering experience functions as a denial of the faith-affirming function of the theophany.

2. But:

$f_y(b) = f_x(b)$ It is the dual role of the mediating term not only to affirm faith but also to deny Job's experience of innocent suffering.

3. Thus:

$f_x(b) * f_x(a)$ The experience-denying function of God's theophany "operates on" and transforms the faith-denying function of Job's suffering. . . .

4. So that:

$f_x(a) \longrightarrow f_{a-1}(y)$ The faith-denying function of Job's suffering is transformed into an affirmation of faith which functions as the inverse of Job's material loss, that is, which functions as Job's spiritual gain $(a \rightarrow f_{a-1})$.

What is central to the Marandas' *adaptation* of Lévi-Strauss' formula is that the Marandas have transformed what appears to be a paradigmatic formula of myth into a formula useful for the *syntagmatic* analysis of folktales. It is precisely the syntagmatic nature of their adaptation that allows me to utlize it in this restatement of the framework of the Book of Job in terms of Lévi-Strauss' formula. My explanation of the following two movements should be understood according to this syntagmatic adaptation. Points 2 to 4 above illustrate the Marandas' graphic illustration (1971: 28):

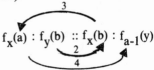

The Third Movement. The Word of God in 42:7-9

As we mentioned earlier, the main battle of the book was fought and decided in the second movement. Consequently we see the third and fourth movements essentially as "mopping-up" operations, short and to the point.

1. Formula: $f_x(a) : f_y(b) \cong f_x(b) : f_{a-1}(y)$
2. Terms and functions:

$a =$ lexemes relating to the theophany of 38-41. A set of all these could be enumerated (for examples see b in 2nd movement): God implies that Job is wrong.

$b =$ lexemes relating to the Word of God found in 42:7-9. A set of all these could be enumerated: b_1 *nᵉkônāh kᵉᶜabdî ᵓiyyôb* (42:7, 8). God asserts that Job has spoken correctly of Him.

$y =$ the affirmation function of this movement becomes a term value: the affirmation of Job's personal experience in suffering.

$f_x =$ negating function of a term. In this movement term a tends to negate Job's interpretation of his suffering experience, e.g. that God is treating him unjustly, and term b, the mediating term, tends to negate elements of the theophanic speeches, e.g. that Job was wrong in accusing God.

$f_y =$ affirmation function of a term. In this movement term b, the mediating term, affirms elements of Job's suffering experience as found in his speeches in 3-37, e.g. that the simplistic 'God rewards the good and punishes the evil' found in traditional sources is not sufficient to validate his experience of suffering.

$f_{a-1} =$ Since a (the theophany) states in part that Job must be wrong in his expressed attitude toward his suffering, $a-1$ is the inverse, that is, God stating that Job has "spoken correctly of (Him)." f_{a-1} is therefore validation by God that Job was correct about Him.

3. Explanation of formula:

The negating function of the theophany (denies Job's experience of his suffering) is related to the affirming function of God's word in 42:7-9 (affirms Job's interpretation of his experience)

JUST AS

the negating function of God's word in 42:7-9 (negates in part the theophany) is related to God's affirmation of Job's experience functioning as proof that Job is correct.

4. Comment. Note here that the mediating term of the previous movement, the theophany of 38-41, has become the initial term of this movement.

The Fourth Movement. The Action of God in 42:10-17

1. The Formula: $f_x(a) : f_y(b) \cong f_x(b) : f_{a-1}(y)$
2. Terms and functions:

a = lexemes relating to the Word of God found in 42.7-9. See term b of third movement.

b = lexemes relating to the act of God toward Job found in 42.10-17. A set of all these could be enumerated:

b_1 *wayyosep YHWH ʾet kol ʾašer leʾiyyôb lᵉmišneh* "and Yahweh increased all Job's possessions twofold" (42.10).

b_2 *waYHWH bērak ʾet ʾaḥᵃrît ʾiyyôb mērēʾšitô* "and Yahweh blessed Job's later life more than his for–mer"

etc.

y = affirmation of theophanic speeches of 38-41. This is one of the two functions of the mediating term of this movement (b) which function acts as a term value.

f_x = negating function of a term. In this movement, term a tends to negate elements of the theophanic speeches, e.g. that Job was wrong in accusing God, and term b, the mediating term, tends to negate Job's material loss by restoring all to him twofold.

f_y = the affirmation function of a term. In this movement, term b, the mediating term, affirms elements of the theophanic speeches, e.g. the awesome power of God.

f_{a-1} = *operative* gain function. Just as *a* is a divine *statement* that Job is correct, *a-1* is a divine *act* showing that Job is correct, viz. twofold blessing. Thus the affirmation by deed of the awesome power of God which is the *function y* of term *b becomes* the term value *y* which functions as an operative gain over *a*.

3. Explanation of formula:

The negating function of the word of God in 42:7-9 (negates elements in vision) is related to the affirmation function of the act of God in 42:10-17 (affirms elements in vision)

JUST AS

the negating function of the Act of God in 42:10-17 (negates material afflictions of Job) is related to the affirmation by deed of the awesome power of God functioning as an operative gain (i.e. God not only *says* Job is correct, he acts accordingly by blessing him twofold).

Chapter III

The Code of the Book of Job

In the previous chapter I investigated the Book of Job as a narrative or story, with a view to dividing it up into its largest analyzable unities. This resulted in a description of a basic *framework* of the book centering around the sequential relationships between Job and God: (1) 1-37, God afflicts Job; (2) 38-42:6, God appears to Job out of the whirlwind; (3) 42:7-9, God states that Job spoke correctly of Him; and (4) 42:10-17, God restores all to Job twofold. This isolating of the largest unities essential to the very framework of the story was conceived as the first step in a three part structural analysis of the Book. The second step in this structural analysis·is the subject of the present chapter: the "code" of the Book of Job. It attempts to offer some remarks on the problems of finding "the invariants in variations," and of discovering aspects of a system operating in and through the framework. As we explained earlier, this second step is the paradigmatic section of a structural analysis (just as the first step was its syntagmatic step). Finally a third task still lies before us after this chapter is completed: a final study on "message" would treat certain aspects of the Book (besides its largest components and the system underlying them) which must be known before its message(s) can be grasped.

The purpose of these three studies goes beyond my inherent interest in structural analysis and its use in the specialized field of Old Testament studies. A goal of these chapters is touched on by J. Piaget as one of the main conclusions of his monograph: "Our second general conclusion is that the search for structures cannot but result in interdisciplinary coordinations" (1970: 137f). I hope to discuss points of contact between biblical studies on one hand and whatever other sciences seem to me, given our inherent limitations, to offer established insights to biblical scholars. Thus my study on the framework of the book attempted to establish connections between linguistics and the study of literature, recalling R. Barthes' desire for developing what he calls a true "linguistics of discourse." I also worked out a short scholion which attempted to relate the framework of the Book of Job to one brand of anthropology: namely to Lévi-Strauss' structural study of myth as interpreted by two scholars in folklore studies, Pierre and Elli K. Maranda.

This present chapter is an attempt to illustrate points of contact between biblical studies and mathematics. However far-fetched this contact between two such disparate disciplines appears on first sight, I must point out that mine is an extremely modest attempt. There is incontrovertible evidence from the history of science that that peculiar multicephalic creature called "structuralism"—which we consider neither a method nor a particular doctrine or philosophy—is indeed responsible for some of the more fruitful interdisciplinary advances of modern time. A short yet profound survey substantiating this point is J. Piaget's already mentioned monograph entitled *Structuralism*. Piaget describes very well the work being done in such diverse disciplines as mathematics, physics, biology, psychology, linguistics, sociology, anthropology, and philosophy. Nevertheless his work is a call to those of us much less gifted and erudite to widen our scholarly vision, to open up our academic interests and to *talk to one another* across the disciplinary fences we ourselves have built for whatever reasons, good *and* bad.

How can we begin to describe the connections that exist between the particular framework of four movements we isolated in the previous chapter and the mathematical concept of group which has played such a key role in many modern advances of science? An example borrowed from A. G. Oettinger and already used in chapter one will help to illustrate the connection (1968: 361-369). You may recall that syntactic analysis by computer of the sentence. "Time flies like an arrow" yields three different structural interpretations which can be represented by conventional sentence-structure diagrams as follows:

(1)

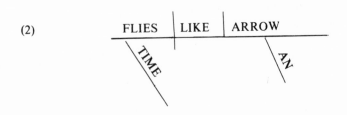

(2)

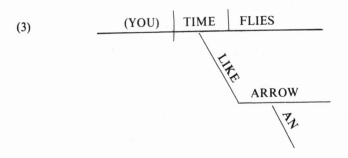

(3)

Confer above, pages 6-7, for the explanation of these three syntactic structures. As Oettınger points out, "Semantics, the all too nebulous notion of what a sentence means, must be invoked to choose among the three structures syntax accepts for 'Time flies like an arrow'" (1968: 367). But here precisely is our problem. Compared with this short syntagm, the syntagm which we are investigating, the Book of Job, is infinitely more complex from a structural point of view. How can we hope to deal successfully with such complexity, given the pitfalls inherent in the syntactic and semantic analysis of even the simplest sentences? Our reaction to these points has been to be as modest as possible in our goals. Thus, in chapter two on the framework of the Book of Job, we attempted to segment the syntagm only into its *largest* structural unities and to describe as concisely as possible the syntactic structure that seemed to emerge from such a segmentation. The *system* underlying the framework was touched on, but not in any organized formal manner. This chapter will attempt to spell out that system (or code) more explicitly. But we have just been reminded how nebulous semantics can be in helping to discover or delineate the particular syntactic structure of an individual sentence. If semantics offers us such relative difficulty in choosing between the three possible syntactic structures of our example, it is obvious that a forty-two chapter syntagm will offer us no easily discovered *semantic* solution. Here precisely is where concepts derived from mathematics may serve as useful guides in discovering and describing a system underlying the elemental structural framework of our book. What then are we to say when we are confronted with the main question of this study: given that the Book of Job is composed of four major unities, *how* are these unities combined and related and what are the implications of these relationships to the *meaning* or message(s) of the book? It seems to us quite realistic and necessary to aim here at the *least* we can say about the structural relationships of these four movements we claim to have discovered in chapter two. What we want to do here is to leave aside as much semantic content from the framework as we can. Of course one may object that bologna is still bologna no matter how thin one slices it. The answer to this waggish objection is simply that scholars clearly deal with objects whose intrinsic nature remains unknown. Sir Arthur Stanley Eddington reminds us that Bertrand Russell's definition of a mathematician is one who never knows what he is talking about nor whether what he is saying is true. Eddington also helps us to have some insight into our present problem:

> Our account of the external world . . . must necessarily be a 'Jabberwocky' of unknowable actors executing unknowable actions. How in these conditions can we arrive at any knowledge at all? We must seek a knowledge which is neither of actors nor of actions, but of which the actors and actions are a vehicle. The knowledge we can acquire is knowledge of a structure or pattern contained in the actions. . . . In mathematics we describe such knowledge as knowledge of group structure. (1956: 1559)

Applying this to our present problem, I think it is possible to see the utility of removing or abstracting from as much as we are able of the interpretation or meaning we claimed to have found in each movement or sequential unit of the framework. We, of course, will not abstract from all content since the movements deal with transformations and we must have *some* idea of what a thing is transformed into, at least with regard to what it was transformed from. As Piaget remarks: "Group structure and transformation go together. But when we speak of transformation, we mean an intelligible change, which does not transform things beyond recognition at one stroke, and which always preserves invariance in certain respects" (1970: 20). What is the pattern or structure of the framework once we have removed as much (often questionable) interpretation as possible from the *semantic content* of each movement? Another image of what we are aiming at here is Lewis Carroll's well-known method of defining a grin as what remains after the Cheshire cat, the vehicle of the grin, has vanished. In reference again to Eddington's remarks, even if we know very little about the actors of our story (Job and God), and even though we put aside for the moment much of the *significance* of their words and actions, these actors and actions are only a vehicle of a structure or pattern contained in the story. It is this structure or pattern behind the framework of the book which is illuminated so well by knowledge derived from the mathematical concept of group structure.

"Groups" in mathematics.

> The Theory of Groups is a branch of mathematics in which one does something to something and then compares the result with the result obtained from doing the same thing to something else, or something else to the same thing. This is a broad definition but it is not trivial. The theory is a supreme example of the art of mathematical abstraction. It is concerned only with the fine filigree of underlying relationships; it is the most powerful instrument yet invented for illuminating structure. (Newman, 1956: 1534)

The following brief description of "groups," it is hoped, will not be too inadequate for our purposes. Marc Barbut (1970: 367-387) utilizes the following example which experimental psychologists often present their subjects:

> take an object, let us say a white disc, and modify one of its characteristics (shape or colour in our example). One may change either the shape, transforming the object into a white square, for example, or the colour, transforming it into a black disc. Lastly one may change both shape and colour, turning it into a black square. If there are but two shapes (round and square) and two colours (black and white) our object has only four possible states, and these are linked by the elementary transformations summarized by the diagram:

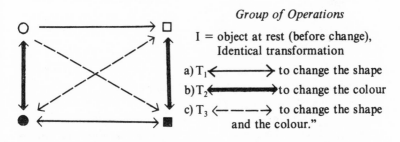

Group of Operations

I = object at rest (before change), Identical transformation

a) $T_1 \longleftrightarrow$ to change the shape

b) $T_2 \longleftrightarrow$ to change the colour

c) $T_3 \longleftarrow - - \rightarrow$ to change the shape and the colour."

Now this is an example of a group (a specific group called the Klein group), composed of four elements which in this case are *transformations.* Our little "game" makes clear that there are only four transformations possible, and when we visualize combining

3 transformations?

or 4 states

transformations, we become aware of four certainties the situation as explained implies:

1) It is certain that if you combine any number of transformations, the result will equal the result of *one* of the group's transformations. (This is called the group property.) Thus, for example, if "0" is used to symbolize a combination of transformations, $T_2 \, 0 \, T_3 = T_1$. In other words, *any* combination of transformations will *always* equal one of the four transformations of the group.

2) It is certain that the result of two transformations plus a third equals the result of the first plus the result of the second and third. (This is the associative property of a group.) Thus $(T_2 \, 0 \, T_3) \, 0 \, T_1 = T_2 \, 0 \, (T_3 \, 0 \, T_1)$. In other words, it does not matter how you group your combinations of transformations, the result is the same. One must remember here that the order of the combinations is either relevant or irrelevant depending on the group in question.

3) It is certain that one of the transformations (here I) when combined with a given transformation will always equal that given transformation. Thus $I \, 0 \, T_1 = T_1$; $I \, 0 \, T_2 = T_2$; $I \, 0 \, T_3 = T_3$. Here I is the *identical* member of the group and every group must have an identical member. Moreover this certainty is commutative, that is, $I \, 0 \, T_1 = T_1 \, 0 \, I$. In other words, when you combine the identical member of a group with another member, the *order* of combination is irrelevant to the results.

4) It is certain that *each member* of the group can be combined with a member of the group (its reciprocal member) to equal the identical member (I). In our example each transformation is its own reciprocal. Thus $T_1 \, 0 \, T_1 = I$; $T_2 \, 0 \, T_2 = I$; $T_3 \, 0 \, T_3 = I$; and $I \, 0 \, I = I$.

These four "certainties" belong to every mathematic group. A Klein group is simply a group of four members whose rules of combination are commutative, that is $T_1 \, 0 \, T_2 = T_2 \, 0 \, T_1$. (Not all groups are commutative; those that are are called Abelian, the others are called non-Abelian.) A Klein group is accordingly an

Abelian group, having four members.

A group is a good example of an algebraic structure. As Barbut notes: "An algebraic structure is a whole made up of any elements whatsoever, so long as they conform to one or more defined *laws of combination* or, synonymously, operations. . . " (1970: 374). But where are structures such as the groups we have been discussing? Here the idea of "representation" is important. A group without specification of its elements is an "abstract group." Once you give a *meaning* to each element of the group, you then have a *representation* of a group. An abstract group then is what two or more specific (specified as to the meaning of its elements) *representations* have in common, once you *erase* the meaning of each element. Their common (group) structure remains on this higher level of abstraction. Thus in the real concrete world we find concrete representations of groups or structures and by *abstracting* from these concrete representations everything except what makes their structure, one obtains an abstract structure or group. As Barbut remarks:

> Clearly there is a constant double process in mathematics from the 'concrete' to the 'abstract' (which is the structure, the syntax), and conversely from the 'abstract' to something 'concrete' (representation, semantics), which offers a strengthening of intuition, if this sense be familiar, by giving meaning to abstract objects, and permits greater efficiency in calculation. (1970: 376)

The example of a Klein group we gave above with its specification of transformations (change colour, change shape, change both), is a *representation* of a group. It is the contention of this chapter that the framework of the Book of Job is made up of a system of transformations, offering us a *representation* of what mathematicians call a Klein group.

The reader is referred to the previous chapter for a more extensive treatment of the framework of the Book of Job. Here we will only review our main conclusions. There are four basic framework unities or movements in the story. Each movement centers around a main sequential function which divides the movement into *before* and *after*. The first segment (= movement) of the story (1-37) centers around the afflicting of Job. Before the affliction (1:1-5), there is equilibrium between two spheres which we called the sphere of *belief* and that of *experience*; both spheres receive general assent. After the affliction (1:6-37:24), a conflict is set up between these two spheres. Job's afflictions enable the dialogues of 3-37 to confront the apparent contradiction between what one *believes* as a member of a religious community and what one *experiences* as an individual. In other words, movement one involves a transformation from general assent to these two spheres (equilibrium) to conflict between them. In his speeches Job takes a stand siding with his personal experience at the expense of denying elements in the sphere of tradition or belief (e.g. God rewards the good and punishes the evil). The second movement comprises God's speeches plus Job's response (38-42:6) and centers around these theophanic speeches. Previous to their appearance, Job assents to one sphere (that of his own suffering experience) and denies elements of the other sphere (that of belief); after the theophany, Job recants and repents, admitting he was wrong. Here as in the first movement, there is a *transformation*: what Job denied he now affirms (the belief sphere) and what he affirmed he now in some way denies (the experience sphere). The third segment or movement is formed in 42:7-9 where God speaks to Eliphaz and states that Job has spoken correctly of him. This word of God is the main sequential function which transforms the state of affairs: before it, the validity of Job's experiences had been denied by Job's general assent to the theophanic speeches; now through God's word in 42:7-9, what was denied in the previous movement (e.g. Job's innocent suffering) is now affirmed and what was affirmed (the theophany of 38-41) is now somehow denied or negated, clearly a twofold transformation like the one in the previous movement. Finally, the last main transformation of the story (involving Job and God) occurs with the fourth sequential function of 42:10-17 in which God restores all to Job twofold. This transforms the negation of the previous movement into a general affirmation: the power of God asserted by *word* in 38-41 and indirectly denied by God's speech to Eliphaz in 42:7-9, is now confirmed by deed: he gives Job twice what he had before. We offer again the diagram we used to summarize these statements:

4th Seq. Function	3rd Seq. Function	2nd Seq. Function	1st Seq. Function	Belief Sphere	Ex- perience Sphere	Read: ↩ Initial Situation
				+ Job is "right- eous"	+ Job is rich	of Story ch. 1:1-5
			Affliction: → −	−	+	Movement One 1:6—37:24
		Vision: →	−	+		Movement Two 38:1—42:6
	Word →	−		+		Movement Three 42:7-9
Act: →	+ Job is "correct"	+ Job is twice blessed				Movement Four 42:10-17

N.B. (1) In movements two and three, the function of the previous movement becomes the denied *term* of the next movement.

(2) Each sphere and function is affirmed before story ends.

Now we can try to remove the cat but keep the grin. Let us return over this familiar territory once again and "erase" as much of the picture as possible without destroying the framework itself. Earlier we wrote "The major contradictions in the story appear to be connected with a major theme of the book: for any thinking person there is a contradiction between what he has been taught to *believe* about divine justice and what he experiences almost daily in his life." But can we step to a higher level of abstraction without destroying a key idea contained in this statement? We would get a statement such as the following: "A major theme of the book is that there is a conflict or contradiction between X and Y." Now let us apply this statement to each of the movements we have isolated.

In the first movement (1-37) the afflictions of Job function as an agent of transformation so that *before* the afflictions, X and Y are not in conflict. We can represent this beginning state of affairs as +X+Y (that is, general affirmation of both the sphere of belief and of the sphere of personal experience). But *after* these afflictions, the speeches of Job with his friends show that, in relation to these two spheres, Job assents to the validity of his suffering experience and must deny elements in the sphere of belief. This first transformation can be expressed as follows: T = +X+Y ——→ -X+Y. This reads: given an initial state +X+Y, the first transformation changes element X but not element Y. (Putting the semantic content back into the statement would result in the following: given the initial state of the book [1:1-5 where Job is described as both righteous and blessed] in which the spheres of belief and experience are affirmed, the afflicting of Job by God transforms the situation so that Job is led to deny elements of the sphere of belief because of his insistent affirmation of the sphere of his suffering experience.) Since we are concerned in the framework only with the mutual relations of God and Job (see reasons in the previous chapter) we will mention here only in passing that whereas the afflictions transform Job's position from +X+Y ——→ -X+Y, the afflictions work the opposite transformation on his friends, so that in general *for them* the transformation is +X+Y ——→ +X-Y.

The second movement's (38-42:6) main transformation is accomplished by the theophanic speeches of 38-41. Now whatever their semantic content, it is very clear what they *do* with regard to Job's previous position. His response in 42:1-6 shows very clearly that, *whatever* he held in his speeches in 3-37, he now admits he was wrong: "I have uttered what I did not understand, things too wonderful for me which I did not know . . . therefore I despise myself and repent in dust and ashes" (42:3,6). Thus, what he affirmed he now denies and what he denied he now affirms. Using our symbols we have the following transformation for this movement: $T = -X+Y \longrightarrow +X-Y$. In other words, whereas he denied elements of the sphere of belief he now affirms them and whereas he had affirmed elements of his suffering experience he now has had to deny them. Now since the *function* of the divine speeches for Job was to affirm the sphere of belief, the divine speeches themselves have become a function of the sphere of belief and serve now to be synonymous with that sphere.

The third movement's (42:7-9) transformation is accomplished by the words of God in these verses. Now whatever their meaning, these verses clearly *do* something: they affirm whatever Job affirmed in his speeches ("You have not spoken correctly of me as my servant Job has"). Since I have represented Job's position in the dialogues as $-X+Y$, we can see, therefore, that the third transformation transforms $+X-Y$ (the position of Job as a result of movement two) into $-X+Y$. Thus we have $T = +X-Y \longrightarrow -X+Y$. Now, since the function of God's words in 42.7-9 was to affirm what Job had affirmed in the second movement viz. the sphere of personal experience, these words of God in 42:7-9 now become a function of the sphere of experience and are now synonymous with that sphere.

The fourth movement's transformation is accomplished by the beneficient acts of God in 42:10-17. Whatever else they do, it is clear that they are in accord with the previous movement in one respect: since Job *was* correct in his speaking about God, God now rewards him twofold. In other words, Job had assented to the sphere of experience ($+Y$ in the first movement). God had said he was correct ($+Y$ in the third movement); now therefore God blesses him twofold in 42:10-17, ($+Y$ in the fourth movement). However, these beneficient acts also *transform* an element of the previous movement: since the effect of the word in 42:7-9 was to *deny* the vision of God (itself standing for or functioning as the sphere of belief) His acts in 42:10-17 transform this denial to an affirmation of the vision (which was an affirmation of the sphere of belief). Thus $T = -X+Y \longrightarrow +X+Y$. The story ends in the same state as it began. Between the beginning and the end (in the second and third transformations), the transforming elements become the denied element of the next movement. And before the story ends, each sphere and function is affirmed.

Redoing our diagram with appropriate changes in terminology and symbols we obtain the following:

4th Transformation	3rd Transformation	2nd Transformation	1st Transformation	X	Y	Read: ↩ Initial Situation
				+	+	of Story ch. 1:1-5
			Affliction: $=Y'$ >	–	+	Movement One 1:6—37:24
		Vision: $=X'$ >	–	+		Movement Two 38:1—42:6
	Word $=Y''$ >	–	+			Movement Three 42:7-9
Act: $=+X+Y$ >	+	+				Movement Four 42:10-17

We can visualize the series of transformations which forms the framework in the following way:

$$
\begin{array}{lllll}
\text{Initial situation or beginning} & I & = & +X+Y \\
\text{First movement} & : & T & = & +X+Y \longrightarrow -X+Y \\
\text{Second movement} & : & T & = & -X+Y \longrightarrow +X-Y \\
\text{Third movement} & : & T & = & +X-Y \longrightarrow -X+Y \\
\text{Fourth movement} & : & T & = & -X+Y \longrightarrow +X+Y = I
\end{array}
$$

Applying our remarks on group analysis, we see that we have a situation analogous to the example we used in explaining the nature of a group. Instead of an object with only two possible shapes and two possible colors, we have a sphere of belief which is either asserted or denied (+X or –X) and a sphere of experience which is either asserted or denied (+Y or –Y). In a series of transformations there are only four possible states:

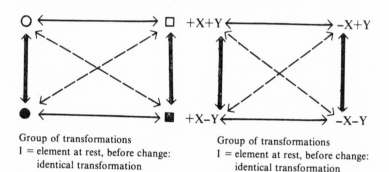

Group of transformations
I = element at rest, before change:
    identical transformation

Group of transformations
I = element at rest, before change:
    identical transformation

a) T_1 = ⟷ to change the SHAPE
b) T_2 = ⟨—⟩ to change the COLOR
c) T_3 = ⟨- - -⟩ to change the SHAPE
                AND THE COLOR

a) T_1 = ⟨—⟩ to change X
b) T_2 = ⟷ to change Y
c) T_3 = ⟨- - -⟩ to change X & Y

Both of the above examples are *representations* of a certain abstract group called a Klein group as we explained above. Each representation contains four transformations, designated I, a, b, c above, and satisfying all the conditions of a Klein group mentioned earlier in this paper.

The first point I want to make is that the structure isolated is not *arbitrary* in the sense that the properties of a structure may or may not be present in the concrete object of study from which it was abstracted (object —→ representation —→ abstract group). One may question whether the *representation* is faithful to the totality or *aspects of the totality* under investigation but once one agrees that the representation is faithful to features found in the concrete object, then it seems necessary to conclude that the properties flowing from that structure also belong necessarily to the concrete object, however little we know about the meaning and significance of the thing we are investigating. Structuralists are often accused of being *selective* in their methodology, therefore preselecting the conclusions at which they arrive ("Of course your conclusion is A and not B: in your investigation of your object, you arbitrarily decided to study only elements a_1, a_2, a_3 etc. and refused to study elements b_1, b_2, b_3 which might have led you to conclude B also, or at least something combining A and B [AB, A-B, A+B, A/B])." The answer to this objection is simply this: selectivity is a necessary feature of even the most irreproachable methodology and is a FACT of scientific investigation; it is not to be confused with arbitrariness. Searching for structures or patterns is necessarily selective in the sense of looking for invariance in variation. It seems to me, therefore, that structural analysis—like all types of analyses—can be carried out in a manner which is good or bad, but as a new approach, its strengths and its weaknesses are today too well established for superficial criticisms of the nature just mentioned to be taken seriously.

What then can an analysis of the group structure of the framework of the Book of Job tell us about the meaning and significance of its "message(s)"? What insights have we gained by bringing our math book to the suffering Job? If we have gone from the concrete to the abstract (text to segmented framework; framework to group representation; group representation to abstract group) it is now time for us to reverse the process and return to the concrete with concrete conclusions derived from our abstract analysis. What might some of these conclusions be?

Notice first of all that there are only four kinds of transformation possible in the framework as we have described it; we have labelled these transformations

I) :   no change, the identical transformation;
a) :   transforming X;
b) :   transforming Y;
c) :   transforming X and Y.

Now not only are there only four kinds of transformation possible, there are only four states that can result from *any* combination of transformations you can think of. These are +X+Y, −X+Y, −X−Y, and +X-Y. We may now ask two questions: (1) how many and which of the four possible transformations are actually found in the framework? and (2) how many and which of the four possible states result from the framework's transformations? To answer these two questions let us "read" the story according to its sequence of transformations. In other words the story is a *combination* of transformations which looks like this:

I a c c a.

We notice in answer to our first question that three out of the four possible transformations occur in the framework, transformation b not occurring. Is there any significance to this? In other words, is there any importance to be attached to the fact that the story allows X to be transformed alone, and XY to be transformed together but Y is never transformed alone? The answer to this question seems to be: no, there does *not* seem to be any significance to this fact. All one has to do is to use the properties of group structure to find that b *is* there. Let us look at the story again:

I 0 a 0 c 0 c 0 a

Recalling the properties of a group, we can "reduce" this sequence to the following by combining the first two transformations (remember I 0 a = a):

a 0 c 0 c 0 a.

Now, let us do the same again by combining a 0 c:

b 0 c 0 a.

In other words (check the representation for verification) the net result of I 0 a 0 c = b, and therefore the movement or transformation from the beginning to the second movement (+X+Y ——→ −X+Y, ——→ +X-Y, two moves), is the same as going directly from the beginning to b (+X+Y ——→ +X-Y, one move). Thus as a transformation is equivalently present in our sequence.

This brings us now to the second question. (2) How many and which of the four possible states or results are actually found in the framework? Looking back at our representation and tracing the path of the transformations we see:

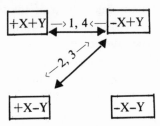

It is immediately obvious that the four movements or successive transformations have avoided altogether the state –X–Y, while resulting along the way in all three of the other possible states. Now, since X represents the sphere of belief and Y the sphere of personal experience, the one state avoided throughout the framework is that state representing somehow a negation both of the sphere of belief and the sphere of experience! It seems to me that this one observation is worth the entire (and tiring) trip. For it appears to me to open up a new set of insights to the story of the Book of Job. Questions immediately clamor for attention. What, in the concrete terms of the story, *might* represent that one state so assiduously avoided in the story? One plausible hypothesis seems to me to be that it is the one state Job vehemently and ceaselessly prayed to Yahweh to grant him: to be sent down to *Sheol*, the land of the dead. Through all the meandering of the story it was never given to Job at his request, its affirmation longed for but never attained. It is the one state avoided by all the transformations of the story and it is hard to avoid the conclusion that this also is in some sense the point of the story. If there was a conflict between Job and God it was ultimately a conflict in which God represents the affirmation +X+Y, while Job keeps begging Him for –X–Y (reread his speeches to see how constant his pleading was). The result of the conflict is that Yahweh won, so that Job stopped demanding Sheol. The concept of Sheol is ultimately the negation of everything (Job's descriptions of it in the book are almost all in negative terms). The message of the book centers around the courageous affirmation of apparently irreconcilable spheres instead of the insane negation of those spheres to avoid conflict and contradiction. The Book of Job is a conflict between God, who affirms life however cruel, and Job, who wanted death to avoid that cruelty. It is the story of how God won.

Chapter IV

The Message of the Book of Job

We now begin the crucial step in our structural analysis of the Book of Job on the plane of content. Chapters two and three lead up to this stage of analysis and find their significance and coherence here, on what Barthes calls "the level of narration" (1966). If what we have been doing so far has any relevance to understanding something about what the Book of Job *means*, it all must fit together somehow, become meaningful and intelligible now, as we attempt to articulate the relationship between what the story says and what the author of the story is saying. Hopefully, therefore, we will now draw closer to the real world of man communicating with man. Formulas, methodologies, formal analyses may all have their place in such an enterprise. But they are valuable only insofar as they help to make what one studies a little more intelligible to whoever employs them. This present chapter is a kind of "test" or "attempt at validation" of the more formal analyses of the two preceding chapters. If it helps to make the Book of Job more meaningful to the reader, it serves its purpose. If not, it will be for such a reader the type of statement Job was talking about when he said to Zophar in 13:12:

> Your maxims are proverbs of ashes
> Your defenses are defenses of clay.

The Book of Job is about a man who has everything that life has to offer and loses it all in a brief series of disasters. At first he voices the instinctive reactions his upbringing has conditioned him to produce: ". . . 'Shall we accept good from God, and not accept evil?' In spite of this Job did not sin with his lips" 2:10; and

"Then Job rose and tore his robe and shaved his head. He fell on the ground, and worshipped. He said: 'Naked I came from my mother's womb, and naked shall I return there. Yahweh gave, Yahweh took away. Blessed be Yahweh's name.' In all this Job did not sin, nor ascribe blame to God" (1:20-22). But what he really feels and thinks comes to the fore during the seven days and seven nights his friends sit on the ground with him, silently. In chapter three the first words Job speaks, after the full impact of his losses has hit him, represent what Job in his present condition wants more than anything else in life: death. He never ceases to give this request the greatest urgency throughout all the myriad facets of the problem which he and his friends examine in the speeches of 3-37. Already here at the beginning of the speeches I am faced with a main problem that in fact remains as I continue on in the story in search of its message: why is it that in the story, Job does not ask to have his health, wealth and family restored to him? In fact not only does he not so request this from God, he steadfastly resists any suggestion on the part of his friends (e.g., Eliphaz's speech in chapter five) that if he is patient and faithful God will in fact restore to him all that he has lost. It is a significant feature of the story, in my opinion, that Job does not consider such a restoration a *desirable* option. At first glance it would seem one of the more likely requests someone in Job's position would make of his God. There is another side to this problem: if Job's most urgent request is death rather than restoration as freedom from his sufferings, why doesn't he somewhere along the line just kill himself or at least consider its possibilities? If I am not mistaken, both a self-initiated suicide and a restoration of his fortunes by God are outside of the possibilities Job considers as a solution to his problem. If one couples this with the fact of Job's insistence upon death as the only solution, there is, I believe, a clear indication of key elements of the message of the story. Before the crucial vision of God in 38-41, what Job does *not* want is that which he has lost. Within the confines of the story this only makes sense if Job's disasters have impressed upon him what he had previously either ignored or, at the most, known only theoretically: to be a man is to be in peril of losing everything at any moment. This *lack* of any insistence or consideration on Job's part that God restore his fortunes is for me a clear *index* of the story on the level of narration: the author wants to portray his protagonist as a person who receives a sudden revelation of the fact of creaturehood and the precariousness of life's gifts and who violently reacts against reality as it has been imposed upon him. The reason Job rejects restoration is because he realizes that he could just as quickly lose *this* restoration as he did his original state in life. Job recognizes this fact in his ashes and decides, "stop the world, I want to get off." But he does not want to get off the world without God's permission and previous sanction. He therefore does not want death or Sheol *per se* but a divinely sanctioned death and passage to Sheol that would constitute God's approval of his "checking-out" of life. The conditions of life involve too much uncertainty; Job wants from God a safe-conduct to Sheol.

> Why gives (God) light to the wretched,
> Life to the bitter of soul . . .
> To a man whose way is hidden
> whom God has fenced about (3:20,23)

Job wants to be

> There where knaves cease strife,
> where the weary are at rest . . . (3:17)

Somehow suicide never enters the picture either because it is not the way to *Sheol* or because, if it is, such a passage would not be according to the plan or will of God. Job wants nothing less than the right to cease being at the mercy of life's capriciousness, to cease being a part of the human condition. As chapter three above attempted to express it: the message of the book centers around a conflict between God, who affirms life however cruel, and Job, who wanted death to avoid that cruelty; it is the story of how God won.

In short, Job is portrayed throughout the book as a man who

always recognizes the power of God and his own subordination to Him, and for this very reason rejects life as God has constituted it. Nowhere in the book is Job the unbeliever; rather he is the supreme realist who rejects not God but life as God has shaped it for man.

The appearance of God out of the whirlwind changes Job's attitude drastically. God's power-play tells Job nothing he does not already know. It is the impact of His appearance before Job that produces the change rather than anything God says. Just as the sufferings convinced Job he no longer wanted to live, the theophany now convinces him he no longer wants to die:

> I talked of things I did not know,
> Wonders beyond my ken . . .
> I had heard of you by hearsay
> But now my own eyes have seen you;
> So I recant and repent
> In dust and ashes. (42:3,5-6)

God now restores to Job twice as much as he had originally. What appears to invest Job's latter good fortune with ultimate significance is not precisely the fact that it is twofold but rather than now this good fortune is possessed with insight (by Job and by the reader) whereas the course of the story has shown so graphically how Job's blessings at the beginning were without such insight.

There is something ruggedly admirable about Job, but still confusing, before and after the theophany. Before his *metanoia* in 42, he knows what he wants and who it is who alone can give it to him. He is not so much scandalized by innocent suffering as by the fact that one has no choice in the matter. He rejects not so much what God *does* but precisely his inability to avoid the consequences of God's actions. It is not the *fact* of evil that really bothers him, it is the human condition in which one has no choice but to suffer what befalls him. For Job, God is still God in spite of His injustice; if only man could cease being man under the circumstances. Yet after the theophany, Job is as definitely *for* as he previously was definitely *against* the human condition.

Part of the story's message therefore centers around the characterization of Job. Yet much of what the story is about comes to us through the author's portrayal of God. In the opening chapters, God is quite clearly in control of everything. But what kind of a person would play games with a man's life as God does? To prove his point with the *Satan,* God allows Job's health, wealth, and family to disappear. To show how Job is worthy of His blessings, God removes them or at least allows them to be removed through the *Satan's* agency. In the Book of Job, God appears insensitive and also cruel. Instead of appearing before Job to comfort him, God brings Job to his knees, demands recognition of His power and removes Job's sufferings only after he forces a cry of repentance from Job's lips. God barters with men's lives and takes advantage of their weaknesses by taunting them with His power.

There is also an apparently arbitrary nature to God's judgments since, as we have already emphasized in chapter two, at one moment Job's speeches appear wrong to God, yet later in 42:7-9, they are deemed to have spoken correctly about Him. If Job vacillates through the course of the story, so does God.

The friends also experience a deep change of heart that allows them to repudiate all they so forcefully said in 3-37. It is simply God's call for repentance that causes them to change their mind.

It is almost as if there is not one major character in the story who has enough strength in his convictions to persevere in them despite opposition. In fact there is no conviction, expressed by any figure in the story, that is so sacred it is not immediately contradicted by someone or something else. God's opinion of Job is quickly doubted by Satan. Job's initial reaction to his sufferings is not the cursing of God his wife had recommended. Job's opening speech is rejected by Eliphaz whose opening words are quickly rejected in turn by Job. A similar pattern of opposition develops with the other friends. Moreover, Job's position in 3-37 is not what God had predicted in chapters one and two. Then God appears out of the whirlwind to correct Job who amazingly accepts correction, only to be portrayed by God's words in 42:7-9 as not needing correction. These same words cause Job's friends to disown their convictions of 3-37 and apparently to embrace what Job had therein expressed to God's immediate displeasure. In chapter one the godfearing Job regularly fears that his sons have sinned and cursed God in their feasting. In chapter two he corrects his wife for talking "like a foolish woman." As for Elihu, his anger "flared up against Job because he held himself to be righteous rather than God. And against his three companions his anger also flared because they had not found an answer and so had made God guilty" (32:2-3). In a word, everyone is in some way *against* someone else and there is no position taken by any figure in the story which is allowed to stand unchallenged.

How then is one to sort through this myriad of opposing figures, convictions and characterizations to arrive at some coherent and persuasive opinion about what the author's own theme, position, or conviction is? Can one assume for example, that the author ultimately represents his own convictions in the person of God? But even in this case God's position changes radically throughout the story. What is the point of a story in which every opposing point is held at one time or another by God, Job and his friends? Is the message of the Book of Job that there is no message? Is the book of Job an exercise in relativity?

To confront questions such as these is to confront the Book with one basic question: what is the *situation* out of which and through which the message of the Book of Job makes sense? Admittedly such a question assumes the Book of Job *does* make sense; indeed this has been a driving assumption of mine throughout this entire investigation.

No message could have affected men's hearts and lives so deeply as the Book of Job has without somehow making sense, without fitting together in a way that avoids meaningless ambiguity. To investigate the *situation* in which the message makes sense is to inquire ultimately about the author of that message, the audience he had in mind, the very code by which his concrete message is formulated. All of this concerns what is called the "situation of discourse" and is the last step in our thematic analysis. Barthes talks about the level of narration, form critics talk about real-life situation, and Roman Jakobson mentions the "context, verbalized or not verbalized but verbalizable."

The reason for the importance of this stage is obvious: without some knowledge of pertinent information concerning the "situation of discourse," both the message of the book and the code that informs it must of necessity remain ambiguous. Without this step, there *is* no clear message received. Thus the title of this chapter, "The Message of the Book of Job."

However, the dichotomy between code and message is not as clear-cut as some would like. Roman Jakobson has already noted the ways in which these two concepts can either overlap or be circular (1971: 130-133) and whatever insights I have to offer in this chapter ultimately find their theoretical base in Jakobson's distinctions (with acknowledgement also to Peirce).

I will limit this discussion of the message of the Book of Job to the meaning and significance of some of the main *figures* of the story as this affects the story's message. T. Todorov explains the three ways by which the semantic contents of figures in a story can be manifested (1972: 286-292): (1) first of all by their name, e.g. the hero is named *ʾiyyôb* and God is called variously *ʾelohîm, ʾelôᵃh,* YHWH; (2) by explicit predication, e.g. Job is "blameless and upright, one who feared God and shunned evil" (1:1); and (3) by indirect means, that is, by what the figure does or does not do in the story, what he says or does not say in the story, the way he perceives or relates to others, the things associated with him in the story. For example, Job sacrifices in behalf of his children (1:5); he will not ascribe blame to God (1:22); he abhors platitudes as worthless in times of crisis (13:12); his dialogues with the comforters takes place on a pile of ashes (2:8).

But in order to avoid ambiguity in any of these manifestations, *something* must be known about the "situation of discourse." This chapter will try to illustrate how this information may be obtained. First we can center our discussion around the two main figures of the story, Job and God.

A discussion of these figures' names in the book will underscore the importance of knowing something àbout the "situation of discourse," the "meaning" of the figure who possesses the name, and ultimately the "meaning" of the story built around this figure. In his discussion concerning the name of our "hero," ⁾iyyôb, Marvin Pope concludes:

> The name Ayyāb > ⁾iyyôb is thus well attested as a fairly common name among western Semites in the second millennium B.C. The name may have been chosen for the hero of the story simply because it was an ordinary name. It may be, however, that some ancient worthy bearing that name actually experienced reversals of fortune and become (sic) the model of the righteous sufferer. The mention of Job (Ezek XIV 14, 20) along with Noah and (the Ugaritic hero) Daniel suggests a hero of great antiquity. (1965: 6)

Pope had previously rejected an etymological interpretation of the name, viz., "that the name was constructed, ad hoc, to characterize the hero of the story" (1965: 5). For example, ⁾iyyôb might mean "inveterate foe." All three of these possibilities directly concern the "situation of discourse:" (1) did the author simply choose a common ordinary name; (2) did the author tell his story about a well-known model of righteous suffering; or (3) did the author construct a name to characterize his hero? Choosing one of these alternatives necessarily affects one's understanding of the book's message. In the first case the name of Job would not affect the message; in the second and third cases it would affect the message. Put a little more technically, in the first case, the name ⁾iyyôb is an index which does not affect the message of the story whereas, in the second and third cases, the name is an index which does affect the message. Now an index is a part of either the code or message which points to the "situation of discourse," that is, either to the giving of the message ("Now he lives in New York"), the sender of the message ("I miss him), or the receiver of the message ("You miss him"). This "pointing toward" the situation of discourse may or may not avoid ambiguity of code or of message. If it does avoid ambiguity, the index may be called pertinent; if it does not, the index is nonpertinent.

Here precisely is the problem: if we need information concerning whether the *name* of Job affects the author's message, and if this information belongs to that sphere we call "situation of discourse," it would seem that we lack any means of deciding this question. The Book of Job, like all ancient texts, speaks to us across the centuries like a voice crying the wilderness: the type of general knowledge of the ancient near-eastern and Israelite *situation* is not specific enough to answer our question concerning the author's choice of the name *ʾiyyôb*. The name of Job would appear to be a non-pertinent *index* of the book's "situation of discourse."

There *is* however a way to remove *some* ambiguity in this regard. I am referring to the not-insignificant fact that (verbal) context is very often what one might call a "contextualized situation."

Let me explain this matter with a sample statement borrowed from Prieto and used with profit by Germain (1973: 25-43). Think of the following statement, "I have just purchased a new book. Would you like to see it?" Now visualize two *situations*. First of all this *statement* is *said* by one person to another whom he has just encountered. Secondly, picture for yourself a situation in which one person writes this statement to a friend who lives across the ocean. The former is an *oral* situation, the latter a *written* one. Now concentrate on various possibilities within each situation. In the first case it is quite conceivable that in such a situation (an encounter between two people) the speaker could point to a book in his hand and say simply, "Would you like to see it?" The other person would immediately understand that "it" refers to the book in the speaker's hand. In this case a non-verbal *situation,* the speaker pointing to the book in his hand, makes absolutely clear what "it" signifies or means. On the other hand such a non-verbal indication is not possible in a letter-writing situation so that it is the *verbal context,* that is, the sentence "I have just purchased a new book," which makes absolutely clear in the letter what "it" means in the sentence which follows: "Would you like to see it?" It is easy to see that the first sentence performs

the same function in the written communication as an aspect of
the *situation* (non-verbal pointing) does in the oral
communication. In other words when one is dealing with written
language, real life situations often have to be verbally
contextualized in order for certain elements of the written
statement to be understood. However, when one deals especially
with written material, a third option is often likely. What if, in the
case of our letter-writing example, there is reference to the author
having purchased a *number of items,* so that his correspondent
reads something like, "I have just purchased a boat, a water-bed,
and a book. Would you like me to mail it to you for your
inspection?" In this case the reader would be able to arrive at the
probable meaning of "it" in the second sentence by a combination
of clues that includes verbal *context,* non-verbal *situation* and
elements not quite one or the other. He might reason that "it"
refers to the book since the book is the last item mentioned in the
preceding sentence (verbal context). He also would conceivably
rule out the probability of his friend referring to either the boat or
the water-bed because of his prior knowledge that boats and
water-beds are usually not mailed from one country to another,
and in any case he knows his friend is not rich enough to pay the
postage for boats or beds, especially having purchased the former
(non-verbal situation). However there might be other elements in
his understanding of "it" as referring to "book" which are like the
context of a statement since they are verbal, yet like the *situation*
of a statement in that more than a "linguistic fact" is involved.
This third example is what Germain calls a "contextual situation"
and is present in any "verbal" element which is not a specific
formal linguistic unity. This is often the case in communications,
especially written ones, since in writing so much more of the real
life situation has to be verbally contextualized to get across what
one means. In the example just given, it might be the "tone" of the
letter not any one specific element which convinces the recipient
that his friend is evidently feeling just crazy enough to send him a
water-bed *air mail.* Or his friend's further statement that he might
like to use "it" "some rainy day" might incline him to suspect the

imminent arrival of a bed or a book but probably not a boat. The important point here is that often there is a fine line between what Germain calls "context" and what he terms "contextual situation" especially when one is dealing with written language; but in both cases one is often enabled to recover a *situation*. A second major point is that all three kinds of information have to be taken into consideration before one can "receive a message."

Applying these linguistic distinctions to the problem at hand we might well ask whether or not there is anything within the message itself (the book of Job) that would comprise that element we call "contextualized situation"? In other words we are looking for an *index* that would both "point at" some aspect of the "situation of discourse" *and* clarify the role which the name of *ᵓiyyôb* plays in the Book of Job. There is some indication in the text itself which points to the fact that in the "situation of discourse" the name of *ᵓiyyôb* was *not* chosen to represent a well-known and ancient model of righteous suffering. Therefore this second of our three possibilities about the role of the name Job is not likely. The reason for this lies in the *context* of the name's use in the text:

> There was a man in the land of Uz, whose name was Job; and that man was blameless and upright, one who feared God, and turned away from evil. (1:1)

Compare this *context* with that found in Ezekiel 14:14,20:

> even if these three men, Noah, Daniel, and Job, were in it, they would deliver but their own lives by their righteousness, says the Lord God. (14:14)

> Even if Noah, Daniel, and Job were in (that land), as I live, says the Lord God, they would deliver neither son nor daughter; they would deliver but their own lives by their righteousness. (14:20)

What is immediately obvious in these two contrasting contexts is that the man named Job is clearly presented in the citation from the Book of Job as *unknown* to the audience in the "situation of discourse" whereas in the citation from the Book of Ezekiel, the man named Job is presented as *well-known* within the "situation of discourse." This type of *index* helps us avoid some ambiguity here and we are left only with the first and third possibilities of the meaning of the name Job, that is, either the name is also part of the message of the book (Job means an "inveterate foe"), or, like most proper names, it refers only to the code of the book ("Job" means the person named Job). Such ambiguity is not further diminished by the pertinent *situational* information pointed out for us by Pope, namely, that this name "is thus well attested as a fairly common name among western Semites in the second millenium B.C." (1965: 6). Such evidence only shows that the first possibility is as likely as the third, and in this sense *situational* information has increased rather than diminished ambiguity.

We can contrast the use of the name of *ʾiyyôb* with those names used to refer to the other major figure in the story, God. "The names used for God are different in the Prologue-Epilogue and the Dialogue; the former uses Yahweh and Elohim while the latter employs variously the terms El, Eloah, Elohim, and Shaddai" (Pope: 1965: XXII). The pertinent contrast is not the *many* names for God versus only *one* name for Job; rather the contrast lies again in the *context* or *contextual situation* surrounding the two cases. As we have just seen, the contextualized situations of Job's name "point at" a "situation of discourse" in which this figure is not well-known to the audience. On the other hand the contextualized situations surrounding the occurrence of God's names always indicate a "situation of discourse" in which God is well-known and presented in the book as one who does not need to be defined, described or clarified in the same way as the figure Job does, in spite of the fact that He possesses six different names. The only other main figure in the story who is presented as a similar figure within the "situation of discourse" is "the *Satan*" who enters the scene and plays his part without any apparent need to be introduced, described or otherwise "fleshed-out" for the audience. Apart from these two figures, every other major figure operates within a contextualized situation indicating the need for

at least an initial introduction and orientation of that figure: Job's
sons, daughters, wife, and friends all find their narrative identity
in their very relationship to Job; and even Elihu must be
introduced as "Elihu, son of Barachel the Buzite of the clan of
Ram" (32:2).

The significance of this crucial difference between the "unknown" aspect of the figure named Job on one hand, and the
"well-known" aspect of the figure named God on the other, as pre-
sumptions in the "situation of discourse" will have profound
effects on our analysis of the remaining narrative features to be
discussed. For now, it is enough to understand the relationship
between these contrasting roles and the function of the names
themselves in the story. If in fact the person named Job is
presented as unknown within the "situation of discourse," we are
now enabled to say something much more definite about the role
of Job's name in the story. Since Job is completely defined by the
message of the book it follows that the question concerning
whether Job's name plays a role *only* in the code of the story (like
most proper names, $^\jmath iyyôb$ would mean the person named
"$^\jmath iyyôb$") or whether his name also overlaps into the message of
the story (e.g. Job's name would carry a message, "inveterate foe,"
similar to part of the message of the story) now receives clearer
articulation. If in fact the author constructed a name to characterize his hero, one can assume that the message of the book will
contain enough information to discover this fact. If however the
author simply chose a common, ordinary name for his "hero" then
it follows that there will be *no information* within the message of
the book concerning the meaning of that name. In both cases the
answer lies within our reach because the answer lies *within the
text*. The key assumption here is that, since Job is not presented as
a known figure in the "situation of discourse," "everything
necessary for the hearer to understand the communication is
present" as Lakoff phrases one of the rules of normal conversa-
tion (1972: 916). With some adjustments, this principle also holds
true in written communication.

This question of the meaning of Job's name may be phrased in

Jakobson's terminology as follows: Is the use of Job's name in the book of Job an example of a duplex structure that is *circular* (C/C: code unit points only to code unit; "Job" means the fellow named Job) or *overlapping* (C/M: code unit cannot be defined without a reference to the message; "Job" is what Jakobson calls a *shifter* since the name deliberately means e.g. "inveterate foe").

Jakobson's terminology as follows: Is the use of Job's name in the book of Job an example of a duplex structure that is *circular* (C/C: code unit points only to code unit; "Job" means the fellow named Job) or *overlapping* (C/M: code unit cannot be defined without a reference to the message; "Job" is what Jakobson calls a *shifter* since the name deliberately means e.g. "inveterate foe").

What this section on the names of the figures shows is how effective for avoiding ambiguities the contextualized situations found within a text can be. Let us look more closely at these contextualized situations in the light of Todorov's ways by which figures are manifested in narration.

The second way by which the semantic contents of figures is made manifest according to Todorov is by *explicit predication*. Here also we see the value of *contextualized situation,* since in a story explicit predication can indeed function as contextualized situation. For example, an investigation of explicit predicates referred to Job on one hand and God on the other tends to confirm our earlier inference that in the "situation of discourse" the figure of Job is portrayed as unknown to the hearers whereas the figure of God is portrayed as well-known to them.

Now an important distinction here is that only explicit predication *not* found in the speech of any figure directly manifests the semantic contents, the significance of the figure so predicated; this is so since any speech in the story which explicitly predicates something of God or Job must first be filtered through, and interpreted by, the author's characterization of the figure making the speech. On the other hand, the function of what the narration itself says is to establish reality "as it really is," which is to say, as the author wants us to understand it. Thus such explicit predications *create* the figures for us. They are small in number since most of the story consists of dialogue.

With regard ʾiyyôb we find out (in 1.1) that he is tām, "blameless," yāšār "upright," yᵉrēʾ ʾᵉlohîm "God-fearing," and sār mērāᶜ "a shunner of evil." In 1:3 we are told that Job is gādôl mikkol bᵉnê qedem "the greatest of all the Easteners." Finally in 42:17 we are told that when Job died he was zaqēn and śᵉbaᶜ yāmîm "old and satisfied with life."

There do not seem to be any direct explicit predications of the figure, God. This category clearly shows, therefore, how that figure named ʾiyyôb appears in contexts which presume him to be unknown to the audience, and how that figure referred to by the various names for God is so well known he needs no introduction by means of explicit predication.

Now we can turn to those implicit means by which a figure's semantic contents are made manifest. I will concentrate only on what God and Job say or do not say. This is at least a good beginning since the story is primarily composed of speeches. (This is true not only of the main dialogue-section of 3–42:6 but even of chapters 1–2 where one finds quite a lot of reported speech.) In general, the fact that the story is largely a series of interrelated speeches bracketed by a preceding and subsequent "situation" shows very clearly that absolutely everything in 3–42:6 must be understood (*on the level of narration*) in relation to the dialogues' "situation" described for us by the author in 1–2 and 42:7–17. In this case, the "situation" of the main dialogues is identified with the verbal *context* of these dialogues taken as a whole. *This means that far from being incidental to the dialogues' message, chapters 1–2 and 42:7–17 are absolutely essential to it.* Not to consider the prose and poetry so related is like considering the first sentence incidental to an understanding of the second sentence in the following written statement, "I just bought a new book. Would you like to see it?" Without the contextualized situation of "I just bought a new book," the specific meaning of "Would you like to see it?" cannot be conveyed. On this point the relationship of the main dialogues of 3–42:6 and their "situation" is reciprocal: just as the prose is the *context* so necessary for understanding the poetry, what is in turn said in the prose must be understood in light of *its* context, the poetry. Each "points to" the other in order to help avoid ambiguity.

What is true concerning the relationship between the main dialogues of 3-42:6 and their *context* is true concerning each and every reported statement in the story. We have here an example of that *circular* duplex structure described by Jakobson: "M/M) 'REPORTED SPEECH is speech within speech, a message within a message and at the same time it is also speech about speech, a message about a message,' as Vološinov formulates it in his study of this crucial linguistic and stylistic problem" (1971: 131). In other words, reported speech, which is a message, is utilized to refer to or "point at" another message of which it is a part and vice-versa. Reported speech is therefore an *index* of the message of which it is a part, and vice-versa. With regard to the figure Job, *his* speeches help to answer the questions: who is the character whom the author designates "*ʾiyyôb*"? To whom is the author referring when he writes "*ʾiyyôb*"? What is the meaning of the figure Job in the story? With regard to the figure God, *his* speeches similarly help to answer the questions: who is the character whom the author calls "God," "Lord" etc.? To whom is the author referring when he writes "God," "Lord," etc.? What is the meaning of the figure, "God," in the story? The reported speeches of Job and God perform the same function in the story as *situation* does in any communication. An example from Peirce writing about indices might be helpful here:

> Suppose two men met upon a country road and one of them says to the other, "The chimney of that house is on fire." The other looks about him and descries a house with green blinds and a verandah having a smoking chimney. He walks on a few miles and meets a second traveller. Like a Simple Simon he says, "The chimney of that house is on fire." "What house?" asks the other. "Oh, a house with green blinds and a verandah," replies the simpleton. "Where is the house?" asks the stranger. He desires some *index* which shall connect his apprehension with the house meant. Words alone cannot do this. The demonstrative pronouns, "this" and "that" are indices. For they

call upon the hearer to use his powers of observation, and so establish a real connection between his mind and the object; and if the demonstrative pronoun does that —without which its meaning is not understood—it goes to establish such a connection; and so is an index. (1932: 162)

In the Book of Job, the speeches define and describe the figures of the story. They can perform the same twofold function as "that" does in Peirce's example. If the figure is not previously known, the speeches help to avoid ambiguity both on the level of code *and* on the level of message. This is the case with the figure Job: "which Job?" "Oh that man who suffered such and such and *spoke such and such* in response." But whereas "a house with green blinds and a verandah" does not indicate *which specific* house with green blinds and a verandah is meant, in the case of the dramatic figure Job, everything the author deemed necessary to understand this figure is "pointed to" in the story; and the speeches of Job play a not-insignificant role in establishing a real connection between the hearer and the object, the figure of Job. On the other hand, if the figure is presented as previously known, there is no need to avoid ambiguity on the level of code. Thus no introductory description or explicit predication of God in the story. Thus no need to answer the question, "What God?" But there *is* need to clarify God's position *vis a vis* the message, "Where does God stand in relation to Job's problem?" Thus the speeches of God play a major role in establishing a real connection between the hearer and the object, the figure of God *in the story*.

The *reported speech* in the book of Job plays an important part in clarifying for us the "situation of discourse" of the book. It does this by pointing to, and avoiding ambiguity about, an aspect of the code by which the discourse was constructed, e.g. the name "Job" signifies or is defined by what the author has "Job" *say* or *not say*. The reported speech also clarifies the "situation of discourse" by clarifying an aspect of the message, e.g. where God (that well-known person) stands with regard to the problem of Job. That is to say, whereas with regard to the figure God, the reported speech functions only as a *circular* duplex structure, M / M, with regard to the figure Job his reported speech functions both as a *circular* duplex structure, M/M, and an *overlapping* duplex structure, M/C. In other words, the reported speech of God helps to avoid ambiguity only on the level of message, since it is the "situation" of God's being already known to the hearers which primarily avoids ambiguity on the level of code. The "situation" of referring to or "pointing at" God would be analogous, in Peirce's example, to talking about the house which is in front of the two men. On the other hand, the "situation" of referring to Job is analogous, in Peirce's example, to the *second* meeting of men, apart from the visible presence of the house. In this case the hearer needs two things, an *index* to know who it is whom the speaker refers to by the name "Job" *and* an index to know what this figure's significance is in the context of the message. "Job" is more completely defined by the message than is God.

Job therefore is defined by his speeches as follows. He represents (in 3-37) a blameless man whose reported acceptance of the trustworthiness of personal experience and whose reported rejection of certain commonly accepted truths are both *validated* by the context of his innocent suffering. However, further along in the story, (38-42:6) Job represents a blameless man whose reported denial of the trustworthiness of personal experience and whose reported acceptance of certain commonly accepted truths are both validated by the context of the theophanic vision, but whose desire for Sheol is not.

"God" is defined by his speeches as follows. Through God's speeches in 1-2 we see that the existence of innocent suffering is *validated* by the context of God's words which effect the pact with Satan. Moreover, further along the way a rejection of Job's position in 3-37 is *validated* by the context of God's words in the theophanic vision. Further on still, an acceptance of Job's position in 3-37 is *validated* by the context of God's words to Eliphaz in 42:7-9.

Putting this "reported speech" information together, we see that since Job's innocent suffering is validated by God's pact with

Satan, every reported speech (of the major figures in the story), which is in some way validated, is done so by the reported speech of God. In other words, God's reported speech identifies itself with every possible permutation of the group structure described in chapter three, except -X-Y (which is taken to represent Sheol).

If in fact the reported speech of God, the Word of God, is the primary means by which one can *validate* or not whatever anyone else in the story is reported to have said, one is left with one last question: what if, as seems the case, God's reported speech seems to be contradictory to itself, since what He affirms in 38-41 he denies in 42:7-9? The answer to this question lies, as we have said in chapter two, in the Act of God reported in the last movement, 42:10-17. For by restoring to Job twice as much as he previously had, God's action validates both what He said in 38-41 ("I am all powerful") and what He said in 42:7-9 ("Job spoke correctly of me").

The conclusion of this discussion of the function of the figures in clarifying the "situation of discourse" of the Book of Job is simply this: if the figure Job is defined and clarified both on the level of code and message (M/C and M/M), the message of the Book is throughout defined and clarified by the figure of God, that is to say, by the reported speech of God; moreover the reported speech of God is in one case clarified by the reported action of God (M/M).

An analysis of the Book of Job's "situation of discourse" reveals that the Book's message is clarified (that is, ambiguity is avoided) by what God is reported to have said and done, which two elements appear to function as validating or non-validating principles of everything else in the story.

The figures of the story, far from being arbitrary, capricious, and mutually contradictory, interrelate with one another to help form a coherent message. There is no absolute answer to the problem of innocent suffering, no stance that is valid for all times and situations of one's life. At certain moments, suffering is so horrendous that any attempt to justify and explain it is "obscene," as Emil Fackenheim has characterized attempts to justify and explain the Holocaust. This is the situation with which Job was confronted as a result of his instantaneous loss of health, wealth and family; it was "obscene" for his friends to explain away the "Holocaust" his life had become. But at another moment in his life, after the vision of God out of the whirlwind, faith in redemption of some sort was once again possible for Job and he could now see his way to a belief he had once lost.

So also with God himself in the story. The "reality" of the story makes very clear that it is the word of God as reported in chapters one and two which brings about, validates, authenticates, the horrible sufferings inflicted upon Job, and it is God's word in 42:7-9 which validates and authenticates Job's defiant response to such afflictions. But it is also God's word in 38-41 which brings about and validates Job's moment of faith in 42:1-6. What God will *not* allow, in all that is said and done in the story, is approve the nihilistic solution so often asked for by Job, to be sent down to the Pit for good, where the values of faith *and* experience are at one and the same time obliterated.

What God says and does determines everything in the story. It has been puzzling to many that God in His theophanic speeches of 38-41 never really addresses Himself to the question at hand, never really attempts to justify Himself in the face of "the Problem" set out for us in the preceding chapters. The theophanic speeches have seemed to many to be "beside the point." But what these speeches *do* in the story is actually to create a moment of faith, a moment of vision for Job in all his horrible afflictions. God does not attempt to justify His actions as Job's friends had obscenely tried to do. Rather He makes it possible for Job to have a moment of vision.

The message of the Book of Job is the message of Auschwitz as Irving Greenberg has explained it:

> After Auschwitz, we have to speak of 'moment faiths,' moments when redeemer and vision of redemption are present, interspersed with times when the flames and smoke of the burning children blot out faith—though it flickers again.

Bibliographic Remarks—Part Two

1. *The Practice of Biblical Structuralism*

A. Concerning the chapters of Part Two. In reference to the kind of diachronic solution to critical problems rejected in chapter two, one can read a brief essay by T. Todorov entitled "Le recit primitif" (1971: 66-77) in which he very well describes this brand of "erudition" in classical studies and comments on its shortcomings.

In order to get a feeling for non-Israelite versions of the widespread traditional retribution theory and opposition to it, one can read, for example, *The Babylonian Theodicy* and the *Ludlul Bel Nemeqi,* both of which center around contradictions similar to those in the Book of Job. A convenient source for these two compositions is Lambert (1960: 21-91). Lévi-Strauss's formula for myth first appeared in 1955 and this article can be conveniently found in Lévi-Strauss (1967: 202-228). Although hardly ever referred to again by Lévi-Strauss himself (see chapter above), this formula has been applied to other kinds of literature besides "myths," e.g. riddles and *Sage*; see for example Maranda (1971: 1-94). On the tripartite distinction of the terms, "framework," "code," and "message," W. O. Hendricks (1973) discusses their meaning in the work of A. J. Greimas (1966) and Lévi-Strauss. "Code" and "message" are concepts derived from communication theory and have been borrowed by linguists because they correspond in general to the classic Saussurean dichotomy of *langue* and *parole,* with the advantage, however, that this latter distinction receives thereby a much clearer, simpler, logically less ambiguous and operationally more productive formulation, as R. Jakobson (1971: 224) points out. "Framework," with regard to this triad, is used in the above chapter to describe the object of the first step in the analysis of a narrative, whereby the discourse is divided up into the basic unities that are to be dealt with in the next two chapters.

Concerning the question as to whether or not the *order* or

sequencing of functional unities of a narrative is essential to their syntax, see on this point Alan Dundes' remarks in Maranda (1970: 171ff) and in the introduction to the second edition of Propp (1968: xi-xvii). For a clear description of the problem and its importance in constructing a syntax of narrative, see R. Barthes (1966: 12-14). See also Ricouer (1975:49-50).

There are a number of sensitive treatments of the Book of Job that attempt to interpret the book in a holistic way: for example, David Robertson (1973) has written a thought-provoking literary study of the Book of Job which produced an equally thoughtful response by Edwin Good (1973).

Concerning chapter three, J. Piaget discusses groups in his monograph on structuralism (1970: 17-28). Two further sources are found in the footnote on page 18. An extremely useful article is Marc Barbut's (1970: 367-387). Any good library will have innumerable books devoted to an introduction to group theory. For example, the success of group theory in the physics of fundamental particles is discussed by F. J. Dyson (1968: 248-257).

Chapter Four illustrates Roland Barthes' contention that, "In fully constituted 'flowing' discourse, the facts function irresistably either as indexes or as links in an indexical sequence" (1970d: 153). Barthes writes this in an article analyzing historical discourse yet it fits equally well with the type of discourse that is the Book of Job: a good part of the Book of Job can be considered as an index pointing to its "situation of discourse."

The references to Emil Fackenheim and Irving Greenberg utilized at the end of this chapter are taken from an article by Israel Shenker in *The New York Times,* Sunday, June 9, 1974, p.E5, which concerns a four-day symposium on Auschwitz, held at New York's Cathedral Church of St. John the Divine during the first week of June 1974.

B. <u>Attempts at structural analysis of the Bible</u>. Besides chapters two through four of this book, one can consult the following:

1. The June 1971 issue of *Langages (22)* contains five articles attempting structural/semiotic analyses of biblical material: E. R. Leach (1971) studies *Genesis* as myth (a translation of Leach [1969]); G. Viullod (1971) analyzes some short *récits* from the Bible, mostly from the New Testament; L. Marin (1971e; 1971f) offers two studies, the first a structural analysis of Matthew 28:1-8, Mark 16:1-8 and Luke 24:1-11, and the second a structural analysis of Matthew 27:1-2 and 11-31 with its synoptic passages; and C. Chabrol (1971b) analyzes the "text" of the Passion.

2. The April 1974 issue of *Interpretation* contains two structural analyses of biblical texts: Polzin (1974) is an earlier version of chapter two of this book; and Dan O. Via (1974) offers a structural approach to Paul's Old Testament hermeneutic.

3. In Bovon, F., ed. (1971a), there are two structural analyses: R. Barthes (1971b) analyzes Genesis 32:23-33 and Jean Starobinski (1971) analyzes Mark 5:1-20.

4. In Léon-Dufour, ed., (1971), Acts 10-11 is "structurally" analyzed in four articles: R. Barthes (1971a); Joseph Courtès (1971); Louis Marin (1971a); and Edgar Haulotte (1971).

5. Paul Beauchamp's book (1969) is advertised as a structural analysis of Genesis 1, although, as he himself admits (1972: 117), one would get a misleading idea of structural analyses were his work considered such. This book is also a central concern of Léon-Dufour, ed. (1971: 55-98).

6. Yehuda T. Radday has published three structural analyses on the plane of expression concerning chiasm in the Hebrew Bible: (1971) discusses chiasm in Samuel; (1972) discusses chiasm in Torah; and (1973) discusses chiasm in Joshua, Judges, and other books.

7. For references to Edmund Leach's structural studies of Old Testament texts, consult R. Culley (1972).

8. Dan O. Via (1973) offers a structural analysis of certain New Testament parables and John D. Crossan (1973) structurally replies to this article.

9. The first three issues of the new journal for biblical criticism, *Semeia,* contain many structural attempts at analyzing biblical texts.

10. A structural analysis of Matthew 13.1-23 is presented by L. Marin (1971d). Daniel Patte (1975) examines the structural network of the good samaritan parable. Luis Alonso Schökel (1975) describes narrative structures in the Book of Judith.

11. There are also many examples on "rhetorical criticism" of biblical texts. *Rhetorical Criticism: Essays in Honor of James*

Muilenburg, edited by Jered Jackson and Martin Kessler (1974) is a recent example.

12. Dan O. Via has published a "structuralist" approach to New Testament hermeneutic (1975) which attempts a new analysis of three Pauline texts on death-resurrection and of the Gospel of Mark. See also his earlier work (1967) on parables.

Part III

Three Classics of Biblical Criticism Analyzed from a Structural Point of View

Introduction

The goal of this section is to examine three classics of modern biblical criticism with a view to answering this question: can any of these three classics properly be termed a structural analysis according to the guidelines outlined in chapter one? My general answer will be that all three are clearly structural with regard both the *objective* aspect of structuralism (viewing the text as a system of structures) and the *self-consciously deductive* aspect of structuralism. With regard to the *subjective* aspect, that self-reflexive feature of structuralism termed "deep subjectivity," some doubts are raised, mostly about Noth's and to a lesser degree about von Rad's and Wellhausen's studies.

Chapter V

The *Prolegomena* of Julius Wellhausen

In what respects are Wellhausen's main stated concerns intimately related to those of the modern structuralist movement? Concerning the aspect of constructed *models*, Wellhausen saw himself firmly stationed on the deductive rather than inductive branch of the hermeneutical tree. Second, concerning the *object-*

ive aspect of structuralism, the structures of the text that concerned Wellhausen, it is an easy matter to place him on the diachronic rather than synchronic branch of that tree. Moreover Wellhausen's classic work is perched almost exclusively on that branch reaching out toward the plane of content rather than the plane of expression. Finally we will offer some reflections on the *Prolegomena* as *signifier:* subjective aspects of one of the greatest works of modern biblical criticism.

Structuralism, as we have seen, involves the study of elements of an object whose relationships one with another make that object to be a whole, a system and not just an aggregate, an *unum per se* as opposed to an *unum per accidens.* As a preliminary description of the "soul" of structuralism this is perhaps too abstract to be of any immediate use without concretely relating it to the actual concerns everywhere apparent in Wellhausen's great work. One of the clearest expressions of these concerns is found in the opening paragraphs of chapter eight, "On the Narrative of the Hexateuch." Beginning this chapter with a reference to the show-piece of higher criticism, the documentary hypothesis, Wellhausen points out that "Critics have shown a disposition, if not in principle yet in fact, to take the independence of these so-called sources of the Hexateuch as if it implied that in point of matter also each is a distinct and independent source" (1965: 295). He then goes on to describe the role of criticism in terms that are amazingly structural in tone:

> Criticism has not done its work when it has completed the mechanical distribution [of the various sources]; it must aim further at bringing the different writings when thus arranged into relation with each other, must seek to render them intelligible as phases of a living process, and thus to make it possible to trace a graduated development of the tradition.(1965: 295)

[handwritten margin note: Wellhausen wishes to show how one source was dependent on the other (previous) one.]

We have here a clear and succinct description of a "structuralist" enterprise written in 1878 and, as such, remarkable only to those who assume that structuralism is something that has arrived upon the scene of biblical studies without any preparation whatsoever. What Wellhausen's statement involves, of course, is a description very close to what is today called genetic or diachronic structuralism. I shall return to this point when I examine in more detail the specific features of Wellhausen's methodology to discover the particular type of structuralist activity the *Prolegomena* represents. What I want to do here is point out the similarities between Wellhausen's method, as he explains it or utilizes it, and those features of structuralism that I discussed in chapter one.

where ?

What is first apparent in the above citations is Wellhausen's insistence that the Hexateuch is to be considered a whole and not an aggregate of sources. It is not enough to discover a number of sources in the Hexateuch, and it is certainly wrong to consider each of them as a distinct or independent source. This would make of the Hexateuch a simple aggregate impossible of being analyzed in a "structural" way, since the various strands are considered to be related only by the fact that they were at some time combined but in no genetic or systematic way. They are more like a heap of stones than a structure of interrelated materials forming an intelligible whole. This view Wellhausen totally rejects, adding that if such a view is not often held in principle, in point of fact it often is. Rather, he tells us, criticism must aim at considering the Hexateuch as a whole. This means making intelligible the various (here genetic) relationships existing between the sources, relationships that help to explain, indeed that *are* the essential explanation of what makes the Hexateuch the systematic and unified whole it actually is. It is because of this primary and crucial distinction of Wellhausen's, a concern that permeates every page of the *Prolegomena,* that his approach can be so easily compared with structural analysis. Another indication of Wellhausen's insistence on wholes not parts is found when we examine how he utilized the data he so laboriously gathered in connection with the main hypothesis of his work: that the Priestly Code is to be dated later than Deuteronomy. For example, when he discusses the relationship between the history of Chronicles and that of Samuel/Kings in chapter six of the *Prolegomena,* he insists, following DeWette, that no matter how many and varied are the specific differences between the two historical sources, it is the total significance or impression of each document that is paramount, " . . . for here the difficulty . . . is not to collect the details of evidence, but so to shape the superabundant material as to convey a right total impression" (1965: 172). He also gives precedence to the general over the specific later on in the chapter: " . . . the problem still really was, as before, how to explain the complete difference of general conception and the multitude of discrepancies of details [between Chronicles and Samuel/Kings]" (1965: 222). Again, when talking about the history of the patriarchs as it is found in JE and P, he begins his section on the Priestly version as follows: "To compare the parallel of the Priestly Code it is necessary to restore it as a whole, for few are aware of the impression it produces" (1965: 327). It is because Wellhausen concentrates on wholes rather than aggregates that he can make general statements such as, "In that book [Deuteronomy] the unity of the cultus is *commanded*; in the Priestly Code it is *presupposed*" (1965: 35). Finally we may note Wellhausen's insistence that relationships between elements rather than the elements themselves are more important than is generally recognized. He is again speaking of the Hexateuchal sources when he writes, "Thus the agreement of the sources in the plan of the narrative is not a matter of course, but a matter requiring explanation, and only to be explained on the ground of the literary dependence of one source on the other. The question how this *relation of dependence* is to be defined is thus a much more pressing one than is commonly assumed" [italics added] (1965: 296).

A second aspect of the "soul" of structural analysis is what we have called an emphasis on *construction*. Piaget insists; "There is no structure apart from construction" (1970: 140). It is clear that Wellhausen himself understood his enterprise to be precisely *constructivist* in nature. In chapter nine of the *Prolegomena,* Wellhausen attempts to answer certain criticisms levelled against him and the methodology by which he arrives at his hypothesis concerning the lateness of P. About the methodology he used in arriving at his hypothesis he writes, "One would imagine that this could not be objected to. But objections have been raised; the procedure which, when applied to Deuteronomy, is called historico-critical method, is called, when applied to the Priestly Code, construction of history. But history, it is well known, has always to be constructed . . . . The question is whether one constructs well or ill" (1965: 367). Wellhausen considered himself a constructivist because he considered all historians constructivists. In his opinion, there is no other way to be a historian. And of course this is what the *Prolegomena* was, that schematic construction of biblical history necessary before one could write a full-fledged history of Ancient Israel. Wellhausen's method does not involve an exaggeraged application of logic, a criticism so often levelled at constructivist analyses: "after laborously collecting the data offered by the historical and prophetical books, we constructed a sketch of the Israelite history of worship; we then compared the Pentateuch with this sketch, and recognized that one element of the Pentateuch bore a definite relation to this phase of the history of worship, and another element of the Pentateuch to that phase of it. This is not putting logic in place of historical investigation" (1965: 367). We can at this point note that Wellhausen's statement that his approach does not involve the idea that the laws follow each other in a certain logical order is certainly accurate insofar as his description of his methodology and often his use of it are concerned. But as I shall have occasion to point out further along the way, Wellhausen is not altogether absolved from such a criticism. This is because of the pervasive influence of Vatke's philosophy of history concerning the development of all religions including Israel's, a philosophy which lies behind some of the *Prolegomena's* argumentation. If, for now, we leave aside those sections of the *Prolegomena* dependent upon Vatke, we shall see that Wellhausen's methodology as an attempt to construct history is in fact often structurally constructive in the sense described in chapter one above. Informative aspects of structuralism's distinctive properties could here be discussed in relation to Wellhausen's *Prolegomena,* for example, its emphasis on laws of transformation or its search for structures that are below or behind empirical reality. I think, however, that these similarities will become apparent as we discuss in some detail the various kinds of structuralism to which the *Prolegomena* is most clearly related.

We have seen in the first chapter in what sense examples of structural analysis are not predominantly "inductive" in approach. This same question can be discussed with regard to the *Prolegomena.* I would like to argue that Wellhausen utilized, and *described himself as utilizing,* a predominantly non-inductive argumentation in the establishment of his hypothesis concerning the lateness of the Priestly Code. That his method was in fact not primarily inductive can be seen not only from an examination of his method in operation and from an examination of his description of that method but also from the fact that he was understood by competent readers to be so arguing. To attend to the last point first, I can mention Robertson Smith's preface to the English translation of the *Prolegomena.* Here we find clear indications that Wellhausen's arguments were not taken by Robertson Smith to be inductive in nature. The terms "inductive," "deductive" are nowhere mentioned by Robertson Smith, but from an examination of certain of his statements one can reasonably infer what his position was in this regard. First of all, we must recall once again certain characteristics which belong to a scientific methodology that can be called inductive. In the inductivist view the only sure basis for a theory or hypothesis is the laborious collecting of data based on scientific observation and experiment. Hence, as Bach describes it, ". . . it is of the utmost importance to give the evidence for any general statement" (1965: 112). "The theory . . . which is based on the widest body of evidence and is thus most probably true is the one most worthy of acceptance" (1965: 112-113). Key notions in this procedure involve "verification" and "based on" (1965: 113). In this view of science one cannot really form his own judgment on the acceptability of a theory unless he controls the data upon which the theory is inductively based. Now when we turn to Robertson Smith's preface we read the following:

> . . . the present volume gives the English reader, for the first time, an opportunity to form his own judgment on questions which are within the scope of anyone who reads the English Bible carefully and is able to think clearly and without prejudice, about its contents. (1965: vii)

What is immediately obvious here is that it is Robertson Smith's conviction that the *Prolegomena* contains everything essential to a proper judgment concerning the question that is the central theme of the book, "Is the Priestly Code earlier or later than Deuteronomy?" All that is necessary on the part of the reader of the English Bible is that he be able to think clearly and without prejudice about its contents. But even a cursory inspection of the book reveals straight off that the discovery and careful dilineation of each of the Hexateuchal Sources, JE, D and P, is already *presumed* by Wellhausen at the start of his book (1965: 12). How then can the English reader, who does not ordinarily control the tools that led to the discovery of the sources themselves, form his own judgment on Wellhausen's theory? Robertson Smith recognizes this problem and answers it for us as follows:

> The process of disentangling the twisted skein of tradition is necessarily a very delicate and complicated one, and involves certain operations for which special scholarship is indispensable. Historical criticism is a comparatively modern science, and in its application to this as to other histories, it has made many false and uncertain steps. But in this, as in other sciences, when the truth has been reached it can generally be presented in a comparatively simple form and the main positions may be justified even to the general reader by methods much less complicated, and much more lucid than those originally followed by the investigators themselves. (1965:vii)

It *is* possible therefore for one who does not control the original "data" upon which the documentary hypothesis was presumably "based" nevertheless to form his own judgment on these questions. One can only conclude, then, that this "scientific data," however helpful it was in the original articulation of the hypothesis, is understood as ultimately non-essential to the *acceptance* of the hypothesis by any unbiased, clear thinking individual. What then are these much less complicated, and much more lucid methods about which Robertson Smith writes? It appears to me that he is describing a method of argumentation that is basically deductive in nature. He is telling his readers, "if you follow Wellhuasen in making a series of plausible *assumptions* (and certainly any clear thinking individual is capable of that), you will see that certain conclusions can be deduced from them." The conclusions form the core of Wellhausen's hypothesis and moreover provide insight that helps one see more clearly the plausibility of the assumptions he originally accepted. It seems to me quite clear that had Robertson Smith understood the *Prolegomena* to be an essentially *inductive* enterprise, he could not have held the view that those readers who did not control the technical aspects of higher criticism could "form their own judgments" on these questions. The inductive compilation of data justifying not only the separation of sources, but also the dating of JE and D, is not argued for but rather only basically assumed throughout the *Prolegomena*. As we shall soon see, these less complicated and more lucid methods to which Robertson Smith refers center around assuming the (inductive?) generalizations to be true and *deducing* from them certain consequences that are so satisfying and coherent that they can confirm in the mind of the non-scholar the rightness of the original assumptions. On the other hand, an inductivist understanding of Wellhausen's project would understand it to be a set of scholarly dogmas, explained to the general reader and intended to be accepted by him in the manner of belief. Once *believed,* however, it would be impossible of the type of personal justification or verification which would allow the reader to form his own judgment on these questions as both Robertson Smith and Wellhausen hoped. "The assumptions

I make will find an ever-recurring justification in the course of the investigation" (1965: 13).

That Robertson Smith's understanding of Wellhausen's methodology as fundamentally non-inductive is accurate is confirmed by an examination of the *Prolegomena* itself, both where Wellhausen uses and where he explains his method. This is immediately clear in his first chapter on "The Place of Worship" in the history of Israel. Wellhausen describes three stages in the historical development of Israelite worship. He "discovers" these three stages by means of an examination of non-hexateuchal sources, namely the historical and prophetic books of the Old Testament. The earliest stage is the pre-prophetic stage when no sanctuary had exclusive legitimacy in Israel. Secondly comes the stage of struggle and transition during the prophetic period, "the course of the Assyrian period," when there is a decline in the power of the sanctuaries and a corresponding rise of Jerusalem as *the* place of worship. This period culminates in the Josianic reform and the Deuteronomic attitude toward centrality of worship as (rediscovered) legislation. Finally there is the post-exilic stage when the centrality of worship is so accepted and unquestioned that it is assumed to have been the case from the beginning. The second part of Wellhausen's argument consists in seeing the correspondence "between the phases of the actual course of events and those of the legislation relating to this subject" (1965: 28). At this point, Wellhausen clearly assumes that JE's legislation on place of worship corresponds to the earliest stage of historical development, and that D's legislation is the culmination of the second or prophetic phase of development. In other words, assuming first of all the reliability of the three phase scheme of historical development and assuming secondly JE's context to be the first phase and D's context the second stage, "what then are we to infer from this as to the historical place of the priestly code, if it be judged necessary to assign it such a place at all?" (1965: 35). Here it is only necessary "to apprehend the whole tenor of Exod. XXV.-Lev.IX. (1965: 34)" to see clearly that whereas in D "unity of the cultus is *commanded;* in the Priestly

Code it is *presupposed* (1965: 35)." This is the minor proposition
of his deductive syllogism. The conclusion follows classically:
"[The Priestly Code's] place then is after Deuteronomy, and in the
third, post-exilian period of the history of the cultus, in which, on
the one hand, the unity of the sanctuary was an established fact
contested by no one and impugned by nothing, and in which, on
the other hand, the natural connection between the present and
the past had been so severed by the exile that there was no obstacle
to prevent an artificial and ideal repristination of the latter" (1965:
38). It remained only for Wellhausen, in the third part of this
chapter to dispose of a few objections that had been raised to such
a conclusion, principally by the great scholar Theodor Nöldeke.
With this his chapter ends. It is this type of deductive
argumentation which makes it clear very early on why the
Prolegomena soon became "the classic and original statement of
the theory of 'higher criticism' of the Old Testament."

Before moving on, I want to emphasize the importance of
chapter one in determining the method Wellhausen used. He
himself tells us in a footnote in chapter nine: "The method is stated
in the introduction (p. 1 seq.): and special pains are taken to bring
it out distinctly in the first chapter, that about the place of
worship" (1965: 366 n. 3). Wellhausen had just previously
described the procedure used in the *Prolegomena*:

> There are in the Pentateuch three strata of law and three strata
> of tradition, and the problem is to place them in their true
> historical order. So far as the Jehovist and Deuteronomy are
> concerned, the problem has found a solution which may be said
> to be accepted universally, and all that remains is to apply to the
> Priestly Code also the procedure by which the succession and
> the date of these two works has been determined—that
> procedure consisting in the comparison of them with the
> ascertained facts of Israelite history. (1965: 366)

Chapters two through five attempt to follow this basic approach
concerning other aspects of Israelite worship which are discovered
in the legislation of the Hexateuch.

In the second part of Wellhausen's book, chapters six through eight, he investigates in considerable detail the independent historical sources used as a control for his deductions in part one, Chronicles, Judges, Samuel and Kings, and applies this analysis to the Narrative of the Hexateuch in chapter eight. The third part "sums up the critical results of the preceding two" (1965: 13).

A crucial question in understanding Wellhausen's method of argumentation is the relationship between parts one and two of the *Prolegomena.* It might, for example, be argued that part two is actually the specific inductive justification for some of the assumptions he uses in part one, namely the threefold schema of historical development and the place of JE and D within this schema. For Wellhausen himself states in his introduction that the two principal assumptions of his work, the dating of JE and of Deuteronomy, "will find an ever-recurring justification in the course of the investigation . . ." (1965: 13). It is, therefore, at first glance possible that he considered part two as the section in which he "justified" in sufficient historical detail the main assumptions forming the schematic backbone of part one. Let us see why this interpretation of part two is not corroborated by an examination of its contents.

The first chapter of part two, chapter six, treats the differences between Chronicles and Samuel/Kings in order to discover the historical influences that moved each period in which the two complexes were composed. If one can delineate the spirit of an age through such writings, one has a historical basis for finding that spirit in other writings, viz., the Pentateuchal sources, less firmly known in their provenance. The method is clear: judgment on the various ages of the Pentateuchal documents is bound up with the independent evidence of the historical books, in which one can assert with greater certainty the aspect of history and influences in ascendancy at one or another time. " . . . we can date the rival histories with tolerable certainty. The Books of Samuel and of Kings were edited in the Babylonian Exile: Chronicles, on the other hand, was composed fully three hundred years later, after the downfall of the Persian Empire, out of the very midst of fully developed Judaism" (1965: 171).

Wellhausen then proceeds in massive detail for fifty pages to spell out the differences between the history of the Babylonian Exile and its counterpart 300 years later. The problem here for Wellhausen is one of *interpretation:* "We shall now proceed to show that the mere difference of date fully accounts for the varying ways in which the two histories represent the same facts and events, and the difference of spirit arises from the influence of the Priestly Code which came into existence in the interval" (1965: 171-172). Wellhausen's clarity of exposition enables us to follow his reasoning step by step. First of all, Samuel/Kings differs from Chronicles in innumerable ways, a,b,c, . . ,n. This fact can be explained by the difference of date between the two sources. Moreover the difference of spirit between the two ages is fully explained by the main conclusion of part one of the *Prolegomena*: The Priestly Code came into existence in the interval. It is precisely here that we see the fundamental precision of Wellhausen's statement in his introduction, that this second part (chapters six through eight) is " . . . in many respects *dependent* [italics added] on the first" (1965: 13). In other words, the *interpretation* Wellhausen gives to the fifty pages of specific differences between the facts and events of Samuel/Kings and those of Chronicles in chapter six is dependent upon the prior establishment of his thesis in part one concerning the intervening "promulgation" of the Priestly Code. Chapter six, then, is another example of a deductive argumentation. If one assumes that the Priestly Code was introduced into, and became the central spirit of, the period between the Babylonian Exile and the writing of Chronicles some three hundred years later, most of the differences between the historical sources of each period can be adequately explained.

This is why part two, as Wellhausen asserts, is dependent on part one, and why moreover it would not be accurate to interpret part two as the *inductive* justification of the assumptions Wellhausen uses for the propositions of his deductive arguments of part one. In reality part two is as deductively argued as part one and moreover *depends on* the conclusion of part one, namely, that the Priestly Code intervened between the writing of Samuel/Kings and that of Chronicles. The subsequent "justification" of his assumptions concerning the date of JE and D about which Wellhausen writes in his introduction is in effect that subsequent insight into the correctness of such assumptions once one has seen the implications of the basic conclusion to which those assumptions lead: the hypothesis that P follows D in Israelite history. In no real sense, then, is part two the presentation of the inductive data supposedly necessary for the propositions used in part one.

Chapter seven, "Judges, Samuel and Kings," serves to confirm our understanding of part two. Here again, all the myriad pericopes from Judges to 2 Kings that he discusses and analyzes are chosen not because they are evidence by which Wellhausen *establishes* an inductive generalization about the various strata of traditions in his material. Rather, his clear intention is to show that the consistently best way to *interpret* the inconsistencies he finds in Judges through 2 Kings is the theory that older historical books have been revised on the basis of the Deuteronomic code, just as it was the Priestly Code that was the basis of the Chronicler's revision of the Deuteronomistic History. We read at the end of this chapter:

> In the Chronicles the pattern according to which the history of ancient Israel is represented is the Pentateuch, i.e. the Priestly Code. In the source of Chronicles, that is, in the older historical books, the revision does not proceed upon the basis of the Priestly Code, which indeed is completely unknown to them, but on the basis of Deuteronomy. (1965: 294)

Chapter eight is the last chapter of part two and is the complement of chapters one through five of part one. Just as they laid bare the diachronic relationship between the Priestly and Jehovistic *legislation,* this chapter has as its aim "to lay the foundation for a history of the development of the Israelite legend by comparing the *narrative* of the Priestly Code with the Jehovistic one. In doing so we shall see . . . that the Jehovistic form of the legend is the earlier of the two" (1965: 296). " . . . Whether tried by the standard of poetry or by that of history, the Priestly Code stands both in value and in time far below the Jehovist" (1965: 360). We shall return to this chapter later on, since it shows quite clearly a fundamental procedural tension existing within the *Prolegomena*. By basing this chapter so strongly on "the standard of poetry and of history," Wellhausen here leaves the realm of his "ascertained facts of history" and enters rather the realm of Vatke's philosophy of history. His great synthesis suffers accordingly.

Part three sums up the critical results of the preceding two parts; and we shall concentrate on chapter nine, "Conclusion of the Criticism of the Law," since it is pivotal in confirming how Wellhausen himself understood the method by which he had argued to the dating of the Priestly Code as later than Deuteronomy rather than earlier. This chapter begins with Wellhausen defending his method and its conclusions against the objections of certain scholars. Before taking up "additional evidence, which has not yet been noticed" (1965: 368), to buttress the argumentation of the preceding pages, Wellhausen in the introduction to chapter nine explains how he conceived himself to have been arguing in the *Prolegomena* and his earlier writings on the subject. He first of all identifies himself with the main elements of the Grafian hypothesis and defends its essential correctness: "What the opponents of Graf's hypothesis call its argument *ex silentio,* is nothing more or less than the universally valid method of historical investigation" (1965: 365). Wellhausen leaves no doubt that the assumptions upon which the hypothesis rests involve an enormous amount of data gathering: "After laboriously collecting the data offered by the historical and prophetical books, we constructed a sketch of the Israelite history of worship . . . " (1965: 367). It cannot be denied that this step involves an inductive phase of his argumentation. It is an attempt to discover in the historical and prophetical books of the Old Testament "the ascertained facts of Israelite history" (1965: 366). Another part of the inductive phase involves data-gathering concerning what is in that stratum of law and tradition called the Priestly Code. By comparing what he calls the ascertained facts of Israelite history with the data he has collected from the Priestly Code, he is able to argue for his Hexateuchal hypothesis the diachronic series: Jehovist, Deuteronomy, Priestly Code. However, this inductive phase of his procedure is by no means considered by him to be *proof* for his hypothesis. Rather, all this inductive data-gathering serves the purpose of setting out in remarkable detail *the basic need for* his hypothesis. This he makes clear: "Not everything that I have brought forward in the history of the cultus and the tradition is a proof of the hypothesis; there is much that merely serves to explain phenomena at the basis of the hypothesis and cannot be used as proving it. . . .Not everything that we have hitherto discussed proves, or is meant to prove Graf's hypothesis" (1965: 367-368). In this statement Wellhausen distinguishes what he considers "proof of" and what he considers "at the basis of" his hypothesis. If, as we have maintained, his inductive data-gathering of the historical and prophetic books on one hand, and of the Priestly Code's contents on the other hand, is taken to be that which "merely serves to explain phenomena at the basis of the hypothesis and cannot be used as proving it," what then in his presentation is the core of what he considers the "proof" of his hypothesis? It appears to me that Wellhausen answers this question when he states how his procedure intentionally has differed from that of Graf: "I differ from Graf chiefly in this, that I always go back to the centralization of the cultus, and deduce from it the particular divergencies. My whole position is contained in my first chapter . . . " (1965: 368). In this lies the distinctiveness of his argumentation: it is proof by deduction and all of the preceding inductive procedures have only served to provide data showing the necessity for his deductive argumentation. His hypothesis concerning the lateness of P is deduced from the ascertained facts of Israelite history as his major proposition and his interpretation of the specific contents of the Priestly Code as his minor proposition. Graf too had gathered material for a similar hypothesis. But "he brought forward his arguments somewhat unconnectedly, not seeking to change the general view which prevailed of the history of Israel" (1965: 368). The result of Graf's work, therefore, was that "he made no impression on the majority of those who study these subjects" (ibid.).

Wellhausen saw himself differing in a second way from Graf's procedure:

> Again I attach much more weight than Graf did to the change of ruling ideas which runs parallel with the change in the institutions and usages of worship; this has been shown mostly in the second part of the present work. *Almost more important to me than the phenomena themselves are the presuppositions which lie behind them.* [Italics added] (1965: 368)

Here we have Wellhausen's awareness of the distinction between his argumentation in part one and that of part two. Centering around "the change of ruling ideas," part two is based upon Vatke's philosophy of history, and it is most revealing that Wellhausen admits that the material discussed in part two is almost more important to him than that of part one. This attitude of Wellhausen's will be important when we discuss chapter eight below. Wellhausen now proceeds in the body of chapter nine to furnish us with additional evidence for his hypothesis, evidence "which has not yet been noticed" (ibid.). Although we do not have space to examine it in detail, this "additional evidence" again confirms the essentially deductive nature of his argumentation. In section one he shows, among other things, that since much of Deuteronomy can be found in JE but not in the Priestly main stock of the Hexateuch (Q) whereas the converse does not occur at all, the Priestly Code must be later than Deuteronomy. Moreover, since "in those narratives which are found both in JE and in Q, Deuteronomy follows, in every case in which there is a distinct divergence, the version of JE," therefore P is later than D (1965: 372). Again, this is an essentially deductive argument however much his major and minor propositions suppose a series of inductive investigations. Section two of chapter nine attempts another proof for his hypothesis through an inductive examination of the contents of the Law of Holiness (Lev. 17-26). After an examination of this corpus revealing traces of JE, D, Ezekiel, and P, he attempts, on pages 379ff, to deduce the correct historical order of literary influences upon it. It is the same method he employed on the Pentateuch, and its results confirm his other arguments: "Lev. XVII-XXVI is incomparably instructive for the knowledge it affords of literary relationships: it is a perfect compendium of the literary history of the Pentateuch" (1965: 376).

We are now in a position to summarize our understanding of Wellhausen's methodology from the point of view of the inductive/deductive dichotomy. His aim was to offer *proof* that the prevailing diachronic scheme concerning Hexateuchal sources, P, JE, D, was incorrect and should be replaced by the scheme, JE, D, P. It was not the mere collecting of data that established his hypothesis. Rather he relied on comparing a construction based on one set of data (the contents of the various Pentateuchal sources) with that construction of history he had built as an interpretation of data found in the historical and prophetic books of the Hebrew Bible. His hypothesis was the logical conclusion of that comparison and essentially an exercise in deductive reasoning. The major proposition of his various syllogisms was, in every case, a constructed sketch of Israelite history (1965: 367). In other words, in order that his data-gathering could be useful in his argument, it was necessary not so much "to collect the details of evidence, but so to shape the superabundant material as to convey a right total impression" (1965: 172). Another way he describes this is to refer to "the ascertained facts of Israelite History" and it is this schema from which he draws the various forms he uses in his major propositions. Notice here that, although in his introduction he may talk about "the data relating to sacred archeology" (1965: 13), his historical schema rests on two main foundations, one explicit, one implicit. Whereas chapter one is *explicitly* based on a close examination of the historical and prophetic books, chapter eight, for example, is *implicitly* based, on a kind of Hegelian philosophy of history.

To his various major propositions he juxtaposed and compared his construction, first of the legislation, then of the tradition (narration) of the Priestly Code. Here again he is not concerned so much with the raw set of data comprising his analysis of the contents of the Priestly Code, "the details of evidence," but rather with "the total impression" of this document. In his own words: "To compare the parallel of the Priestly Code it is necessary to restore it as a whole for few are aware of the impression it produces" (1965: 327). Time and time again, we see that it is not the mass of individual instances that constitutes the main argument, but rather the general impression he has of a particular source. The mass of individual instances is precisely Wellhausen's attempt at conveying a correct total impression for the minor proposition of his deductive argument. Once we accept the essential truth of his major premise, a structure he has constructed, and put in comparison to it the truth of his minor premise, another structure he has constructed, we can deduce what logically follows: P is subsequent to D. This conclusion, which is the main hypothesis of the *Prolegomena*, is not *proven* by the wealth of detail found in the book; rather this hypothesis best *interprets,* Wellhausen believes, all the data he has collected. In short, then, all the specific data he brings together so masterfully are nothing more nor less than the full articulation of his *interpretation* which forms the major and minor propositions of his basic syllogism: The contents of JE and D are such and such. But the contents of P are such and such. Therefore P is later than both JE and D. In chapter one this argument is unassailable because it rests on a specific historical reconstruction. In part two, especially chapter eight, this argument collapses because it rests on the fragile shoulders of Vatke, as we shall see shortly.

Deductive rather than inductive, diachronic rather than synchronic, the *Prolegomena* is lastly an analysis on the plane of content rather than on the plane of expression. Wellhausen argues for the diachronic scheme, JE———→ D———→ P, almost exclusively by means of the semantic material contained therein. Even in that one small section where he deals with the *language* of the Priestly Code (pp. 385-391) and its relation to dating, he spends most of his time dealing with lexicographic material. He believed that "the destructive efforts of tendency-criticism" (1965: 385) would demolish the supposed priority of the Priestly Source, whereas "the study of the history of language is still at a very elementary stage in Hebrew" (1965: 390).

In my first chapter I attempted to characterize content-plane and expression-plane analyses as neither of them more "objective" than the other, yet each needing the other to complement and corroborate an analysis. Since the time of the *Prolegomena's* publication, much work has been done analyzing the Priestly Code on the plane of expression. In fact in 1878, the very same year the *Prolegomena* was published, Ryssel published a monograph attempting to date P early on the basis of its language alone (lexicography and grammar). Three years later, Giesebrecht attempted to argue the opposite. The present writer in 1971 attempted to clarify the issue on the basis of the expansion of our knowledge of the historical development of biblical Hebrew. By now, enough research has been done on the plane of expression to corroborate Wellhausen's thesis based on his content-plane analysis of biblical sources: P is definitely later than the other major Hexateuchal material.

Since Wellhausen's diachronic concerns and methodology are by this time self-evident, I will use his main diachronic conclusions to offer some reflections on whether the *Prolegomena* as *signifier* can be called structural. In talking about the deep subjectivity of structuralism, I wrote in the first chapter that for an analysis to be structural there had to be a self-conscious awareness (Polanyi's subsidiary awareness) of the law-like relationships between the analyst's model, the structure as constructed, and the personal structures within the analyst, (the structure as structuring) which enabled him to construct or "find" such a structure in his object in the first place. I argued that it was this conscious awareness, within the analyst, of the relation between the object constructed and subject constructing that constitutes an important indicator of whether an analysis is structural or not. Since such an awareness admits of degrees, my suspicion that Wellhausen's *Prolegomena* exhibits some tension concerning its author's self-awareness casts some doubt about whether his great work can be considered truly structural. At the same time it, as few other major works since published in Old Testament studies, comes very close, in my opinion, to what structural analysis is all about.

The crucial distinction here is between Wellhausen's "ascertained facts of history," on one hand, and his *philosophy* of history, on the other. The latter is derived from Vatke, from whom, Wellhausen writes, "indeed I gratefully acknowledge myself to have learnt best and most" (1965: 13). Wellhausen's arguments are based upon one or another of these two foundations but he does not seem to have clearly seen, or at least expressed, the difference between them. For example, whereas he spells out admirably the "ascertained facts of history" upon which his first chapter is based, concerning chapter eight the Vatkean philosophy of history upon which it is based is only implicitly assumed and never explicitly referred to. It is hard for me not to conclude that there is some tension at least in Wellhausen's self awareness of key internal structures within himself (i.e. structures structuring) by which he reconstructed the history of Ancient Israel.

First let me briefly comment on chapter eight. Here we find the type of interpretations of data which are, as Frank Moore Cross has implied, ". . . content with a simple interpretation in terms of a unilinear, diachronic development: the historicizing of myth" (1973: 82). Chapter eight is entitled "The Narrative of the Pentateuch," and in it Wellhausen tells us he wants "to lay the foundation for [a history of the development of the Israelite legend] by comparing the narrative of the Priestly Code with the Jehovistic one. In doing so we shall see . . . that the Jehovistic form of the legend is the earlier of the two" (1965: 296). Why is JE earlier, more primitive, than P? We find in Wellhausen's answer, perhaps more clearly than anywhere else in the *Prolegomena*, that his argumentation for P's lateness is intimately bound up with what he considers an unassailable truth: the progression of outward culture in a certain unalterable fashion. It is beyond doubt, he believes, that in any culture, narratives develop diachronically from marvel and myth to rationalistic explanation and speculative cosmology, from universal ethnic origins to specific ethnic modifications, from a many-coloured poetic charm to pedantry, from the freedom of myth to the slavery of morality, from concrete to purified notions of God, in short, by means of the gradual removal of all notions too childish, superstitious or mythical. Thus the Jehovistic narrative is earlier because it "does shine by the absence of all efforts after rationalistic speculation, by its contempt for every kind of cosmological speculation" (1965: 303); because in it, "we are on the ground of marvel and myth" (1965: 304); because its materials have "a universal ethnic origin" and are suffused with ". . . a kind of antique philosophy of history" (1965: 314); because its narratives are adorned with a "many-coloured poetic charm . . . the springs from which legend arises" (1965: 335); because in it, "the very notion of the law is absent" (1965: 347). On the other hand, the Priestly narrative is much later than the Jehovistic one. The reasons are numerous but consistent. In P, "we stand before the first beginnings of sober reflections about nature" (1965: 304). "Intimately connected with the advanced views of nature . . . is the 'purified' notion of God found there" (1965: 305). In P "the mythical mode of view is destroyed by the autonomy of morality" (1965: 315). "The removal of colour from the myths is the same thing as the process of Hebraising them" and "in fact (P) Hebraises much more" (1965: 315). Moreover, P in Genesis "deals in no etymology, no proverbs nor songs, no miracles, theophanies nor dreams, and is destitute of all that many-coloured poetic charm which adorns the Jehovistic narratives" (1965: 335). In P "moral and religious culture is further advanced; and hence the removal . . . of notions which are too childish, or superstitious, or even mythical" (1965: 337). In P, " . . . art-products of pedantry take the place of the living poetic detail of the Jehovist narrative" (1965: 337). In P one finds "that which brings forth nothing but numbers and games" (1965: 361). All these factors are "beyond doubt signs of progress in outward culture" (1965: 307). Thus, with regard P's age "there can be no question at least of youthful freshness" (1965: 361).

Such a basic diachronic structure is one of the chief arguments upon which Wellhausen's great synthesis, and especially its eighth chapter, rests. By means of what was to him an indisputable pattern of development, so fundamental it need not be explicitly referred to as an assumption, Wellhausen rearranged the various parts of the Hexateuchal puzzle into a genetic structure mirroring this archetypal pattern. Wellhausen's grand synthesis was marred by that type of philosophy of history about which Morton White writes, "a philosophy of history. . . associated almost exclusively with grand speculation about the development of society, with pretentious volumes on the laws of civilization and its decay" (1969: 1). From Hegel to Vatke to Wellhausen. Fortunately, as White remarks, "the speculative philosophy of history has not endured as a serious intellectual enterprise in the age of analysis" (1969: 2). But if it has not endured, it still influences scholarly activity in biblical studies. For example, as Frank Moore Cross has pointed out, with regard to most myth-and-ritualists "the idealistic framework of the evolution (of the Hegelian system) is kept" (1973: 82). We shall have occasion to return to this point when we discuss the diachronic enterprises of Von Rad's form criticism and M. Noth's tradition-history in the following chapters.

Certainly there is much in the *Prolegomena* that is not argued for after the manner of chapter eight. It seems to me worth repeating that, although the bankruptcy of the general philosophy of history that permeated much of Wellhausen's great synthesis has often been pointed out by scholars, the *Prolegomena* is still in many ways a hypothesis whose value can be termed inestimable in terms of fruitfulness, simplicity and elegance. As he himself admits, he is concerned with "the construction of history" and "the question is whether one constructs well or ill" (1965: 367).

Wellhausen's construction of history was not everywhere so dependent on Vatke's Hegelian schema. Often we find the elegant simplicity of historical deduction. As I have already noted, the chapter he specifically singled out as representative of his methodology is chapter one on the places of worship in Israel's history. It seems to me that we have here the carving out of a hypothesis that is as fruitful, simple and elegant as one could hope for. Whether the argumentation is essentially Wellhausen's or merely the classic restatement of his predecessors, one looks in vain in chapter one for echoes of Vatke's philosophic speculations and finds instead the brilliant construction of a typological progression from the sources themselves and not from any philosophy of history. Here one can touch most palpably the creative nature of Wellhausen's diachronic reconstruction. Instead of that sterile explanation of the documentary hypothesis as an inductive enterprise, we have a classic example of what F.S.C. Northrop called "deductively formulated theory" (1947). Since the heart of the documentary hypothesis is diachronic in nature, the long difficult process of data-gathering and even of initial segmentation of the Hexateuch into sources is only preliminary to the actual hypothesis itself, which attempts to interpret and explain in genetic terms the material one has segmented and reshaped (Wellhausen 1965: 295). Taken by itself, I have little hesitation in viewing chapter one as a good example of diachronic structural analysis. But there are indications that he placed more importance on the subject matter and proofs of part two. The following quotation bears repeating:

> Again I attach much more weight than Graf did to the change of ruling ideas which runs parallel with the change in the institutions and usages of worship; this has been shown mostly in the second part of the present work. *Almost more important to me than the phenomena themselves, are the presuppositions which lie behind them.* (1965: 368) [Italics added]

It is ironic that Wellhausen here discusses priorities, using language that is very close to the "deep structures" so sought after by modern structuralists; ironic because in the very section of the *Prolegomena* where he is most concerned about "deep structures," (part two), he relies most heavily on the Vatkean schema concerning "the change in ruling ideas." Whereas he clearly expresses the difference of subject matter between part one, "the change in the institutions and usages of worship" and part two, "the change of ruling ideas"—"the phenomena themselves" as opposed to "the presuppositions which lie behind them"—a clear self-awareness of the Hegelian structure of history upon which his argument in chapter eight squarely but implicitly rests is to my knowledge nowhere expressed.

Vatke's Hegelian philosophy no longer obtains, but many elements of Wellhausen's brilliant reconstruction of the history of the religion of Israel *do* remain. The heart of Wellhausen's method of higher criticism was a deductive approach, diachronic in nature and restricted primarily to the plane of content. Frank Moore Cross summarizes all this very well: "Had Wellhausen proceeded purely as a positivistic historian, his great synthesis would never have been written, and he would not have become the powerful figure he was and is" (1973: 82n.9). It is only my doubt about a clear and distinct awareness of the "structures structuring" within Wellhausen himself which makes me somewhat hesitant in describing without qualification his great work as a structural synthesis. At the same time there are few structuralist works that surpass its clarity and brilliance.

Chapter VI

Gerhard von Rad's *The Form-Critical Problem of the Hexateuch*

Gerhard von Rad published this provocative study in 1938. Despite the very strong reactions for and against its main conclusions, *The Form-Critical Problem* was already twenty-eight years old when an English translation was made (von Rad 1966). In his foreword to the English translation, von Rad advised:

> I must therefore beg the reader to exercise a certain historical discretion in making use of the present volume, and to bear in mind the state of our knowledge of a given topic at the time when each particular essay was written. (1966: V)

I will try to heed his advice and aim therefore at the assumptions behind the article rather than the specific conclusions reached. I have chosen this study because it seems to me to be representative of form-critical studies and quite influential among Old Testament scholars as a carrier of biblical concerns along the narrowly diachronic paths marked out by the major modern studies that preceded it. There is a certain irony in this last point, for unlike many of his predecessors and contemporaries, von Rad was very sensitive to the ultimate, disintegrating effects of the diachronic approaches of source and form-critical studies upon the Hebrew Bible.

I want to discuss this point in greater detail, but for now it is sufficient to point out that the assumptions upon which *The Form-Critical Problem* is based unfortunately acted *against* von Rad's instincts in this regard, so that the predominant thrust of the article, indeed of his work in general, led him finally toward the very diachronic disintegration of the biblical message he sometimes reacted against in print. *The Form-Critical Problem* illustrates my contention that the stages prior to the final forms of the text in *practice* remained for von Rad the most urgent and fundamental areas of research. In theory and by protestation the final stage of the text was for von Rad last but not least; in point of fact, the bulk of his work, in spite of his sincere assertions to the contrary, reveals an absolutely crucial dimension of his interest in the final stage of the biblical text: the last is not least precisely because the last has not obliterated any of the essential stages that came before it. He himself ends *The Form-Critical Problem* by emphasizing the following statement in italics: "None of the stages in the age-long development of this work has been wholly superseded; something has been preserved of each phase, and its influence has persisted right down to the final form of the Hexateuch" (1966: 78).

But there is a more specific reason for analyzing *The Form-Critical Problem* at this point. It more than any other work of which I am acquainted is a preview of that particular kind of diachronic research into Pentateuchal themes that finds its ultimate realization in Martin Noth's *A History of Pentateuchal Traditions,* the subject of my next chapter. The brilliant beginnings of a diachronic thematics of the Pentateuch (Hexateuch, Tetrateuch) best exemplified by Wellhausen's classic exercise in source criticism are carried along in similarly brilliant fashion by von Rad's form criticism, finally to receive their ultimate apotheosis in Martin Noth's tradition-historical study of the Tetrateuch. Thus *The Form-Critical Problem* can be seen as a crucial link between two of the most important stages in the development of the diachronic analysis of the Hebrew Bible. Just as the Torah became for the Jews the standard against which to measure the remaining scriptures, so too in the world of scholarship it has been the classic approaches to the Penta- (Hexa-Tetra-) teuch which have for good or ill largely determined the direction in which the remainder of the Hebrew Bible has been studied.

Any deviation from this basic diachronic approach drew down upon its perpetrators the ultimate punishment: academic ostracism akin to excommunication in the religious sphere. No wonder then, that in 1924 the editor of *ZAW* could write:

> We must stress with the utmost emphasis that there is no school
> of Biblical scholarship today that is not founded on the critical
> analysis of the sources in the Hexateuch . . . and anyone who
> does not accept the division of the text according to the sources
> and the results flowing therefrom has to discharge the onus, if
> he wishes to be a collaborator in our scientific work, of proving
> that all the research work done till now was futile. (quoted in
> Cassuto 1961:7)

When finally it was generally recognized that source criticism
had gone as far as it could go in solving the Pentateuchal problem,
indeed had gone *too* far, the scholarly world began to turn its
attention and approval toward a methodology that both built
upon and was a reaction *against* source-critical study. Form
criticism came into its own largely through the genius of Hermann
Gunkel. The *excesses* of source criticism were eschewed while its
fundamental elements were retained. The problem of the Hebrew
Bible's four-, five-, or six-headed beginning was taken up anew by
a new generation of form critics. Certainly von Rad can be
considered to have given an archetypal solution to this problem in
the present article. His form-critical banner is raised once again in
behalf of and in fundamental allegiance to the primacy of the
diachronic approach to the Pentateuchal problem. He will carry
this banner as far as he can go, to the pre-literary background of
the earliest literary source of the Pentateuch, the Yahwist. Shying
away from a *detailed* and systematic explanation of the oral prehistory of the main Pentateuchal themes, von Rad is unable or
unwilling to carry his form-critical explorations very far into the
period of the tribal confederacy. But this wilderness must also be
subdued, and we shall see in the next chapter how Martin Noth
continues the pioneering explorations of scholars such as
Wellhausen and von Rad. Noth's vehicle will be the tradition-
historical method and it will be my contention that the results of
that journey question seriously whether it should have been
continued so far in the direction it went.

There are eleven sections in *The Form-Critical Problem.* In this article von Rad begins to outline for us how and why the Hexateuch is for him the end product of a series of stages of which the following are essential: First of all, traditional narrative material "in its canonical form" (1966: 21) is the basis for, specifically prior to, and normative for various cultic ceremonies in the history of Israel. The two cultic events about which von Rad is most concerned center around the originally separate Settlement and Sinai traditions. Once these traditional narrative traditions are taken over as the basis for cultic retelling, their form precisely as cultic becomes the basis for the present *literary* form of the various traditions. The Hexateuch itself as the product of a long *literary* development has as its core the Settlement traditions. It was the Yahwist, an individual collector or editor of these traditions, who is largely responsible for *combining* the cultic narratives centering around the events of Sinai with the main cultic traditions of the Settlement. Even prior to this Yahwistic marriage of traditions, the respective cultic traditions had "become detached from the cultic places in which they had grown up" (1966: 48). This detaching "caused their content to become highly spiritualized" (1966: 49) so that their " . . . historical recollection has been seriously eroded" (1966: 50). This stage is what von Rad calls "from tradition to literature." But with the formative influence of the Yahwist upon the Hexateuchal material comes a process of "historicization" which is complementary to the "de-historicization" that preceded the Yahwist's activity. Just as the cult transformed the traditional narratives for its own purposes, these cultified traditions were once more transformed by a gradual detachment from their original cult centers, finally to be transformed once again at the main literary stage of this development by the historicizing influence of the Yahwist, the main architect of the Hexateuchal structure.

In part one, von Rad lays the foundation for his analysis by examining three texts, Deut 26: 5b-9, Deut 6: 20-24, and Josh 24: 2b-13. His aim is to examine the implications of assuming that the Hexateuch is a creed, representative of a type of literature (a *genre*) concerning which one can point to various of its *stages*. The three texts mentioned seem to be miniature forms of the Hexateuchal material. Since they vary in only insignificant details and seem to represent no casual recollection but "a recital in exalted pregnant form, pronounced in a situation of lofty significance in the setting of a cultic ceremony" (1966: 8), von Rad concludes that "the solemn recital of the main parts of the redemption narrative must have been an invariable feature of the ancient Israelite cultus, either as a straightforward credal statement or as a hortatory address to the congregation" (1966: 8). Moreover, two essential things can be said about the three texts here isolated. First of all they represent comparatively early stages in the development of this traditional material and secondly, the stage they represent makes no mention of the revelation of Yahweh at Mt. Sinai. What follows part one is an attempt to show "the principal stages of the process by which this cultic material developed into the Hexateuch as we have it" (1966: 8).

Part two examines a set of texts which von Rad calls "free adaptations of the Creed in cult-lyrics." These are 1 Sam 12:8, Ps 136, Exod 15, Pss 76, 78, 105, 135. The significant feature of all these accounts of the redemption story is a lack of reference to the Sinai events. Only with Neh 9:6ff and the post-exilic Ps 106 do we have interpolation of the Sinai story into the redemptive history. Von Rad summarizes part two for us:

> . . . even the more or less free accounts of the redemption-story which follow the canonical scheme do not mention the events of Sinai. These events seem rather to have given rise to a tradition of their own, which remained separate from the canonical pattern and only at a very late date became combined with it. (1966: 13)

Parts three through six investigate the origin and nature of the Sinai tradition; part seven investigates the origin of the central Hexateuchal tradition, the Settlement tradition; parts eight through ten discuss the role of the Yahwist in the main stages of the development of the Hexateuch; and part eleven concludes with a few remarks on the development of the Hexateuch *after* J.

Part three examines the nature and role of the Sinai tradition within the larger complex of the Hexateuch. Three things become clear in this part. First of all, following Gressman, there are obviously *two* traditions of law-giving within the Hexateuch: the Kadesh narratives of Exod 17-18 and Num 10-14, and the Sinai narratives of Exod 19-24; 32-34. Secondly it is only the Kadesh narratives which have been closely interwoven with the Exodus story proper; the Sinai narratives form obvious breaks in the story line. Thirdly, von Rad here finds a corroboration of his conclusion of parts one and two, namely that none of the major elements of the Exodus and Wandering traditions or Settlement traditions are found in the main section of the Sinai traditions, Exod 19-24.

Part four examines the *Sitz im Leben* of the Sinai traditions and concludes that they have their origin "in the public religious activity of the community, that is to say, in the cultus" (1966: 21). Just as the separate Settlement tradition was cultic in origin, so also the Sinai tradition. Von Rad, following Mowinckel's lead, utilizes Pss 50 and 81 to "confirm and fill out our thesis. We could not perhaps regard either of them in their present state as direct accounts of a cultic ceremony: they are not liturgical manuals but secondary poetical compositions which retain their characteristics of original *genre* only in their form" (1966: 24). Von Rad shows that just as Pss 50 and 81 illustrate an indirect connection with a cultic ritual, so also does the Sinai material. "Nevertheless, taken in conjunction with the Sinai narrative, [Pss 50 and 81] compel us to recognize the existence of a great cultic drama, the distinctive features of which are undoubtedly the divine self-revelation and the subsequent communication of God's purpose in the form of apodeictic commandments" (1966: 24).

Part five examines the *genre* of the book of Deuteronomy and serves "to corroborate duly the belief that the Sinai tradition is a cultic tradition" (1966: 33). For when one examines Deuteronomy, it "as a unity reveals itself to us in a new light as a rather baroque agglomeration of cultic materials, which nevertheless reflects throughout one and the same cultic occasion" (1966: 33).

Once the existence of a covenantal cultic occasion lying behind the Exodus Sinai material, the Book of Deuteronomy, and Pss 50 and 81, is made probable, part six confronts an even more difficult problem: ". . . the question of what the historical antecedants of this festival are. What, so far as we can tell, was its earliest setting in the history of Israel, both in time and place?" (1966: 34). We have information concerning an ancient covenantal rite (ancient Feast of Booths) at Shechem, and von Rad reconstructs this ancient festival from pieces of evidence found in Josh 24, Deut 27, Deut 11: 29ff, and Josh 8:30ff. "We have only to compare the separate cultic elements of the Shechem ritual with those of the Sinai narrative as we have found them to be in our study of Ex 19ff and Deuteronomy" (1966: 38). We have then the following structural similarities between Exod 19-24, Deuteronomy, and the Shechem covenant ceremony reconstruction:

EXODUS 19	DEUTERONOMY	SHECHEM RECONSTRUCTION
1. Exhortation (Exod 19: 4-6) and historical recital of Sinai events (Exod 19ff.)	1. Historical presentation of Sinai events and paraenetic material (Deut 1-11)	1. Joshua's allocution (Josh 24:14ff) and assent of congregation (Josh 24:16ff,24)
2. Reading of the Law (Decalogue and Book of the Covenant)	2. Reading of the Law (Deut 12-26:15) 3. Sealing of the Covenant (Deut 26:16-19)	2. Proclamation of the Law (Josh 24:25; Deut 27:15)
3. Promise of blessing (Exod 33:20ff)	4. Blessing and Curses (Deut 27ff)	3. Sealing of the Covenant (Josh 24:27)
4. Sealing of the Covenant (Exod 24)		4. Blessing and Curses (Deut 27:12ff; Josh 8:34)

"We would hold that our contention that the Sinai tradition had its cultic setting in the ancient covenantal festival at Shechem is as certain as such matters ever can be" (1966: 38).

But the core tradition of the Hexateuch, the Settlement

tradition, is also a cultic tradition and part seven deals with this matter. Von Rad holds that ". . . the creed as we have it in Deut 26:5ff is the cult legend of the Feast of Weeks—that is, it contains those elements of Yahwistic faith which were celebrated at the Feast of Weeks" (1966: 43). The place was not Shechem but Gilgal and the tradition is of great antiquity since ". . . the settlement tradition must have originated and have had its historical setting in a place where the ownership of the land really was a live issue." Another way to date the Settlement tradition is to investigate its earliest literary version (J) and see if this version "may yet preserve a solid deposit of the ancient tradition" (1966: 44). This is the topic of parts eight through ten.

Part eight is a brief preface to parts nine and ten. It describes the subsequent analysis as an attempt to "to look for a moment *at the whole process* by which tradition grows into literature" (1966: 50). This is a process whereby the cult legends become detached from their cultic origins, become highly spiritualized or rationalized, so that historical recollection has been seriously eroded" (1966: 50).

Part nine describes this process from tradition to literature from the point of view of the chief architect of the Hexateuch's basic structure, the Yahwist. The settlement tradition is the framework supporting the whole of the Yahwist's work. He subordinates all the traditions he incorporates to this tradition. The Yahwist is a great editor not a long process (1966: 52) who is responsible for the interpolation of the Sinai tradition into the Settlement tradition . . . "since even at a time later than that of the Yahwist it had not taken root in the traditional account of the history of redemption" (1966: 53-54). Moreover had this fusion taken place earlier in a pre-literary stage, one would have expected the two traditions to be better fused and organically interwoven than they are (1966: 54). The fusion therefore was "a purely literary process" (1966: 54). In addition to adding the Sinai material, the Yahwist developed the Patriarchal History, already present in the Settlement tradition from the beginning as "a simple reference to Jacob" (1966: 56). Finally the Yahwist took the truly revolutionary step of adding the Primaeval History. Von Rad employs the term "revolutionary" because ". . . one cannot avoid the feeling that the looseness of the composition as a whole stems from the fact that this is the first trial of a new venture" (1966: 67).

Part ten poses the theological problem of the Yahwist: why in J there is "not one single instance in which the original cultic interest [of its main traditions] has been preserved" (1966: 68). The reason is because these traditions took on new theological associations concerning a new-found recognition of the hidden activity of God in history. The cultic materials have become newly historicized just as they had become de-historicized when first taken over by the various cults. Von Rad sees this new process as "more related to David than hitherto supposed" (1966: 72).

Part eleven concludes the article with observations on the post-Yahwistic phases of the formation of the Hexateuch. These remarks include opinions that E never had a primaeval history, that P aims at a validation of sacral institutions and lacks the religious naïvete of the ancient cultic traditions, and that the Hexateuch achieved its present form at the hands of redactors (1966: 77). Most importantly he points out that "The process by which E and P are superimposed on J, as well as their relationship to one another, is a purely literary question, which adds nothing essentially new to the discussion as far as form-criticism is concerned" (1966: 74).

When one attempts to assess the methodology underlying *The Form-Critical Problem* one is immediately struck by its concern for the discovery and articulation of structures within the Hexateuch. Von Rad's article is of course an exercise in *form* criticism and it is quite obvious that a *genre* is a kind of structure discovered within or behind certain biblical texts. Any comparison therefore between form criticism and structural analysis must carefully distinguish "structure" as understood in form critical studies from "structure" as understood in structural analysis. One common manner of distinguishing the two kinds of structure is to say that structuralism investigates the "hidden or underlying" configuration of a text rather than "the more or less visible or obvious pattern in a text." Such a distinction, according to Jean

Pouillon (1966) and Dan O. Via (1974), for example, differenti-
ates the reality from the appearance of structuralism. This is a
rather popular way of describing the self-identity of structural
analysis and is based upon the already widely accepted distinction between "deep" and "surface" structures. I suppose there is a
certain comfort available to the structuralist when he believes that
he investigates "hidden" structures whereas non-structuralists
investigate only "surface" or "obvious" patterns in a text. Who is
doing the more important and crucial analysis: he who barely
scratches the surface of a text or he who digs deep into its layers
discovering what is there but not obvious? Who would not rather
be profound than topical in his approach? Which methodology is
more powerful: one which aims at discovering the subtle meaning
of a text or one which is content to analyze its superficial meaning?
It is this (unfortunate) choice of words the structuralist uses to
map out his own territory which both provides him with a false
sense of satisfaction and ensures that his more traditional
colleagues will react negatively to his assertions. One does not
immediately gain the attention of another person by talking down
to him.

But more importantly, this distinction between deep and
surface structures is not just an error in tactics, a crisis in
communication; it is my strong conviction that such a distinction
unless correctly understood, distorts the basic difference in
approach between the "structuralist" and the "non-structuralist."
All analysis to some degree draws the hidden from the obvious,
attacks the superficial aspects of an object and attempts to get to
the heart of the matter. Once one realizes that "deep" vs. "surface"
structure is a *metaphor,* one can understand the strategic power it
wields but also the degree of heat not light with which it can invest
a discussion. When it is *not* recognized for its metaphoric value
but taken to be somehow literally meaningful, it misleads rather
than clarifies. For those scholars who see themselves as trying to
conquer Everest in their work, to descend to the depths of
structuralism holds no attraction whatsoever.

In this regard I can certainly be accused of using the same

strategic metaphor when I choose to describe a key aspect of structuralism with the phrase, "deep subjectivity." Here however there is no danger that I will be accused of talking down to other scholars since "subjectivity" is one characteristic scholars often try to avoid, not emulate. So that in many eyes, I suspect, the fact that I call this subjectivity "deep" is the same as calling the scholarship upon which it rests superficial. From this point of view I probably would be seen as talking up to them.

There is one specific effect that unfortunately follows from *not* understanding the deep/surface dichotomy as metaphor: a whole branch of present-day structural analysis is lopped off the structuralist tree and cast into a pile containing only "surface analyses of biblical texts." I am thinking now of synchronic analysis on the expression-plane of language about which I wrote in the first chapter. For convenience one can refer to it here as rhetorical criticism. Given the deep/surface metaphor by which such an amputation is accomplished, I do not know whether to call it a de-grading or up-grading of rhetorical criticism. In any case, it is my conviction that structural analysis can just as appropriately be concerned with surface structures as deep structures, so that the question arises: how does structural analysis on the plane of expression, that is, rhetorical analysis, differ from other types of analysis conceived of by some structuralists as dealing only with surface structures? Form criticism would indeed fit this latter category so that we are now back to the initial question of the relationship between form criticism and structural analysis. Is a genre a deep form or a surface form, a deep structure or a surface structure, a pattern on the plane of content or a pattern on the plane of expression?

Even a superficial knowledge of form criticism leads one to realize that such questions ultimately lead to a *cul-de-sac*. Essential steps in every form-critical analysis call for the discovery and description of the form of a genre, the content of a genre and the *Sitz im Leben* of a genre. If the form of a genre concentrates on the expression plane of language and the content of a genre focuses on the content plane of language, then is there a correlation between expression plane and surface structure on one hand and content plane and deep structure on the other hand? Or if, as we have maintained from the beginning, structural analysis can operate on the expression plane of language, as well as the content plane, is there then a surface structure *and* a deep structure belonging to the content of a genre? Would one then have to hold that some form critics are structuralists whereas others are not? Moreover since it is our contention that structuralism can operate in the diachronic as well as the synchronic sphere, would it follow that form criticism with its emphasis on history and development of genres deals with the surface history of a genre whereas structural analysis would concentrate on the deep history of a genre? Is there in other words a useful distinction in deep versus surface diachrony? Looking at the problem from the point of view of *Sitz im Leben* of a text, are there such things as deep situations in life as opposed to surface situations in life?

In reality all of these questions, however intriguing in themselves, are unable to help us solve our basic question: how does form criticism differ from structural analysis? The reason for this lies in the fundamental assertion of the present book, already discussed at length in the first chapter. If it is true that structuralism concentrates on the relations between objects, that is, on their *context* rather than on the inherent nature of the objects themselves, then it follows necessarily that the *structural* distinction between one object, structuralism, and another object, form criticism, cannot lie in the inherent quality or nature of the structures they variously isolate and describe but rather in the *context* or *way* such structures are isolated and analyzed. To look therefore at the quality of patterns investigated by form criticism ("surface") as opposed to the quality of patterns investigated by structuralism ("deep") is to search *in a non-structural way* for a distinction between two approaches. *The Form-Critical Problem* is as concerned with discovering and articulating basic structures within the Hexateuch, as any structural analysis we could conceive of.

Let us return to the article itself to see first of all how it is like structural analysis insofar as it is *deductive* in approach, and concentrates on *structures* in the text that are diachronic both on the plane of expression and on the plane of content.

Like Wellhausen's *Prolegomena, The Form-Critical Problem* is an outstandingly clear example of deductive reasoning. One might recast the main argumentation in the following syllogism:

Deut 6, 26 and Josh 24 contain the essential features of a cultic recital of an invariable creed.

But they are also clearly seen as the earliest forms of the Hexateuchal narrative in miniature.

Therefore The Hexateuch is a decultified later stage or elaboration of these creeds to which has been added, chiefly by the Yahwist, the decultified Sinai traditions plus other material.

One sees quite clearly how, if the major and minor propositions are accepted, the conclusion which is the main contention of the article plausibly follows. The major contention states that three texts segmented from the Bible represent the same genre: a cultic recital of an invariable creed. The minor states that in addition to these texts, the Hexateuch itself is a *creed,* the earliest form of whose genre is precisely the three texts in question. The conclusion plausibly follows that the Sinai traditions form an originally separate tradition not found in the earlier creeds and therefore added by the Yahwist to this genre in the course of its development.

In accordance with the major preoccupations of form criticism, von Rad's analysis of the various genres discussed in the article alternates between a description of their form and of their content. In other words he examines the genre which he isolates both on the plane of expression and on the plane of content. Both features of his genre are necessary for his argument. For example on the plane of expression these cultic creeds are "short," they are "recitals in exalted pregnant form." In speaking of Deut 26.5b-9 he points out "the rhythmical and alliterative character of (its) opening phrases" (1966: 4n.3). On the plane of content he isolates the *constant* elements of the historical creeds, of which the most noteworthy feature is *the complete absence of any mention of the revelation of Yahweh at Mount Sinai.*

> *None of the stages in the age-long development of this work has been wholly superseded; something has been preserved of each phase, and its influence has persisted right down to the final form of the Hexateuch.* (1966: 78)

When I think of the form critical work of von Rad (as well as the tradition-historical work of Noth) the best image that comes to mind is that of a laboriously careful textual archeologist digging up the ancient site of *Tell el Tanach* in order to reveal to the world the various stages in the long and glorious history of that city. In part one von Rad describes for us the earliest stratum of the Hexateuchal narrative as it is embodied in Deut 26: 5b-9, Deut 6:20-24, and Josh 24: 2b-13. This stratum of the text allows von Rad to reconstruct certain aspects of the ancient Israelite credal system, the most amazing of which, given the later development of the site, is the complete absence of signs of occupation by that later citizen of the site, *homo Sinaiticus*. The excitement of such a discovery can scarcely be concealed and the main thrust of von Rad's investigation is already clear: what were the principal stages of the process by which the native population of the earliest stratum developed into the heterogeneous population everywhere apparent on the surface of the site? How did *homo Sinaiticus* come to enjoy a central role in the life of the hexateuchal city? The beliefs of the original citizens were characterized by an emphasis on Gospel: how Yahweh's saving acts brought them to this holy city they then inhabited. With the coming of *homo Sinaiticus* however a new dimension was added to the life of the city: an emphasis on Law: how Yahweh revealed himself through his covenant. And indeed soundings throughout the site with its many and varied artifacts reveal everywhere the style of that architectural and political genius who integrated (but not completely) both populations with their respective traditions. That master builder was the Yahwist.

Von Rad's reconstruction of the principle stages in the life of this leading biblical city rests upon his discovery of the *terminus a quo* of its history as seen in the stratum containing Deut 6, 26 and Josh 24, and to a certain extent the cult lyrics of 1 Sam 12:8, Exod 15, Pss 105, 76, 78, 135, 136. But by what means does he date this stratum? Modern archeology uses controls such as typological pottery dating or the less accurate and less useful principle that what is deeper in the ground is often older. Von Rad has a similar dating method: "To discover the minimum content of a creed *one must turn to the simplest possible versions of the creed since only these versions can properly be expected to tell us what is the historical starting point of the tradition"* (italics added) (1966: 55). This earliest stratum consists of the biblical texts mentioned earlier in this paragraph, and the question arises as to which of these various *loci* represent most accurately this earliest stratum. Von Rad tells us which and why in the following words:

> There are of of course, no fixed points of reference which would enable us to say with certainty that this text (*Deut* xxvi.5ff) is prior to all other examples of its *genre;* but both its concise, simple form and its connection with a cultic act of great antiquity justify our belief that it is among the examples of the *genre* which approximate most closely to the original. (1966: 55)
>
> . . . everything in this creed is so tightly knit . . . that there is no trace whatever of inconsistencies which might indicate the fusion of originally independent traditions. (1966: 56)

Moreover

> . . . *1 Sam.* xii.8 . . . is equally distinguished by extreme conciseness. (1966: 56)

Earlier in the article we had a diachronic indication of another kind: concerning Deut 26:5b-9:

The rhythmical and alliterative character of the opening
phrases in particular reveals its antiquity. (1966: 4n3)

In the above quotations we have clear examples of von Rad's
principle diachronic indicators of genre development. First of all
are those that concern *form* of a genre: *the more concise, the
simpler; the shorter a particular genre example is, the older it is.*
This is the central *formal* criterion of age utilized by von Rad in
this article. It is of course based upon Gunkel's pioneering form-
critical theory, central to most form-critical work since attempted
(as is everywhere apparent in Koch's useful monograph of the
form-critical method [1969]), and utterly without any justification
whatsoever. In fact key studies of living oral tradition such as
Albert Lord's *The Singer of Tales* (1968) tend to cast serious
doubt upon the validity, let alone usefulness, of this central
diachronic principle of form criticism. A second example of a
formal criterion of age in genre development plays a relatively
insignificant role in the dating of von Rad's earliest creeds: "the
rhythmical and alliterative character of the opening phrases" of
Deut 26:5ff is consigned to a footnote on page four.

These *formal* diachronic criteria certainly involve (but are not
confined to) the plane of expression of a genre-text, especially the
second, insignificant criterion. However, the principle of simplicity and conciseness is so central to form-critical methodology
that it plays a major role in dating genre-representatives according
to their *content* especially when the genre in question is a content-
oriented genre, a *creed*. If a *creed* is " . . . a summary of the
principal facts of God's redemptive activity" (1966: 2), those texts
which are shorter and more concise with respect to the *number* of
principal facts are from the point of view of *content* the earlier
representatives of the credal *genre* that eventually reaches its final
stage in the Hexateuch itself. Therefore any stage of the
Hexateuch-creed *with* the principal Sinai traditions is definitely
later than a stage of the creed *without* these traditions. Any locus
without traces of *homo Sinaiticus* belongs therefore to a stratum
earlier than strata showing signs of his intermingling with the

native population. Thus we see how "the more concise the earlier" plays its central role also as a *content*-oriented criterion of age in genre studies and we shall see in the next chapter how Noth stretches this principle to the greatest length possible as he pursues his great thematic study of the Pentateuchal traditions.

A third diachronic criterion utilized by von Rad in *The Form-Critical Problem* concerns the third major aspect of a genre, its *Sitz im Leben*. Deut 26:5ff is one of the earliest examples of the Hexateuchal creed because of "its connection with a cultic act of great antiquity" (1966: 55). Now why does the *Sitz im Leben* of Deut 26:5ff oblige us ". . . to reckon the tradition to be of very great antiquity?" (1966: 44). Since it is essentially a tradition of Settlement, it ". . . *must have originated and have had its historical setting in a place where the ownership of the land really was a live issue.* . . .The tradition must point to a place and a time at which the question of the legality of the settlement was of such a pressing concern that the faith itself was under compulsion to give an account of it. . . .At what later stage, once the settlement was an accomplished fact of long standing, would there have been any necessity to make this particular question a matter of religious belief?" (1966: 44). Here then is the diachronic criterion of *Sitz im Leben* operating to determine the relative age of a particular textual stratum. We have only to think of a situation in life *after the fall of Jerusalem* at the other end of the diachronic pole when the question of who rightly should control the land, the Israelites or Babylonians, to see just how slippery a criterion a text's *Sitz im Leben* can be.

The *Form-Critical Problem of the Hexateuch* is a diachronic investigation of the Hexateuch, a study that rests upon three kinds of principles operative in form-critical studies, principles of *form, content,* and *real life context.* To get a new perspective on the methodology utilized by von Rad, let me now superimpose this methodological scheme upon a similar scheme developed by the concerns of modern linguistics. Roman Jakobson has written:

However, it is not enough to know the code in order to grasp the message. When I say "he did," you may be familiar with the words *he* and *did* and with the rules of word order, and you will then realize that I speak about some man who performed some action, but in order to learn who this person is and what the action which is he performed, you need to know the context, verbalized or non-verbalized, but verbalizable. Here we again enter the field of contiguity. The components of any message are necessarily linked with the code by an internal relation of equivalence and with the context by an external relation of contiguity. (1971: 233)

What Jakobson is saying is that in every language product there are three aspects to be analyzed: internal relations of metonymy or contiguity (the discourse viewed as a syntagm), internal relations of metaphor or equivalence (the discourse viewed as a paradigm) and external relations of metonymy (the real life context of a discourse). All three analyses are necessary before one can "grasp the message." Now von Rad's article is a study in *genre,* that particular form of discourse he calls a historical creed. Amazingly enough he frames his study on genre in terms that allow us to formulate categories similar to those delineated by Jakobson. The basic difference between the two approaches is that whereas Jakobson is talking about a synchronic analysis of language, von Rad is concerned with a diachronic analysis. Nevertheless von Rad formulates Jakobson's internal aspects of language in the following way:

In the absence of much of the firm evidence one would have wished to find, our investigation will be able to point only remotely to the stages in the development of this *genre,* and it will have to take account of both constant and variable elements. The constant element is that of the historical creed as such. It occurs from the earliest times onwards, and in its basic constituents is not subject to change. The variable element is the external expression, the outward form; and not only this external appearance, but above all the degree of theological penetrations and manipulations of the traditional deposit. (1966: 3)

In other words, given numerous, Hexateuchal examples of the genre: *historical credo,* those elements which are constant are those elements without which it would not be a historical creed of God's redemptive activity. These can be on the expression plane of language such as those which indicate "a recital in exalted, pregnant form . . ." (1966: 8) or they may be on the content plane of language so that one can conclude what is not appropriate within such a summary of the principal facts of God's redemptive activity: "All three texts (Deut 6, 26, Josh 24) were evidently compiled according to the same plan, a fact which was made clear *by the absence of any reference to the events of Mt. Sinai*" (1966: 8). All of these necessary elements of the genre under discussion whether they be from the plane of expression or from the plane of content constitute *paradigmatic* elements of this genre, its code. That is, they constitute its internal relations of metaphor.

On the other hand von Rad mentions variable elements of the genre, elements which need not be constant along the diachronic axis of the genre's development. Again such variables may be found on the expression plane of language; examples would include "The rhythmical and alliterative character of the opening phrases [of *Deut.* xxvi.5ff] . . ." (1966: 4) and other unnecessary aspects of the external appearance of genre representatives. Moreover these variable elements would be found on the content plane of language, for example "minor accretions—details concerning the Miracle of the Red Sea, the meeting with Balaam and so on" (1966: 7) which were not " . . . so fundamental an alteration as would have been occasioned by the introduction of the events of Mount Sinai" (1966: 7-8). All of these variable elements of the genre under discussion constitute what Jakobson might call the level of internal variance in discourse. They are bound together in analysis only by internal relations of contiguity or metonymy, that is solely by the fact that they are found joined together as components of a message or messages.

We are here in the familiar territory of *langue/parole,* competence/performance, code/message. Although von Rad's description is not so precise as these linguistic and information-theory categories, I do not believe I am reading too much into his statements to see them as reflective of and largely similar to their very useful linguistic counterparts.

The final aspect of analysis mentioned by Jakobson is the *context* of a statement: "The components of any message are necessarily linked . . . with the context by an external relation of contiguity" (1971a: 233). Here one would analyze discourse in its external relations of metonymy and it is precisely here where I would situate von Rad's statements concerning the *Sitz im Leben* of the historical credos he analyzes.

Jakobson's synchronic scheme of message, code and context of language is similar to von Rad's diachronic scheme of variable elements, constant elements and *Sitz im Leben* of a genre. What von Rad has attempted to do in *The Form-Critical Problem* is tease out the code of a genre from the external message of its various representations so that the various contexts in which the genre developed could thereby be discovered. Von Rad discovered and described phases of a genre, he discovered and described phases of a pattern, he discovered and described *structural* changes. And it seems clear to me that the ease with which one can superimpose Jakobson's structural scheme upon von Rad's *Form-Critical Problem* goes a long way toward its being understood as a structural analysis.

There is another reason why I believe *The Form-Critical Problem* comes very close to being the best example of structural analysis among the three works we are analyzing in this section. I can best describe why this appears to me to be so by offering some remarks on *The Form-Critical Problem* as *signified* (of the text about which von Rad wrote, the Hexateuch). At the end of chapter one I asserted that every statement about a text was actually a statement about the source or author of that text. It appears to me that von Rad recognized this very well in *The Form-Critical Problem* by concentrating his efforts toward delineating for us the characteristics of the person who was for him the chief architect of the Hexateuch, the Yahwist. It is ironic that if von Rad does not seem always to be conscious of what he himself was doing in writing *The Form-Critical Problem* he is very conscious of what he believes the Yahwist appeared to be doing when he fleshed out the main outline of the Hexateuch. Von Rad takes this "structural" approach primarily in part ten: "The Theological Problem of the Yahwist." Some of the more salient features of the Yahwist are said to be these: concerning the saving ordinances, his attitude of tolerance rather than of conviction that they are indispensable; a remarkable faith that is midway between a one-sided spirituality and a one-sided emphasis on cult; a conviction that God's dealings with his people are not to be found in the sacral institutions but in the events of history. In this section von Rad is telling us how very important it is to analyze the Bible as *signifier*.

But *The Form-Critical Problem* is also a *signifier* of structures within *its* author. In chapter one I wrote that an analysis is structural in the sense that there should be a self-conscious awareness (Polanyi's subsidiary awareness) of the law-like relationship between the analyst's model, the structure as con-structed, and the personal structures (the structures-structuring, within the analyst) which enable him to construct or "find" such a structure of the text in the first place. We can here single out one example of a "structure-structuring" within von Rad which is apparent from an examination of his text considered as *signifier;* this structure involves the consistent pattern by which he arrives at the third aspect of genre, its *Sitz im Leben.* This, as I have emphasized, involves that aspect of an analysis which concerns an object's (here a genre's) external relations of contiguity or metonymy. As Jakobson points out, to grasp any message "you need to know the context, verbalized or non-verbalized, but verbalizable" (1971: 233). Von Rad attempts to verbalize the various contexts of the genre representatives discussed in *The Form-Critical Problem* and the "structure structuring" of his verbalization is best seen in his treatment of the Sinai traditions of the Hexateuch in parts three through six.

As Jakobson emphasizes, this context may be verbalized or

non-verbalized and von Rad treats both kinds when he discusses the origin of the Sinai traditions. With respect to the *verbalized context* of the Sinai traditions we are in the area of the present literary context of Exod 19-24; 32-34: von Rad acknowledges in part three the well-known intrusive nature of these materials within the larger story-line of the Hexateuchal narrative. As had been long recognized, these chapters' literary context argues strongly for their being an interpolation artificially separating the Kadesh locale of Exod 17-18 on one hand and of Num 10:29 on the other. This type of analysis of literary context is a source-critical device taken over by form critics. One can see this example of form-critical "structure-structuring" in even clearer relief in K. Koch's form-critical analysis of Gen 12, 20 and 26 (1969: 111-118).

The second kind of context is the non-verbalized type which is clearly form criticism's concept of *Sitz im Leben*. Here von Rad's treatment of the non-verbalized origins of the Sinai traditions is found in parts four through six of *The Form-Critical Problem*. When one is discussing the "situation in life" of a particular genre, what one is doing is articulating the non-verbalized but verbalizable context about which Jakobson writes. Here again von Rad's exposition reveals a "structure- structuring" within him which consistently allows him to verbalize such a context.

Von Rad's procedure is here carried out three times successively in parts four, five, and six, and it is briefly this: What is the *Sitz im Leben* of genre representative A? One has only to look at another or other similar genre representatives and postulate *their Sitz im Leben*. Since *their Sitz im Leben* is probably such and such, genre representative A's *Sitz im Leben* is thereby established or confirmed. Thus in part four von Rad wants to establish that the Sinai traditions of Exod 19-24; 32-34 have a cultic *Sitz im Leben*. Following Mowinckel's lead, von Rad examines Pss 50 and 81 "to confirm and fill out our thesis" (1966: 24). His conclusion follows: "Nevertheless, taken in conjunction with the Sinai narrative, they compel us to recognize the existence of a great cultic drama, the distinctive features of which are undoubtedly the divine self-revelation and the subsequent communication of God's purpose in the form of apodeictic commandments" (1966: 24). In part five, von Rad follows the same procedure. He wants to study the genre of Deuteronomy and establish its original cultic *Sitz im Leben* in order " . . . to corroborate duly the belief that the Sinai tradition is a cultic tradition (1966: 33). His conclusion is clear ". . . *Deuteronomy* belongs to precisely the same cultic tradition with regard both to its form and to its content [as the Exodus Sinai tradition]" (1966: 28). Again in part six, by examining another genre representative (von Rad's *reconstruction* of the ancient Shechem covenant ceremony based on Josh 24, Josh 8, and Deut 27), von Rad is able to specify in greater detail the *Sitz im Leben* of the Exodus Sinai traditions. "We have only to compare the separate cultic elements of the Shechem ritual with those of the Sinai narratives as we have found them to be in our study of *Exod.* xixf and *Deuteronomy!*" (1966:38). His conclusion follows immediately: "We would hold that our contention that the Sinai tradition had its cultic setting in the ancient covenantal festival at Shechem is as certain as such matters ever can be" (*ibid.*). Now the point of this analysis of von Rad's pattern of argumentation in parts four through six is not to dispute his conclusions. Rather it is to pinpoint what I consider an extremely important "structure-structuring" utilized by von Rad to establish his thesis. His procedure is an odd one. He confirms one thesis by postulating similar theses concerning other texts *no more clear in their* Sitz im Leben *than his original text.* Thus he corroborates the cultic context of Exod 19-24; 32-34 by postulating the cultic context of Ps 50. He then corroborates these contexts by postulating the cultic context of Ps 81. He then corroborates all *these* contexts by postulating the cultic context of Deuteronomy. Finally he corroborates all these contexts by postulating their connection with the cultic context of his reconstructed Shechem ritual.

It is because of von Rad's apparently non-reflexive acceptance of his "proof by postulation" principle concerning the *Sitz im Leben* of relevant genres, (as well as his "shorter is older" principle) that I have some reservations about the subjective aspect of his analysis.

Even with this article's tremendous strengths the theological problem of the Yahwist remains after von Rad has finished his analysis of the form-critical problem of the Hexateuch. The reason for this appears to me to be von Rad's strategic choice of attempting to *solve* the problem of the Hexateuch through a purely *diachronic* analysis of the Hexateuch's message. When all is said and done, we are still left with a large part of the problem with which we began: what are the *synchronic* structures of the Hexateuch that help to clarify for us what its main message is. By framing his fundamental study on a diachronic axis, von Rad is actually no closer to understanding what the Hexateuch *as a whole* signifies.

One finishes his reading of *The Form-Critical Problem* realizing that von Rad has not succeeded in avoiding " . . . the profoundly disintegrating effect which has been one result of this method of hexateuchal criticism" (1966: 1). Had von Rad better heeded his own cautious warnings, perhaps he would have been more successful:

> One can but sound a note of warning with regard to all reconstructions which derive from one single line of descent where questions of sacral history are at issue. What do we *really* know—especially in a tradition of such crucial theological significance—of the various stages through which it passed in the history of the cultus? (1966: 47)

And writing about the Book of Deuteronomy, von Rad offers sound advice applicable to the interpretation of *all* biblical texts:

> This resolute synchronism is a fact which may serve to temper our own strongly marked interest in history and in the passage of time in matters of religion. (1966: 29)

Chapter VII

Martin Noth's *A History of Pentateuchal Traditions*

Claude Lévi-Strauss in his remarkable work, *The Savage Mind,* explained the myth-making faculty in man with the image of the "bricoleur," a man who builds whatever he has to build with whatever materials are at hand; this ingenious fellow exploits a haphazard collection of materials in a truly creative but limited way. He is constrained in what he may build by the physical limitations of the building materials at his disposal and differs in this respect from, say an engineer, in that his *materiel* is not collected from the start for specific purposes or functions but rather "builds up" through all the odds and ends of one's life. Mythical thought is an intellectual form of of *bricolage* and it is immensely important for Lévi-Strauss that this image be understood not only in its limiting characteristics but especially in its liberating functions. Be that as it may, mythical thought *does* limit and constrain, and it is in light of this that I would like to borrow Lévi-Strauss's image to characterize the *bricolage* aspects of all hermeneutical quests and to assert that the supreme *bricoleur* of modern Old Testament Studies is in my opinion Martin Noth.

> Mythical thought for its part is imprisoned in the events and experiences which it never tires of ordering and reordering in its search to find them a meaning. (Lévi-Strauss, 1966: 22)

The building blocks of any hermeneutics are sections of the various texts one attempts to interpret. In the course of the biblical scholarship we have so far been discussing—first

Wellhausen, then von Rad, and now Noth—we find a diachronic quest behind and beyond our present biblical texts. Far too often such a quest finds itself imprisoned in those textual "events and experiences" which it never tires of diachronically ordering and reordering in its search to find in them a meaning. *No* attempt at explaining what this or that language product means escapes these bars, but it is this book's thesis that no biblical hermeneutics better exemplifies these 'mythical' aspects than the diachronic constructions which reach their ultimate stage in Martin Noth's *A History of Pentateuchal Traditions,* hereafter *Pentateuchal Traditions.*

Another comparison comes to mind. When Mircea Eliade discusses myths of creation and origins (1968: 76-79), one becomes aware of an irony in Sigmund Freud's views on myth and religion. How deliciously ironic it is that Freud, who prided himself on his rational and methodical approach to the study of his object, constantly *explains* phenomena by appealing to origins or beginnings within the human psyche, a mechanism which is at the heart of all *myth* and which is commonly held to be what largely distinguishes *mythical* explanations of the nature of things from rational or philosophic explanations! This comparison is immediately relevant to anyone who has followed the course of biblical studies over the last one hundred years. The fundamental drive that has produced the greatest insights into the biblical message so far is fueled by the myth of origins. As Eliade so often puts it when explaining an essential characteristic of myth: it is the first manifestation of a thing that is significant and valid, not its successive appearances or epiphanies. Eliade uses the following words to describe man in his myth-making capacity, yet they apply equally well to the biblical scholars about whom we have been writing and especially to M. Noth: "Knowledge of the origin of each thing . . . confers a kind of magical mastery over it; he knows where to find it and how to make it reappear in the future" (1968: 76).

It would be unfair to Noth to claim he felt he obtained any definitive *answers* in *Pentateuchal Traditions*, for he makes it quite clear that he is interested primarily in asking the right questions (1972: xxxv; 3-4). My analysis of his work will concentrate on whether or not he did ask the right questions and whether the way in which he formulated these questions and pointed toward their eventual solution can be called structural in the sense in which we have been describing it. It will be the contention of this chapter that *Pentateuchal Traditions* is the least structural work of the three we have investigated, in spite of or perhaps because of its being the most structured of all.

Noth's central *questions* are similar to the questions myths attempt to answer: "knowledge of the origin of each thing . . . confers a kind of magical mastery over it; he knows where to find it and how to make it reappear in the future." Who can fail to be impressed with the diachronic skill by which Noth carries us back from the text in its final form to its thematic beginnings *over 500 years earlier*? And once we attain all we can hope to know about the Pentateuch's oral stages during the period of the tribal confederacy, given the paucity of material available to us, Noth knows how to make these oral beginnings "reappear in the future" in the Pentateuchal narrative as a whole. He writes at the end of his book:

> *Question:* The question still remains as to whether the combination of the sources . . . actually did not give rise to something new, which transcended the individual sources and their particular content and put them in a peculiar light, beyond the conscious intentions of the redactors. (1972: 250)
>
> *Answer:* Partly in consequence of a common harking back to a fully developed oral narrative tradition, and partly in consequence of mutual literary dependence, the course of history was narrated so much the same in all the sources that even their combination with one another could change nothing essential in this regard. (1972: 251)

Notice how Noth's explanation of the nature of the Pentateuchal narrative is based upon his explanation of its origins. It is the first manifestation of a thing that is significant and valid, not its successive appearances or epiphanies.

Pentateuchal Traditions is a transposition of the myth of origins onto the academic mode. Noth attempts to destroy time by invoking it. He is the supreme biblical *bricoleur* who places the diachronic efforts of Wellhausen and von Rad within the immense shadow his presence casts upon the entire biblical scene. Of all three, he is the "master builder" of the myth of origins.

First a brief look at salient features in the book. Such a tightly packed work will not allow a summary or synopsis of its chief points without robbing it of much that contributes to its greatness. What follows is a brief taste of what one may find who works through the book in detail.

The task Noth sets out for himself is an explanation of the origins of the growth of the Pentateuch in its preliterary first stages. Within this historical perspective, the *basic themes* must be isolated, related and assessed. Noth bases his study squarely upon the main conclusions of the documentary hypothesis and chapters two through five give us an *introductory orientation* to the literary-critical analysis which he assumes in his tradition-historical investigation. Anderson has a useful summary on this point (Noth 1972: xvii-xviii). Before embarking on his main thematic journey, Noth describes for us his main historical presupposition, namely that the creative formation of the Pentateuchal traditions was in the " . . . sphere of Israelite tribes living on the soil of the arable land of Palestine between the time of the occupation of the land and the beginning of the formation of the state" (1972: 45). We thus have a location, Palestine, a *terminus a quo,* the beginning of the occupation, and a *terminus ad quem,* the formation of the Israelite state. These are the spatial and temporal limits of the problem.

Chapter seven discusses the major Pentateuchal themes and their origins, and Noth is specific at the very outset of this chapter: the history of Pentateuchal traditions is understood and presented under the assumption that the major themes isolated were not united all at once but "joined together step by step in a definite sequence which can still be determined in general" (1972: 46). It is accepted by Noth as fundamental that the primeval history is a *literary* addition to the Pentateuch, that the patriarchal history was only secondarily placed before the following themes, and that as von Rad has shown the Sinai tradition was added on rather late in the formation of the Pentateuch. Thus, the Exodus, Wandering, and Occupation traditions are the only major themes left among which to look for the origins of the Pentateuchal tradition. But since the Occupation tradition does not have as much weight as the Exodus-from-Egypt tradition, and the Wandering tradition depends upon elements from both of them, it follows that the "guidance out of Egypt" theme is *"the kernel of the whole subsequent Pentateuchal tradition"* (1972: 49). It is a *"primary confession of Israel,* one that is expressed rather strictly in hymnic form . . . "* (ibid.). It was an all-Israelite theme *from the beginning.* The second theme is "guidance into the arable land" and is the first essential secondary expansion of the "guidance from Egypt" theme, accomplished in the (earlier) central Palestinian stage of the Pentateuchal formation. Thirdly, the "promise to the patriarchs" theme arose independently, but when it was combined with the two prior traditions there was accomplished an identification of the God of the Patriarchs with that God who led Israel out of Egypt into the arable land. This process of combination emphasized the promise aspect of the Patriarchal traditions while its fulfillment aspect was deferred to the "guidance into arable land" theme. First the Jacob traditions and then the Joseph story both belong to the earlier central Palestinian stage of the Pentateuch's formation. Then the later southern Palestinian stage incorporated the Isaac and Abraham traditions. The fourth theme, "guidance in the wilderness" "is not a very important or really independent theme" (1972: 58). However, it is treated in an imposing number of individual narratives. In contrast to the prior themes it has no cultic rootage and belongs to the same circle as the "promise to the patriarchs" theme. Moreover it is a contribution of the *Southern tribes.* Noth at this point joins up with the path earlier carved out for us by von

Rad: "This traces the growth of the Pentateuchal tradition essentially up to the point represented by the relatively fixed form found in the summary outline in Josh 24: 2-13 as well as the concise hymnic recital of the great acts of God in Ps 135: 8-12 and Ps 136 : 10-22" (1972: 59). Finally "revelation at Sinai" completes the five basic Pentateuchal themes. Von Rad's convincing demonstration that this tradition was added to the Pentateuchal corpus *secondarily* and *late* poses additional questions for Noth: why is this theme so infrequent outside Pentateuchally related sources? Why was it added so late when it is so ancient and important an event? Noth's position is clear: newer traditions had come to the fore and dominated the field. These newer traditions were of course "the comparatively more recent themes of the 'guidance out of Egypt' and the 'guidance into the arable land' . . ." (1972: 61). The sphere of this theme was the Southern Palestinian tribes since the theme was added late; in fact it was "the latest to be added to the series of the other themes" (1972: 62). Not only von Rad's thesis shows this but also the fact that it was inserted between elements of the wandering theme, a theme which itself was added to the other themes among the Southern tribes. Noth concludes this section by stressing that his arguments are not conclusive but should be understood "only in terms of a certain probability" (1972: 62).

Noth up to now has only been dealing with "basic materials," that is, narrative material comprising an *indispensable* fund of themes narrated in a vivid and concrete manner in order to communicate an event not an abstract statement. To this indispensable fund of narrative themes there were added all sorts of "enriching supplements." Noth will now devote roughly one-third of his book (83 out of 259 pages) to the separating out of "the supplements" from "the basic material." This he does in chapter eight: "The Filling-out of the Given Thematic Outline with Narrative Materials." This chapter is especially important to Noth's thesis since it treats in detail the secondary stage in which his basic schemes and motifs have been elaborated. Noth begins by making it clear that he is *not* about to "inquire into the universal narrative schemes and motifs which have given shape and color to the individual Pentateuchal narratives" (1972: 63) since these matters "pervade the narrative material of all peoples" (1972: 64). Noth's rationale here is important in understanding his methodology. Having put aside these universal questions of narrative analysis, he is ready to state the main position of this chapter: the relationship between "the great themes given in this tradition, together with the individual figures already contained in them" (1972: 64-65) and their narrative elaboration through the application of certain schemes and motifs is clearly that the former is diachronically primary and the latter secondary. Thus, the subject matter of this chapter is specific, definite, and concrete on two counts: its basic material, the great themes, is concrete and non-recurring insofar as it has been made vivid and concrete through the narrative form (1972: 62); moreover here in chapter eight " . . . we are dealing chiefly with that which is concrete and non-recurring, with definite persons, places, and events in the narrative, and not so much with general narrative schemes and motifs which by their nature are tied neither to place nor time" (1972: 65). Moreover, "it must be emphasized that . . . the development of the various major themes took place concurrently . . . " (1972: 65).

First of all, the indispensable narrative core of the theme, "guidance out of Egypt," was enriched by the story of the Egyptian Plagues, which was automatically added to the basic material when the Passover material itself was added. This process produced a tension which is somewhat relaxed in the text by the Pharoah having changed his mind but which is still discernible: did the Israelites leave Egypt unnoticed (older version) or as a direct result of the plagues (elaborated version)? The only material basic to this theme of "guidance out of Egypt" was "information about the 'oppression' of the Israelites in Egypt, about their departure, and their deliverance through the destruction of the Egyptians in the Sea . . . " (1972: 65-66), preserved in a relatively original form in Exod 1 and 14.

The core material of the theme "guidance into the arable land" included information concerning the occupation of the territories subsequently held by the Israelite tribes. This material was elaborated with all kinds of episodes going back to ancient memories and etiological legends but unfortunately "this material is almost totally lost to us" (1972: 73) except for the Sihon story of Num 21: 21-31. Other elaborative material of this second theme included a number of narratives dealing with the sanctuary of Baal Peor in Num 25 and the Balaam story of Num 22-24.

The basic core of the third major theme, "promise to the patriarchs" was the Jacob tradition. Whatever material is in the present Jacob traditions can be *prior* to the theme itself (traditions about Jacob *before* he "was elevated to the dignity of father of the twelve Israelite tribal ancestors [1972: 81]), basic to the theme itself, or subsequent elaborations of the theme. It is not clear to me which material involving Jacob at Shechem, Bethel, and in East-Jordan in Noth's view is basic and which is supplementary. It is at least clear that most of the Shechem and Bethel material is prior to the "worldly" Jacob material involving the East Jordan and Laban/Esau. Moreover all this material belongs to the central Palestinian stage of the Pentateuchal tradition. The southern Palestinian stage of its development comprises the incorporation of the figures of Isaac and Abraham into the patriarchal theme. "The major traditio-historical problem with regard to Isaac and Abraham is *the question of priority* . . . Now the fact that Isaac recedes into the background in contrast to Abraham, the figure that manifestly evolved later, speaks for Isaac's priority" (1972: 103). Therefore duplicate material belongs originally to Isaac rather than to Abraham. Moreover the Isaac stories are "closer to the origin of the 'patriarchal' tradition" (1972: 106) than the stories of the West Jordan Jacob! In general the Abrahamic material is the *latest* patriarchal material.

The fourth major theme, "guidance in the wilderness," was not "an independent theme inasmuch as it does not seem to be rooted . . . in cultic institutions and celebrations of the arable land, but probably presupposes an already well-advanced stage in the expansion of the Pentateuchal narrative" (1972: 115). This theme "took shape in the circles of the southern group of tribes, the same circles that elaborated the 'patriarchal' theme by adding the figures of Isaac and Abraham" (1972: 115). It is given special treatment here because "it cannot be regarded as merely a further unfolding of one of the other themes . . ." (1972: 115). These traditions involve the problems of thirst, hunger, enemies, and the murmuring of the people. The tradition of Caleb in Hebron (Num 13-14) belongs to the Southern stage of Pentateuchal development and represents therefore an *abortive* attempt at occupation since, tradition-historically, the shape of the Occupation tradition had already been determined in the prior central Palestinian stage of development. To the periphery of the Wilderness theme belongs also the meeting at the "mountain of God" found in Exod 18.

The final major theme is "revelation at Sinai"; " . . . the old Pentateuchal material belonging to this theme is remarkably small in extent, indeed quite meager. This theme manifestly did not receive narrative elaboration worthy of mention" (1972: 141). In fact it "appeared altogether late, and clearly was the last theme to be included in the circle of the Pentateuchal themes" (1972: 141). The basic core of this material is the contents of a festival legend of the making of the covenant as von Rad had pointed out; narrative elaboration of this theme is small: the story of the golden calf in Exod 32. This discussion brings Noth's long chapter to an abrupt end. It is easily the most difficult chapter to understand.

Chapter Nine treats the origin of various *figures* in the Pentateuchal tradition not already discussed. These include figures in the circle of the "patriarchs," both women and men; the main subject of the chapter, Moses; and finally figures alongside of Moses. Anderson has discussed the implications of Noth's views on the figure of Moses (Noth: 1972: xxviii-xxxii). Chapter ten is a chapter of retrospect and summary in which Noth attempts to articulate the *Sitz im Leben* of the elaborated material, thus clarifying its substantive relation to the core material. In distinguishing the two materials here, Noth clearly states they are *not* the products of discrete stages which can be strictly separated chronologically (1972: 190). This is difficult to understand since Noth's main thesis is precisely that the core material was largely united *before* elaboration took place. In any case, the real-life situation of the core material was *cultic* whereas that of the elaboration was far broader: *everyday life*. The core material was, generally speaking, cultic in character, issuing from the mouth of the priests of the worshipping community, and dealing with unique historical events. On the other hand, the elaborated material deals with day-to-day realities and issues from the mouth of popular narrators who concern themselves with the abiding and everyday conditions of life. The only exception to this is with regard to the first theme in which the Passover tradition is a cultic-historical elaboration. The elaboration of the other themes, however, took a different course, emphasizing everyday spheres of life: the inhabitants of the Canaanite city-states, huntsmen living in the woods of southern Transjordan, other fringe-area inhabitants, the exciting areas of civilization in Mesopotamia and Egypt, and even strange phenomena within the Israelite tribes' own sphere. The substantive relation of core to elaboration is basically cult versus popular narrative, unique historical events versus day-to-day life, and emphasis on the divine giver versus emphasis on the gift.

Chapters eleven through fourteen discuss the merging of the themes and individual traditions. Chapter eleven largely repeats what Noth has already written concerning the gradual interweaving of the thematic materials. Chapter twelve concerns the Joseph story's function as a connecting piece between the themes "promise to the patriarchs" and "guidance out of Egypt." Such a story does not belong to any of the fundamental themes but represents the broad and artistic narrative development of a cluster of themes. It is an imaginative story used to elaborate the already formed sequence, Jacob and his sons in Palestine ——> in Egypt. It "evolved out of the sentence, 'Jacob and his sons went down to Egypt.'" Chapter thirteen discusses examples of the merging of themes through genealogical means (artificial ties of kinship between the acting persons) and chapter fourteen treats

examples of mergings through itineraries (artificial ties of
originally independent traditions). These genealogies and
itineraries are therefore *secondary* and are to be distinguished
from *authentic* genealogies and itineraries whose connected
elements are not artificial but original from a tradition-historical
point of view. For example the *patriarchal* genealogies and
itineraries are largely secondary since they are based on the
contents of the traditions merged together, whereas there are
examples of authentic itineraries in the narrations of the themes,
Exodus, Wilderness, Sinai, and Occupation.

If the sphere of the cult was essential to the *formation* of the
Pentateuchal themes, and if the sphere of popular narrative was
essential to their *elaboration,* the sphere of theological reflection
and of the synoptic view was essential to the *literary form* of this
material. This latter topic forms the subject matter of chapter
fifteen. For Noth, each literary source of the Pentateuch is an
individual author. The time and place of each composition,
however, is not too important from a traditio-historical point of
view. This is fortunate because "sure clues for the precise dating of
the individual sources are far fewer than people commonly want
to believe" (1972: 229). Moreover, G as the basis for J and E could
be either oral or written. Either J or E could be earlier or later than
the other. Although it is clear that J is of southern provenance, E
could be just as easily of southern as of northern provenance. P is
definitely post-Deuteronomic, but precisely how late we do not
know. P may have been composed in Judea or in the circle of the
Babylonian diaspora. All of these questions are necessary for a
history of Israelite literature, Noth emphasizes, but not too
important from a tradition-historical point of view. Tradition-
historically, the important thing is "to establish in what way and
with what purpose the literary versions reworked and shaped the
received narrative materials" (1972: 231). Noth's general position
is that the older sources are "great literary synopses" which have
modified the oral material far less than one might suppose. The
key question here is what were "the basic ideas which were
determinative in the Pentateuchal sources at the time the material

of the traditions was given literary formulation?" (1972: 236). Noth precludes discussing the entity G and the source E because of lack of evidence and concentrates therefore on the theology of J and the theology of P. J's theology concerning the nature of man is contained predominantly in the material he added to the old material, his *Urgeschichte,* and the rest of his narrative is to be interpreted accordingly. For J, man from the beginning lives as one who continually strives to be like God, is continually disobedient to God, and thus is subjected to the curse of God. J presents his theology not in general formulations but in a popular way. P's theology is more difficult to perceive since he used so many *termini technici* for objects and institutions. In any case, some things can be said about P's viewpoint: 1) like the older sources it is *theological;* 2) it envisions an "ideal" cultic order by portraying it as having been realized at one time in remote antiquity; 3) it is directed toward P's conception of the sanctuary and God's relation to the sanctuary; and 4) thus the theology of P "is separated a great distance, both chronologically and substantively, from the theology of history of the old Pentateuchal sources" (1972: 247). Chapter seventeen concludes Noth's treatment of the literary sources' relevance for tradition-history with the following question and answer which may be considered a major conclusion of his study: Did the combining of the sources give rise to something new beyond the conscious intentions of the redactors? Is the whole greater than merely the sum of its parts? Noth's answer is a definite No! "Partly in consequence of a common harking back to a fully developed oral narrative tradition, and partly in consequence of mutual literary dependence, the course of history was narrated so much the same in all the sources that even their combination with one another could change nothing essential in this regard" (1972: 251).

Noth finishes his study by articulating in chapters seventeen and eighteen its historical implications for the ancient history of Israel and the prehistory of the Israelite tribes. By way of conclusion, he indicates how in the Pentateuchal narrative there " . . . is reflected a stage of the life and behaviour of the united

tribes of ancient Israel . . . " (1972: 252). *Cultic action* stands at
the beginning stage of the Pentateuchal tradition whose
comprehensive theme was the *divine guidance into the possession
of the arable land of Palestine.* In the Pentateuchal narrative, the
making of the Sinai covenant appears merely as an episode so
that, although it *could* be the first tenet of faith of Early Israel,
Noth's earliest identifiable material indicates "guidance into the
arable land" as pre-eminent. Moreover a common Israelite
consciousness is older than even this oldest tradition and is its
fundamental premise. The core material of the Pentateuchal
traditions testifies to this all-Israelite consciousness, and the
elaborated material shows us how Israel viewed herself within the
context of her earliest environment: life in Palestine in the tribal
confederacy. She saw herself as an intermediary between the
strange nomads of the desert and the weak and corrupt
inhabitants of the cities.

Noth's final conclusion is clear from chapter eighteen. Each of
the elemental themes *separately* rests upon an historical basis,
later cultified. However, the connection and interweaving of these
themes is "completely secondary . . . whereas we touch the
bedrock of the tradition only in the fundamental content of the
individual themes as still disconnected from one another" (1972:
257). Moreover, the connecting and interweaving of the original
historical events is even more secondary than that of the traditions
about each one of them. Noth believes that " . . . the further we
move back in the traditio-historical analysis of the Pentateuchal
narrative the more we come to separate items of information . . .
It is no longer possible for us to ascertain any *connections* between
these initial stages" (1972: 258). Whatever connections *are* present
in the narrative are secondary and vastly simplify actual historical
developments. Noth prefers these negative results of his study to
an artificial reconstruction that fits everything in neatly. He
concludes his book with a question: if a common history was not
responsible for Israel's earliest common consciousness, what in
fact *was* the formative element of that consciousness?

What shall we say of the approach that erected such a massive superstructure? In the course of this discussion I shall have occasion to analyze some of the guidelines used by Noth to distinguish early from late material and I must disagree with B. Anderson when he writes:

> We have noted previously that these guidelines, . . . work hand in hand and mutually reinforce one another. It is facile to point out weaknesses in any one of these clues when it is taken by itself. (1972: xxv)

Moreover:

> It would be unfair to regard these as principles derived from the supposed evolution of genres according to laws. (1972: xxiii)

First of all, Anderson's caution on criticism of any single clue is relevant only for guidelines that *by themselves* add some weight to a multiply corroborative argumentation. However, if an individual guideline can be shown to be not only weak but *erroneous* it is not only facile but valid to reject its probative force. Thus, as we shall see, it is not the *weakness* of the "shorter is older" guideline that is the target of criticism but rather its absolute uselessness as any kind of a guideline, corroborative or otherwise. It is certainly true, as Anderson points out, that "the historian of traditions perhaps may be compared to a detective who cannot rely upon a single clue, since it is ambivalent, but must weigh the total evidence and then must use creative imagination in solving the problem" (1972: xxvi). But truly ambivalent evidence is no evidence at all and Anderson's description of the ambivalence of the "shorter is older" guideline (1972: xxv) shows that he holds it, among others, to be truly ambivalent: shorter can just as easily be younger as older. It is as if Anderson is telling us that when a detective combines the two signs of fingerprints and of a whiff of perfume found at the scene of a crime, the evidence taken together points to a female culprit. But fingerprints may be indicative of either man *or* woman and they do not corroborate at all the feminine evidence of a *woman's* presence; they are simply irrelevant to the question of gender.

There is an additional reason for rejecting certain of Noth's guidelines from a methodological point of view. Noth apparently used one and the same guideline at times to argue for lateness and at times to argue for antiquity. We will point this out in detail as the relevant guidelines are discussed.

The importance of these diachronic guidelines in Noth's study can scarcely be exaggerated. Anderson points out perhaps the fundamental weakness of Noth's approach: concentration upon units rather than configurations of material. He writes "It is not *a priori* impossible that the earliest core of the Israelite tradition was an integrated whole or configuration of material, to which various individual genres and narrative elaborations were added as the tradition was further transmitted during the historical pilgrimage of Israel" (1972: xxx). Such a criticism had earlier been levelled against Noth's approach by Frank M. Cross and repeated recently (Cross: 1973: 88). Since the issue of individual versus connected themes is central to Noth's thesis it is important to emphasize here that it is by means of the diachronic guidelines which we are shortly to discuss that Noth argues for the early existence of separate rather than connected Pentateuchal themes. We can repeat what Noth writes in the last chapter of *Pentateuchal Traditions:*

> . . . then the further we move back in the traditio-historical analysis of the Pentateuchal narrative the more we come to separate items of information. The implications for the reconstruction and presentation of the historical beginnings of Israel are obvious. It is no longer possible for us to ascertain any *connections* between these initial stages. (1972: 258)

What is clear from this statement and indeed from Noth's entire book is that the existence of originally separate themes is not a conscious assumption on Noth's part but a *conclusion* of his diachronic analysis of the Pentateuchal material. Thus Anderson's statement about the *a priori* possibility of early configurations is true but may be beside the point since Noth is, at least explicitly, arguing not from principle but from an interpretation of fact. On the other hand, Anderson and Cross may have hit upon Noth's implicit and perhaps even unconscious predisposition toward judging discrete units as *a priori* earlier than their configuration. It is my opinion that they indeed are correct in this regard, and an analysis of Noth's use of diachronic guidelines will underline this point in some detail. For the sake of uniformity I will discuss the guidelines wherever possible as articulated by Anderson.

> Earliest traditions are formulated in small units and in concise style in contrast to later material which tends to appear in large units composed in discursive [*ausgeführt*] style. (1972: xxiv)

This indeed is an ubiquitous guideline in Noth's study. We are told, for example, that the Balaam story in Num 22-24 ". . . exhibits the later 'discursive' saga style and is doubtless one of the latest fruits to mature on the tree of the old oral Pentateuchal tradition" (1972: 75). Again, the "discursive saga-style" and "complicated saga composition" of the East Jordan Jacob stories show that such a narrative ". . . is a relatively late growth in the process of the formation of the Pentateuch" (1972: 88). Further on we read, "The discursive narrative in Gen. 24 (J) concerning the search for a bride for Isaac is, however, a late connective piece . . . " whereas "Gen. 26 (J) . . . is completely devoid of passages composed in the later discursive saga style" (1972: 104). Noth tells us that the Abrahamic narratives attached to the region of Hebron appeared " . . . only at a relatively late stage in the formation of the tradition. In accordance with this is the fact that they exhibit the later, discursive saga style" (1972: 110). A final example is the Joseph story which "shows itself to be a traditio-historically late construction by its discursive narrative style . . . " (1972: 208).

This "shorter is older" guideline is certainly one of those "theoretical conceptions of oral transmission presently ruling

certain circles of both Old and New Testament scholars" which
Frank Cross believes has been undercut by such research as A. B.
Lord's *The Singer of Tales* (Cross 1973: 112n.3). Since also this
guideline is simply an application of Noth's concentration upon
units rather than configurations, Anderson's remark is pertinent
here: such concentration "is understandable within the context of
an earlier period of research that was heavily influenced by the
romanticism of Herder" (1972: xxx). That elements of themes are
older than their combination is actually a transformation of the
"shorter is older" guideline applied on the level of content. Noth's
term, "discursive saga style" emphasizes the level of expression;
Noth's priority of thematic units over configurations of themes
emphasizes the level of content. In both cases the same
evolutionary principle is at work, and in both cases Noth does not
seem to have been sufficiently aware of how deeply this
assumption was imbedded in his conclusions. But such a criticism
rests upon the belief that Noth's assumption was wrong, not weak,
and I repeat my opinion that it is not unfair to criticize such
guidelines individually.

> 'Cultic' or 'religious' traditions are earlier than comparable
> 'secular' or 'worldly' traditions.
>
> Earlier traditions usually lie in the background whereas later
> traditions are usually more prominent in the present
> Pentateuchal narrative.
>
> Earliest traditions tend to be anonymous and to deal with
> typical figures, while later traditions are more specific and
> individualized. (1972: xxxiv)

I shall discuss these three guidelines together because they
illustrate most clearly the total ambiguity of Noth's diachronic
criteria and therefore the uselessness of his main conclusions. I do
not wish here to emphasize that they are invalid principles—even
though the "cultic versus worldly" guideline certainly is—but
rather that Noth constantly uses them *at the same time as he uses,
in other places, their mirror image to arrive at exactly the opposite*

conclusion. In other words, by sometimes reasoning that the more prominent tradition is later and at other times reasoning that the more prominent tradition is older, Noth is able to arrive at whichever diachronic conclusion his intuition tells him is correct. Moreover, by sometimes reasoning that the sacral or religious tradition is later and at other times reasoning that the sacral or religious tradition is earlier, Noth can arrive at any convenient diachronic conclusion he wishes. He works in similar fashion with the typical/specific dichotomy. I do not maintain that Noth did this consciously, and this is precisely the point. Noth possesses a methodological rifle that allows him to hit squarely whichever diachronic pole he aims at. A few examples will illustrate Noth's diachronic procedures in this regard.

The "religious" or "cultic" versus "secular" or "worldly" guideline is clearly operating (in conjunction with ' the "shorter is older" guideline) when Noth discusses the diachronic relationship of the Jacob traditions of Shechem and Bethel and the Jacob stories of East Jordan:

> So it happens that the East Jordan Jacob appears to be much more 'worldly' than his West Jordan prototype. That is true both with regard to the content and the manner of the stories which circulated about him . . . Obviously we have here a later kind of narrative which is distinct from the older sacral style of tersely composed narratives concerning God's revelations and promises to the 'patriarchs.' (1972: 91)

Here it is quite clear that Noth is dealing with an older "sacral" style versus a younger "worldly" *(weltlicher)* style. From his statement that the later worldly style is one in which "everyday human behaviour now comes openly into the foreground" (ibid.), we are able to infer, I think, the same kind of distinction that separates for him the "cultic" *core* material from the popularized narrative that formed its *elaboration* (1972: 189-197). In short, this guideline is a crucial one for Noth in his attempt to separate out what is original core material from that which is later elaboration. However, as I mentioned earlier, I am not at all clear,

from my reading of chapter eight, about which Jacob material
from West Jordan is basic and which is supplementary elaboration. In any case, Noth's use of this guideline to relate the Jacob
material diachronically is otherwise quite clear-cut: "sacral-
cultic" is early and "worldly" *(weltlicher)* or "secular" is late.
Moreover this principle is directly related to Noth's view on the
Sitz im Leben of the core versus elaborated material of the
Pentateuch. Noth makes the point that the later "worldly"
elaboration of the core material does not make such material
"profane" *(profan)*:

> Now the fact that the Pentateuchal narrative in its detailed
> exposition abandoned the cultic sphere, in which the origins
> determinative of the structure of the whole were rooted, does
> not mean that it thereby became 'profane' *(profan)*. (1972: 197)

We are forced therefore to infer that the diachronic sequence,
cultic ——› worldly, does *not* include or imply the sequence.
cultic ——› profane. Where then are we to place a tradition done
in a "profane" style?

Noth provides us with some indications for an answer when he
discusses the three variations of the "ancestress of Israel in
danger" tradition found in Gen 12, 20 and 26. Speaking about Gen
26, Noth states:

> Finally, we find in verses 7-11 the story of Isaac's apprehension
> about the possible consequences for himself and his beautiful
> wife of living in the vicinity of the pleasure-loving Canaanite
> inhabitants of the arable land. This story, as distinct from the
> two variants in the corresponding Abraham story (Gen. 12: 10-
> 20 [J]; 20: 1b-18 [E]), appears here in a still completely
> 'profane' form . . . It may be that here we find ourselves
> relatively close to the original form of this frequently utilized
> narrative material. (1972: 105)

Noth repeats his assertion:

> In any case this story, as its still 'profane' early form shows . . .
> (1972: 106)

Now Noth allows us to make a connection with the Jacob stories we have just discussed:

> On the whole these Isaac stories give the impression of being even more original traditio-historically than the stories of the West Jordan Jacob. They stand, as a matter of fact, closer to the origin of the 'patriarchal' tradition than do the latter. (ibid.)

Apart from the fact that it is difficult to understand how the Isaac stories are closer to the origin of the patriarchal tradition than the West-Jordan Jacob stories (Noth had earlier stated that Jacob "was the only patriarch to be directly connected with the older Pentateuchal themes, while the other patriarchs were connected with the rest of the Pentateuchal themes only through Jacob"[1972:56]), we are at least able now to set up a diachronic typology of narrative content/style as follows:

1. "still profane"   :   the Isaac stories
                                          then
2. "cultic, religious"   :   the West Jordan Jacob stories
                                          then
3. "worldly, secular"   :   the East Jordan Jacob stories.

What is significant to me from this example is the quite ambiguous distinction between thematic and stylistic elements of a *very early* "profane tradition" and those elements of a *very late* "worldly or secular tradition." What precisely distinguishes an early, still profane characteristic of a tradition from an already worldly or secular characteristic? Given such ambiguity, it is my contention that Noth is always able to point out certain characteristics of a tradition and either by calling them "still profane" judge the tradition to be more original, or else by calling them "worldly or secular" judge the tradition to be quite late. Here again it is of no use to involve Anderson's *caveat* that Noth uses this type of guideline in conjunction with other guidelines and thus corroborates his judgments. For, in reality, the other guidelines are either *invalid* (as the "shorter is older" guideline is) or equally ambiguous or irrelevant (as the "less prominent is earlier" or the "more typical is earlier" guidelines are). Since in fact, at least *three* of Noth's diachronic guidelines are totally ambiguous (i.e. both the guideline and its mirror image are used at various times by Noth to arrive at exactly opposite diachronic conclusions) it will be more and more apparent as this discussion proceeds why I believe Noth's *Pentateuchal Traditions* is the best example I can give of myth in the scholarly mode as it is practised in biblical studies today.

The second totally ambiguous (and therefore totally convenient and "efficient") guideline is that which states "the more anonymous and typical, the earlier; the more specific and individualized, the later." This guideline is used by Noth, (as Anderson points out [1972: xxiv]), when Noth discusses Exod 5 and concludes that the earliest stage of this tradition involved the more anonymous and typical "foremen of the people of Israel" stated in verses 15-19. Again, when Noth analyzes the covenant meal tradition of Exod 24, he finds the earliest figures of the tradition to be the anonymous and typical representatives of the people. Later are added Nadab and Abihu, then Moses, and finally Aaron. We could not ask for clearer examples of Noth's use of this guideline. However, the ambiguity of Noth's diachronic methodology becomes immediately evident when he is (once again) sorting out the temporal relationship of the West- versus East-Jordan Jacob stories. Here we seem to find a mirror-image of the guideline under discussion:

> The East Jordan Jacob is really no longer a 'patriarch' at all in the original sense; nor is he a tribal personification in the sense formerly presumed in scholarly circles, for a 'tribe of Jacob' is not involved. *He is, rather, a type that characterizes the whole people and their life.* (1972: 91) (italics added)

Here the diachronic scheme is exactly the opposite of the guideline under discussion; instead of typical ——> specific we have specific ——> typical. Moreover we have an added similarity in our two examples insofar as they both concern "figures" of a tradition. If, on one hand, we can go diachronically from an earlier anonymous figure to later specific ones in Exod 5 and 24, here in the Jacob stories we go from the earlier specific "patriarch" (the West-Jordan Jacob) to the later typical figure (the East-Jordan Jacob). It is not helpful to object that Noth bases his diachronic judgment here squarely on his understanding of the tribal movement of the Central tribes from east to west, since, even in this case, one would expect some indication of surprise on Noth's part that the specific ——› typical diachrony of this material is at odds with his usual understanding of the guideline. However, this is not the case here, and Noth gives every indication of viewing the sequence, "patriarch" ——› "type," as normal and expected. Given this state of affairs it is again easy to see how Noth can go in whichever diachronic direction he chooses whenever he discusses traditions that involve an anonymous/typical versus specific/individualized dichotomy.

A third ambiguous guideline in Noth's procedure is the one that states "earlier traditions usually lie in the background in the present Pentateuchal narrative whereas later traditions are usually more prominent in the present narrative." This is an especially ubiquitous guideline in *Pentateuchal Traditions*. Noth explicitly refers to this guideline (see for example: 1972: 101 n. 299 and p. 81) and utilizes it constantly in his diachronic judgments. Because of this guideline Noth is able to show how Abraham as a patriarchal figure belongs to a late stage in Pentateuchal development. Similarly, the extensive space given to the theme "revelation at Sinai" in the present form of the Pentateuch is explained by "the fact that here in the final, already advanced, literary stage of the growth of the Pentateuch, a tremendous amount of material has accumulated" (1972: 141). Not only figures or themes but also other *elements* of a narrative that stand out in the present text have every right to be regarded as later (1972: 101n. 299). He is here criticizing Gunkel's position concerning prominent features of the Jacob tradition.

It is at this point that we must ask of Noth a crucial question:

why then does Noth appeal to Moses being, with the possible exception of Jacob, the oldest figure of the Pentateuchal narrative as an explanation of why he became in the end the most prominent human figure of the present Pentateuchal narrative? Noth writes:

> Indeed, with the possible exception of Jacob, who belongs to the 'patriarchal' theme which stands by itself, Moses traditio-historically would have been absolutely the oldest Israelite figure of the Pentateuchal narrative. It is no wonder, then, that as the Pentateuchal narrative evolved he constantly grew in importance and finally came to be *the* overwhelmingly prominent human figure of the Pentateuchal narrative. (1972: 174)

Noth's position on the place of Moses in the Pentateuchal narrative is certainly not an insignificant part of his thematic study so that our question goes to the heart of the matter with regard to this guideline. What precisely is it about a prominent theme, figure, or element of a tradition that *sometimes* leads Noth to judge it, *because of its very prominence,* to be relatively early (Moses), and at other times leads him to judge it, *because of its very prominence,* to be relatively late (Abraham)? Here again I do not feel it is useful to appeal to corroborative guidelines leading Noth to make his varied judgments, for in the specific examples I have chosen (the *late* prominent features of the Abraham stories and the *early* prominent figure of Moses) Noth explicitly and primarily bases his diachronic judgment on precisely the guideline under discussion.

If there is ambiguity surrounding this guideline when applied to figures and features of the Pentateuchal narratives, there is equal confusion concerning Noth's understanding of this guideline when applied to major themes themselves. For if prominence is usually a sign of lateness why is it that Noth bases his opinion concerning the theme "guidance out of Egypt" being "the kernel of the whole subsequent Pentateuchal tradition" (1972: 49) upon the prominence of the *fixed formula,* "Yahweh who brought Israel out of Egypt," not only in the Pentateuch but also in the rest of the

Old Testament? This, in fact, is the major thrust of his treatment of this theme on pages 48-51 of *Pentateuchal Traditions,* and of course his analysis of this theme is the kernel of his subsequent analyses of the remaining major themes. We again ask our question: what in Noth's methodology distinguishes an *early* prominent element from a *late* prominent element when analyzing narratives? Why did not the prominence of the "guidance out of Egypt" theme lead Noth to conclude rather that it was the *latest* of the major themes? Or why at least did not Noth confront this prominence as an objection to be explained away if in fact he felt *for other reasons* this theme to be the original core of the Pentateuchal narrative? I therefore am led to the same conclusion on this guideline as on the two preceding ones; by using both it and its mirror image, Noth is able to draw either early or late assessments of similar if not identical elements of the narratives he is so insistent on ordering diachronically.

If the above guidelines taken separately are to be rejected, there is also some doubt about their *mutual* significance and relationship. For example we have not yet mentioned another guideline articulated by Anderson:

> Earliest traditions are attached to places and frequently end with an etiology of the place name. (1972: xxiv)

This is Noth's well-known clue of *Ortsgebundenheit.* A major problem I have here is that this guideline seems to be a frequent counter-indicator of the guideline concerning early-anonymous vs. late-specific tradition. If in fact earliest traditions tend to be anonymous why is this usually not the case with traditions explicitly attached to places? Again, to use another guideline, if *"connections* are later traditio-historically than the tradition-units which are connected" (1972: xxv), what is a more frequent connector of traditions, in Noth's view, than the local cult shrines of Palestine? Why then should not more explicitly local traditions turn out in Noth's view to be late rather than early? Why in fact does he consistently place cultic (and therefore localized) traditions earlier than "worldly" traditions, not essentially bound to a particular place?

In reality, when one investigates the relationships of the guidelines isolated by Anderson, it becomes obvious that their *combined* use sometimes enables Noth to conclude that the tradition he is analyzing is either early or late. Thus if an element of a tradition is a specific local place, the *Ortsgebundenheit* clue will allow him to argue for an *early* stage: however the anonymous versus specific guideline allows him equal latitude to argue for a late date. Again if it is a particular figure's *location* in a specific place that allows him to experience separate traditional events, that locale can be an early sign following the *Ortsbegundheit* principle, or a late sign following the bracketing guideline.

Another aspect of Noth's approach worth mentioning here is the relationship between his diachronic analysis of texts and his historical reconstruction of events in Israel's early history. The former is influenced to a great extent by the latter. As Anderson points out "His judgments about the relative age of materials are heavily influenced by historical considerations such as the presumed existence of a six-tribe league at Hebron which was immediately exposed to the conditions of the southern wilderness, or the ascendancy of the central Palestinian tribes in the early period of the twelve-tribe covenant league, or the activities of central Palestinian tribes in colonizing East Jordan" (1972: xxvii-xxviii). Such a procedure does not appear to be bothersome until one realizes what Anderson immediately points out about it: "Of course, Noth's historical understanding of the early period is based primarily upon a study of the primary evidence of Old Testament traditions themselves" (1972: xxviii). Perhaps one might object that this type of approach is too often vulnerable to the formulation of diachronic analyses of texts which are *petitiones principii* in which Noth simply begs the question. Thus Noth will base his reconstruction of certain phases of Israel's early history on a detailed investigation of "layers of traditions" in various *specific* parts of the Hebrew Bible, e.g. Josh 1-11 or the patriarchal traditions. But then he will use these historical reconstructions as a basis for his judgments concerning various "layers of tradition" in the Hebrew Bible. In other words, hypotheses concerning various layers of tradition in the Hebrew Bible lead him toward other hypotheses concerning Israel's early history. These latter hypotheses then lead him toward further hypotheses concerning various layers of tradition in the Hebrew Bible. These further hypotheses then lead him toward more hypotheses concerning Israel's early history . . . and so on *ad infinitum*. Concerning *Pentateuchal Traditions,* there is some question about which comes first in Noth's deductive argumentation: does he reconstruct his history of the tribal confederacy period and then dissect his Pentateuchal traditions diachronically, or vice-versa? In either case he must *first* dissect (at least part of) his Pentateuchal traditions diachronically. But then his judgments about the relative age of materials are not really based on methodologically prior historical reconstructions. So the criticism goes. I find this type of critique of Noth's methodology less disquieting than one might suppose. There is some validity to the point that all historical reconstruction operates in a kind of reciprocal "groping" such as we have just described. There is actually a great deal of this in most problem-solving situations, as the work of Michael Polanyi has so admirably shown.

What is important here is Noth's degree of self-awareness. He consistently employs his tradition-historical method in a manner that is ironically similar to procedures he has criticized when assessing certain historical reconstructions of the Albright school. For example, Noth criticizes the American School for correlating certain biblical texts with archeological investigations to obtain a historical reconstruction of the conquest. He tells us that "one must be very cautious in explaining a situation ascertained by means of archeology as applying to a definite historical event without relevant written evidence" (1966: 144). What Noth is specifically objecting to is the interpretation of destruction layers of Hazor, Lachish, Debir, and Eglon *as caused by the "Israelites"* even though there is no *archeological* textual evidence to corroborate this interpretation, only *biblical* textual evidence. Now, taken by itself, this criticism carries some weight since, as Kathleen Kenyon has also recognized (1960: 219-220), the possibility that such destruction layers might be related to the punitive raids of Merneptah or the advance of the Sea Peoples in the area at this time cannot be ruled out as competing interpretations of the archeological evidence. However, what is relevant here is that Noth does a remarkably similar thing as does the Albright school when he bases his history of early Israel on the detailed investigation of "layers of traditions" in various parts of the Hebrew Bible. The degree of "historical hypothesis" that is necessary to construct a framework into which and by which to interpret the biblical traditions is as hypothetical in Noth's *textual* reconstruction as it is in the American School's *archeological* reconstructions. And in a certain sense the American School can be said to have the better of the argument here since the two sources it correlates are dissimilar and objectively unconnected, i.e. textual biblical evidence and non-textual archeological remains. The degree therefore that one hypothesis can methodologically *control* the other hypothesis is far greater than in Noth's procedure in which he relies principally on the reciprocal interaction of textual reconstruction and the historical reconstruction based primarily on it.

We are now in a position to understand why *Pentateuchal Traditions* is, of the three classic diachronic works we have been discussing, the furthest removed from structural analysis as we have described it. In spite of the fact that Noth's great work is by far the most "structured" of all, he appears to me to have been least aware of the significant relationship between the structures he constructed and the "structures-structuring" within himself by which his hypotheses were formed. All of the diachronic guidelines we have analyzed are examples of such "structures-structuring" within Noth himself. Moreover his reciprocal use of historical and textual reconstruction is another such example. In both cases, I believe there are enough indications of a serious lack of that self-awareness which I have, called "deep subjectivity."

It is obvious that Pentateuchal Traditions is the most structured of our three examples. Diachronically, Noth leads us further back than either the literary stages of Wellhausen's reconstruction or the proto-oral stages of von Rad's form critical reconstruction. Thematically, Noth investigates the formative content of the Pentateuchal traditions in a much more structured and sophisticated analysis than do his predecessors. Methodologically, Noth believes his structures are more "powerful" than others since, unlike the scholars before him, he has been enabled finally thereby to discover " . . . the right way of posing the question . . . which is above all the most important matter and the fundamental presupposition for correct solutions" (1972: 4). Noth's major thematic categories are all diachronically oriented. Insofar as this is clearly what Noth *intended* to do, his categories are clear, concise and stimulating. Insofar, however, as an exploitation of the major themes of the present Pentateuchal narrative is concerned, it must be said that a truly synchronic thematics of the Pentateuch has yet to be accomplished. Moreover, it is doubtful whether such a thematics can be accomplished as long as it is accepted among biblical scholars that Noth's *diachronic* thematics, or attempts similar to it, are after all, "the fundamental presupposition for correct solutions" on the synchronic level as well. What was expressed above in the first chapter is especially relevant here: diachronic and synchronic analysis are complementary and co-equal. Neither provides the exclusive basis for the other. This is perhaps the most important area for communication today between the established biblical methodologies and new currents of interest such as biblical structuralism.

Bibliographic Remarks—Part Three

I am not aware of any studies on the relationship of structural analysis to source-criticism or tradition-history. The best treatment of von Rad's methodology in relation to structural analysis is found in a number of conferences and communications by Paul Ricouer to be found in Leon-Dufour, ed, (1971). This volume reproduces the conferences, discussions and communications of the French Catholic Association for the study of the Bible's second national conference at Chantilly in September 1969. Paul Ricouer, in the introductory paper of the conference (Ricouer 1971c), offers a splendid introduction to methodology in biblical exegesis. Then on the first day of the conference he speaks on the interpretation of Gen 1:1-2:4a in an attempt to show how the traditional genetic methodologies exemplified by those of von Rad and Werner H. Schmidt converge toward and complement the structural approach (Ricouer: 1971d). This paper articulates very well many of the relationships between the two approaches. Then in a concluding conference (Ricouer: 1971a), Ricouer attempts to spell out both the strengths and weaknesses of genetic and structural approaches. Most recently, however, see Ricouer: (1975). Hugh White (1975) has compared the structural approach of Roland Barthes (1971b) with the literary-critical approach of Hermann Gunkel with regard to Gen. 32. 23-33.

BIBLIOGRAPHY

Alonso Schökel, Luis
  1975 "Narrative Structures in the Book of Judith," *The Center for Hermeneutical Studies Colloquy 11*, Berkeley, California.

Bach, Emmon
  1965 "Structural Linguistics and the Philosophy of Science," *Diogenes 51*, pp. 111-128.

Barbut, Marc
  1970 "On the Meaning of the Word 'Structure' in Mathematics," in *Structuralism: A Reader*, Michael Lane, ed., London, pp. 367-387.

Barthes, Roland
  1966 "Introduction à l'ánalyse structurale des récits," *Communications 8*, pp. 1-27.

  1970a *Elements of Semiology. Writing Degree Zero*, Beacon Press.

  1970b "La linguistique du discours," in *Sign. Language. Culture*, Mouton, pp. 580-584.

  1970c "Science Versus Literature" in *Structuralism: A Reader*, edited by Michael Lane, London, pp. 410-416.

  1970d "Historical Discourse" in *Structuralism: A Reader*, edited by Michael Lane, London, pp. 145-155.

  1971a "L'analyse structurale du récit a propos d'actes X-XI" in *Exégèse et herméneutique*, X. Leon-Dufour ed., Paris, pp. 181-204.

  1971b "La lutte avec l'ange: analyse textuelle de Genèse 32.23-33" in *Analyse structurale et exégèse biblique*, Neuchâtel, pp. 27-39.

Beauchamp, Paul
  1969 *Création et séparation. Etude exegetique du chapitre premier de la Genèse*, Aubier.

  1970 "Propositions su l'Alliance de l'Ancien Testament comme structure centrale," *Recherches de science religieuse 58*, pp. 161-193.

  1971 "Autour du premier chapitre de la Genèse" in *Exégèse et herméneutique*, X. Leon-Dufour, ed., Paris, pp. 59-65.

  1972 "L'analyse structurale et l'exégèse biblique," in *Supplement to Vetus Testamentum* Congress volume, Uppsala, Vol. 22, pp. 113-128.

  1973 "État et méthodes de l'exégèse," *Esprit*, May, pp. 843-858.

Benveniste, Emile
  1971a "The Levels of Linguistic Analysis," *Problems in General Linguistics*, Coral Gables, University of Miami Press (translation of *Problèmes de linguistique générale*, Paris, Gallimard, 1966), pp. 101-111.

1971b "'Structure' in Linguistics," *Problems in General Linguistics,* Coral Gables, University of Miami Press (translation of *Problèmes de linguistique generale,* Paris, Gallimard, 1966), pp. 79-83.

Bergonzi, Bernard
1975 "A Grid of Codes, Views of Structuralism" *Encounter 45,* pp. 52-58.

Blancy, Alain
1973 "Structuralisme et herméneutique," *Etudes théologiques et religieuses 48,* pp. 49-60.

Blenkinsopp, Joseph
1975 "The Search for the Prickly Plant: Structure and Function in the Gilgamesh Epic," *Soundings,* Vol. LVIII, No. 2, Summer 1975, pp. 200-220.

Bloomfield, Leonard
1933 *Language,* New York

Boudon, Raymond
1971 *The Uses of Structuralism,* London (translation of *A quoi sert la notion de structure,* Editions Gallimard, 1968).

Bouillard, Henri
1971 "Exégèse, herméneutique et théologie. Problèmes de méthode" in *Exégèse et herméneutique,* X. Leon-Dufour ed., Paris, pp. 271-283.

Bovon, F., ed.
1971a *Analyse structurale et exégèse biblique,* Neuchâtel.

1971b "Le structuralisme francais et l'exégèse biblique" in *Analyse structurale et exégèse biblique,* Francois Bovon ed., Neuchâtel, pp. 9-25.

Cassuto, Umberto
1961 *The Documentary Hypothesis and the Composition of the Pentateuch: Eight Lectures,* Jerusalem.

Caws, Peter
1970 "What is Structuralism," in E. Nelson Hayes and Tanya Hayes, eds. (1970), pp. 196-214.

Chabrol, C.
1971a "Problèmes de la semiotique narrative des récits bibliques," *Langages 22,* pp. 3-12.

1971b "Analyse du 'texte' de la Passion" in *Langages 22,* pp. 75-96.

Courtes, Joseph
1971 "Actes 10, 1-11, 18 comme système de représentations mythiques" in *Exégèse et herméneutiques,* X. Leon-Dufour ed., Paris, pp. 205-211.

Cross, Frank Moore
    1966   "The Divine Warrior in Israel's Early Cult" in *Biblical Motifs. Origins and Transformations,* edited by Alexander Altmann, Harvard University Press.

    1973   *Canaanite Myth and Hebrew Epic,* Harvard University Press, Cambridge, Massachusetts.

Crossan, John Dominic
    1973   "Structuralist Analysis and the Parables of Jesus," *Linguistica Biblica* 29/30, pp. 41-51.

    1975   editor *Semeia 4*: Paul Ricouer and Biblical Hermeneutics.

Culler, Jonathan
    1975   *Structuralist Poetics,* Cornell University Press.

    1973   "The Linguistic Basic of Structuralism" in *Structuralism: An Introduction,* David Robey ed., Oxford, pp. 20-35.

Culley, Robert
    1972   "Some comments on structural analysis and Biblical studies" in *Supplement to Vetus Testamentum,* Volume 22, (Congress volume, Uppsala), pp. 129-142.

    1974   "Structural Analysis: Is it Done with Mirrors?" *Interpretation 28,* pp. 165-181.

    1975   "Themes and Variations in Three Groups of Narratives," *Semeia 3,* pp. 3-13.

Doty, William G.
    1972   "Fundamental Questions about Literary-Critical Methodology," *Journal of American Academy of Religion 40,* pp. 521-527.

    1973   "Linguistics and Biblical Criticism," *Journal of the American Academy of Religion 41* pp. 114-121.

Ducrot, Oswald, et al.
    1968   *Qu'est-ce que le structuralisme?* Paris.

Dyson, F. J.
    1968   "Mathematics in the Physical Sciences," in *Mathematics in the Modern World. Readings from Scientific American,* San Francisco and London, pp. 248-257.

Eddington, Arthur Stanley
    1956   "The Theory of Groups" in *The World of Mathematics,* James R. Newman, ed., New York, pp. 1558-1573.

Ehrmann, Jacques, ed.
    1970   *Structuralism,* Doubleday, New York.

Eissfeldt, Otto
1965 *The Old Testament. An Introduction,* New York and Evanston, (Translated from the 3rd German edition).

Eliade, Mircea
1968 *Myth and Reality,* New York and Evanston, (Harper Torchbook edition).

Esbroeck, M. Van
1968 *Herméneutique, structuralisme et exégèse,* Paris.

Funk, Robert W.
1966 *Language, Hermeneutic and the Word of God,* New York.

Gardin, Jean Claude
1967, "Analyse semiologique et littérature," *Nuovo 75,* pp. 4-8.

Genette, Gérard
1966 *Figures,* Paris.

1969 *Figures II,* Paris.

1972 *Figures III,* Paris.

Germain, Claude
1973 *La notion de situation en linguistique,* Ottawa.

Giard, Luce
1973 "Lectures plurielles" *Esprit (May),* pp. 859-876.

Good, Edwin M.
1973 "Job and the Literary Task: A Response" *Soundings 56,* pp. 470-484.

Granger, G. G.
1965 "Objet, structure et signification," *Revue internationale de philosophie,* Vol. 19, No. 73-74, pp. 251-290.

Greimas, A. J.
1966 "Eléments pour une théorie de l'interpretation du récit mythique," *Communications* (Ecole Pratique des Hautes Etudes) 8, pp. 28-59.

Gunn, David M.
1975 "David and the Gift of the Kingdom (2 Sam. 2-4, 9-20, 1 Kings, 1-2)," *Semeia 3,* pp. 14-45.

Haulotte, Edgar
1971 "Fondation d'une communauté de type universal. Etude critique sur la rédaction, la 'structure' et la 'tradition' du récit" in *Exégèse et herméneutique,* X. Leon-Dufour, ed., Paris, pp. 321-362.

Hayes, E. Nelson and Hayes, Tanya, eds.
1970 *Claude Lévi-Strauss: The Anthropologist as Hero,* Cambridge and London.

Hendricks, William O.
    1973   "Verbal Art and the Structuralist Synthesis," *Semiotica*, Vol. 8, pp. 239-
           262.

Hirsch, E. D.
    1975   "Current Issues in Theory of Interpretation" *The Journal of Religion 55*,
           pp. 298-312.

Hjelmslev, Louis
    1953   *Prolegomena to a Theory of Language* (Translated from the Danish, 1943,
           by Francis J. Whitfield), Bloomington.

Horkheimer, Max
    1972   *Critical Theory: Selected Essays,* New York.

Ingarden, Roman
    1973   *The Cognition of the Literary Work of Art,* Evanston (Translation from   *ρ 47*
           German Edition 1968).

Interpretation 28
    April Issue devoted to "Structuralism" as a way of investigating the literature of
    1974   the Bible." Articles by R. Spivey (1974), R. Jacobson (1974), R. Culley
           (1974), R. Polzin (1974), and D. Via Jr. (1974).

Iser, Wolfgang
    1974   *The Implied Reader.*

Jackson, Jered and Kessler, Martin, editors
    1974   *Rhetorical Criticism, Essays in Honor of James Muilenburg*, Pittsburgh
           (Pittsburgh Theological Monograph Series).

Jacobson, Richard
    1974   "The Structuralists and the Bible," *Interpretation 28,* pp. 146-164.

Jakobson, Roman
    1971   *Selected Writings,* Vol. II, The Hague, Mouton.

Kenyon, Kathleen
    1960   *Archeology in the Holy Land,* New York.

Kikawada, Isaac M.
    1974   "The Shape of Genesis 11. 1-9," *Rhetorical Criticism: Essays in Honor of
           James Muilenburg,* Pittsburg, pp. 18-32.

Koch, Klaus
    1969   *The Growth of the Biblical Tradition. The Form-critical Method,*
           (translated from the second German edition (1967) by S. M. Cupitt), New
           York.

Kropat, A.
    1909   *Die Syntax des Autors der Chronik,* BZAW XVI, Giessen.

Lakoff, Robin
1972 "Language in Context," *Language 48,* pp. 907-927.

Lambert, W. G.
1960 *Babylonian Wisdom Literature,* Oxford.

Lane, Michael, ed.
1970 *Structuralism: A Reader,* London.

Langages 22
June Issue devoted to: "Semiotique narrative; recits
1971 bibliques."

Leach, E. R.
1969 *Genesis as Myth and Other Essays,* London.

1971 "La Genèse comme mythe" in *Langages 22,* pp. 13-23.

Léon-DuFour, X.
1970 "Exégètes et Structuralistes," *Recherches de Science Religieuse 58,* pp. 5-15.

1971 *Exégèse et herméneutique,* Paris.

Lévi-Strauss, Claude
1963 "Réponses à quelques questions," *Esprit 31,* pp. 628ff.

1966 *The Savage Mind,* University of Chicago Press (translated from the French, *La Pensée Sauvage* 1962).

1967 *Structural Anthropology,* Doubleday Anchor Book (translated from the French edition of 1958).

1970 *The Raw the the Cooked,* Harper Torchbooks (translation of *Le Cru et le Cuit,* Librairie Plon, 1964).

Long, Burke O.
1975 "The Social Setting for Prophetic Miracle Stories" *Semeia 3,* pp. 46-63.

Lord, Albert B.
1968 *The Singer of Tales,* Atheneum, New York.

Lyons, John
1971 *Introduction to Theoretical Linguistics,* Cambridge.

1973 "Structuralism and Linguistics" in *Structuralism: an introduction,* David Robey, ed., Oxford, pp. 5-19.

Macherey, Pierre
1966 "L'Analyse littéraire tombeau des structures" *Les Temps Modernes,* Vol. 22, No. 246, pp. 907-928.

Mallac, Guy de, and Eberbach, Margaret
1971 *Barthes,* Éditions Universitaires, Paris.

Maranda, Elli Köngas and Pierre
  1970 *Structural Analysis of Oral Tradition,* Philadelphia.

  1971 *Structural Models in Folklore and Transformational Essays,* The Hague.

Marin, Louis
  1971a "Essai d'analyse structurale d'Actes 10, 1-1118" in *Exégèse et herméneutique,* X. Leon-Dufour, ed., Paris, pp. 213-238.

  1971b "En guise de conclusion," *Langages 22,* pp. 119-127.

  1971c *Sémiotique de la Passion. Topiques et figures,* Aubier

  1971d "Essai d'analyse structurale d'un recit-parabole: Mat 13. 1-23," *Etudes, Théologiques et Religieuses 46,* pp. 35-74.

  1971e "Les femmes au tombeau," in *Langages 22,* pp. 39-50.

  1971f "Jésus devant Pilate," in *Langages 22,* pp. 51-74.

  1973 "Du corps au texte," in *Esprit (May),* No. 423, pp. 913-928.

Martinet, André
  1953 "Structural Linguistics" in *Anthropology Today,* A. L.
Kroeber (ed.), Chicago, pp. 574-586.
  1965 "Structure et langue," *Revue internationale de philosophie 73-74,* pp. 291-299.

McEvenue, Sean E.
  1975 "A Comparison of Narrative Styles in the Hagar Stories" *Semeia 3,* pp. 64-80.
Minnis, Noel, ed.
  1973 *Linguistics at Large,* St. Albans.

Molino, Jean
  1969 "Sur la méthode de Barthes," *La Linguistique,* pp. 141-154.

Mounin, George
  1966 "La notion de situation en linguistique et la poésie" *Les Temps Modernes,* Vol. 22, No. 247, pp. 1065-1084.

  1970 *Introduction à la semiologie,* Ed. de Minuit, pp. 189-197.

  1972 *Clefs pour la semantique,* Paris.

Muilenberg, James
  1969 "Form Criticism and Beyond," *Journal of Biblical Literature 88,* pp. 1-18.

Nattiez, Jean-Jacques
  1973 "De la semiologie a la semantique," *Cahier de linguistique 2,* pp. 219-239. (Vol. 2 is devoted to "Problèmes de Semantique." The series is published by Les presses de L'Université du Quebec).

Newman, James R., ed.
   1956   *The World of Mathematics,* New York, 4 volumes.

Noth, Martin
   1966   *The Old Testament World,* Fortress Press. (translation of the fourth
          edition of *Die Welt des Alten Testaments,* Berlin 1964).

   1972   *A History of Pentateuchal Traditions,* Englewood Cliffs, N.J.,
          (Translation of German edition of 1948).

Oettinger, A. G.
   1968   "The Uses of Computers in Science," *Mathematics in the Modern World,*
          San Francisco and London, pp. 361-369.

Orlinsky, Harry M.
   1971   "Whither Biblical Research," *Journal of Biblical Literature 90,* 1-14.

Paillet, Jean-Pierre
   1973   "Prérequis pour l'analyse semantique" *Problèmes de semantique* (No. 2 of
          the series *Cahier de linguistique* published by University of Quebec Press),
          pp. 1-18.

Palmer, Richard E.
   1975   "Toward a Postmodern Interpretive Self-Awareness" *The Journal of
          Religion 55,* pp. 313-326.

Parret, Herman
   1971   *Language and Discourse,* The Hague, Mouton.

Patte, Daniel
   1975   "Structural Network in Narrative: The Good Samaritan," *Soundings,* Vol.
          LVIII, No. 2, Summer 1975, pp. 221-242.

Peirce, Charles Sanders
   1932   *Collected Papers of Charles Sanders Peirce,* edited by Charles Hartshorne
          and Paul Weiss, Harvard University Press, Volume II.

Perrin, Norman
   1975   "The Editor's Bookshelf," *The Journal of Religion 55,* pp. 371-372.

Piaget, Jean
   1970   *Structuralism,* New York, Basic Books (translation of *Le Structuralisme,*
          Paris, 1968).

Petersen, Norman R.
   1974   "On the Notion of Genre in Via's 'Parable and Example Story: A literary-
          structuralist Approach'" *Semeia 1,* pp. 134-181.

Polanyi, Michael
   1962   *Personal Knowledge,* New York.

Polzin, Robert
1967   "Notes on the Dating of the Non-massoretic Psalms of 11QPs*," *HTR 60*, pp. 468-476.

1974   "The Framework of the Book of Job," *Interpretation (April)*, pp. 182-200.

1976   *Late Biblical Hebrew*, Harvard Semitic Monographs, Fortress Press and Scholars Press.

1975   "'The Ancestress of Israel in Danger' in Danger" *Semeia 3*, pp. 81-98.

Poole, Roger
1972   *Towards Deep Subjectivity*, Harper Torchbooks.

Pope, Marvin
1965   *Job. The Anchor Bible*, Garden City, N.Y., Doubleday.

Popper, Karl
1968   *The Logic of Scientific Discovery*, New York, Harper and Row (2nd Harper Torchbook edition).

Pouillon, Jean
1966   "Présentation: un essai de définition," *Les Temps Modernes*, Vol. 22, No. 246, pp. 769-790.

Propp, V.
1968   *Morphology of the Folktale*, Austin.

Rad, Gerhard von
1962   *Old Testament Theology*, Volume One, Harper and Row (translation of *Theologie des Alten Testaments* 1957 with revisions for 2nd German edition).

Radday, Yehuda T.
1971   "Chiasm in Samuel," *Linguistica Biblica 9/10*, pp. 21-31.

1972   "Chiasm in Tora," *Linguistica Biblica 19*, pp. 12-23.

1973   "Chiasm in Joshua, Judges and Others," *Linguistica Biblica 27/28*, pp. 6-13.

Ricoeur, Paul
1969   *Le Conflit des interprétations*, Paris.

1971a "Esquisse de conclusion," in *Exégèse et herméneutique*, X. Leon-Dufour, ed., Paris, pp. 285-295.

1971b "Contribution d'une réflexion sur le langage à une théologie de la parole," in *Exégèse et herméneutique*, X. Leon-Dufour, ed., Paris, pp. 301-319.

1971c Conférence d'introduction: du conflit a la convergence des méthodes en exégèse biblique," in *Exégèse et Herméneutique*, X. Leon Dufour, ed., Paris, pp. 35-53.

1971d "Sur l'exégèse de Genèse 1, 1-2,4a" in *Exégèse et herméneutique,* X. Leon Dufour, ed., Paris, pp. 67-84.

1974 *The Conflict of Interpretations: Essays in Hermeneutics* Evanston: Northwestern (translation of French edition, 1969).

1975 "Biblical Hermeneutics" in *Semeia 4,* pp. 29-148.

1975-76 "Philosophical Hermeneutics and Theological Hermeneutics" *Studies in Religion Sciences Religieuses,* Vol. 5, No. 1, pp. 14-44.

Robertson, David
1973 "The Book of Job: A Literary Study" *Soundings 56,* pp. 446-469.

Robey, David, ed.
1973 *Structuralism: an introduction,* Oxford.

Ryssel, C. F.
1878 *De Elohistae Pentateuchici Sermone,* Lipsiae.

Saussure, F. de
1966 *Course in General Linguistics,* New York (1915 from 1906).

Schiwy, Günther
1969 *Der französische Structuralismus,* Rowohlt.

1971 *Neue Aspekte des Structuralismus,* München.

Scholes, Robert
1974 *Structuralism in Literature. An Introduction.* New Haven and London.

Spivey, Robert A.
1974 "Structuralism and Biblical Studies: The Uninvited Guest," *Interpretation 28,* pp. 133-145.

Starobinski, Jean
1971 "Le démoniaque de Gérasa: analyse littéraire de Marc 5 p. 1-20," in Bovon (1971a: 63-94).

Steiner, George
1973 "Linguistics and Literature" in *Linguistics at Large,* Noel Minnis ed., St. Albans, Paladin, pp. 111-136.

Todorov, Tsvetan
1971 *Poétique de la prose,* Paris.

1972 "Personage" in *Dictionnaire encyclopédique des sciences du langage,* edited by O. Ducrot and T. Todorov, Paris, pp. 286-292.

1973a "Artistic Language and Ordinary Language," *Times Literary Supplement,* October 5, pp. 1169-1170.

1973b "The Structural Analysis of Literature: The Tales of Henry James" in *Structuralism: an introduction* edited by David Robey, Oxford, pp. 73-103.

1969   *Grammaire du Décaméron,* The Hague.

Tucker, Gene M.
1971   *Form Criticism of the Old Testament,* Fortress Press.

Ullman, Stephen
1973   "Semantics" in *Linguistics at Large,* Noel Minnis, ed., St. Albans.

Updike, John
1975, "Roland Barthes," *The New Yorker,* Nov. 24, 1975, pp. 189-194.

Via, Dan O.
1967   *The Parables,* Philadelphia, Fortress Press.

1971   "The Relation of Form and Content in the Parables: The Wedding Feast," *Interpretation 25,* pp. 171-184.

1973   "Parable and Example Story: A Literary-Structuralist Approach," *Linguistica Biblica 25/26,* pp. 21-30.

1974   "A Structuralist Approach to Paul's Old Testament Hermeneutic," *Interpretation 28,* pp. 201-220.

1975   *Kerygma and Comedy in the New Testament,* Philadelphia: Fortress Press.

Viullod, G.
1971   "Exercices sur de courts récits" in *Langages 22,* pp. 24-38.

Watkins, Evan
1975   "Criticism and Method: Hirsch, Frye, Barthes" *Soundings,* Vol. LVIII, No. 2, Summer 1975, pp. 257-280.

Watson, George
1975   "Old Furniture and 'Nouvelle Critique'" *Encounter* February.

Wellhausen, Julius
1965   *Prolegomena to the History of Ancient Israel,* Meridian Books, Cleveland and New York (first published in German in 1878).

White, Hugh C.
1975   "French Structuralism and OT Narrative Analysis: Roland Barthes" *Semeia 3,* pp. 99-127.

White, Morton
1969   *Foundations of Historical Knowledge,* Harper Torchbook, New York.

Wittig, Susan
1975a "The Historical Development of Structuralism" *Soundings,* Vol. LVIII, No. 2, Summer 1975, pp. 145-166.

1975b "Meaning and Modes of Signification: Toward a Semiotic of the Parable." (Paper given at Conference on Semiology and Parables, Vanderbilt University, Nashville, Tennessee, 15-17 May, 1975).

p 47

Wright, Addison
    1968   "The Riddle of the Sphinx: The Structure of the Book of Qoheleth,"
           Catholic Biblical Quarterly 30, pp. 313-334.

Zacklad, J.
    1971   "Création, péché originel et formalisme (Gen. I-III)," *Revue d'histoire et*
           de philosophie religieuses 51, pp. 1-30.

INDEX OF MODERN AUTHORS